Native American Worldviews

Native American Worldviews

An Introduction

Jerry H. Gill

Humanity Books

an imprint of Prometheus Books
59 John Glenn Drive, Amherst, New York 14228-2197

Published 2002 by Humanity Books, an imprint of Prometheus Books

Inquiries should be addressed to
Humanity Books
59 John Glenn Drive
Amherst, New York 14228–2197
VOICE: 716–691–0133, ext. 207
FAX: 716–564–2711

06 05 04 03 02   5 4 3 2 1

Library of Congress Cataloging-in-Publication Data

Gill, Jerry H.
    Native American worldviews : an introduction / Jerry H. Gill.
        p. cm.
    Includes bibliographical references and index.
    ISBN 1–59102–051–4 (paper : alk. paper)
    1. Indian cosmology—North America. 2. Indian philosophy—North America.
3. Indians of North America—Rites and ceremonies. I. Title.

E98.C79 G56 2002
191'.089'97—dc21

                                                            2002027253

Printed in the United States of America on acid-free paper

In memory of Dale Keith McGinnis

"Brings Horses"

Uncle, Friend, and Teacher

Contents

List of Figures

Preface

A preface provides the writer with an opportunity to do two important things. One is to explain why the book was written and what it does and does not seek to accomplish. The other is to acknowledge and thank those persons who have helped to make the book a reality.

This book aims at providing a clear, representative, and faithful introduction, and only an introduction, to what are called the "worldviews" of Native American peoples. This term is meant to designate a people's basic understandings of the world as a whole, along with their own place in it. Worldviews comprise a synthesis of philosophical and religious beliefs as they are commonly understood in Euro-American culture.

Since I am not myself of Native American descent I have done my best to gather and present the combined wisdom of many scholars, ethnographers, and Native Americans in an accessible and clear format that does justice to both the complexity and the concrete character of their beliefs and practices. For the experts there is nothing new in these pages, but for those who desire an overview of the subject there is a good deal of information and useful structuring.

The book stands in between firsthand scholarship and a mere narrative summary of this scholarship; it seeks to offer a reliable and clear presentation of appropriate and relevant material within broad conceptual categories. At the most basic level this entire project is dependent on the work of ethnographers who have compiled information about Native American beliefs and practices, and thus I have found it both necessary and wise to quote extensively from their publications. Where possible, I have drawn on the work of Native American scholars.

Clearly, then, I am deeply indebted to those scholars on whose reports I have relied for details and insight into Native American beliefs and behavior. Since this book grew out of my teaching of courses at several colleges, I have profited greatly from interaction with my students as well. I am also very grateful to Ann O'Hear, my editor, for her unflagging enthusiasm and many helpful suggestions. In a real sense this book has been "co-authored" by her. Thanks also to Lucas Guthrie for help with the illustrations. As always, I gratefully acknowledge the support of my wife and colleague, Mari Sorri. She makes it all worthwhile.

Finally, let me add that the primary inspiration for writing this book came from the Spirit of the Native American worldviews themselves. We Euro-Americans have a great deal to learn from the values and perspectives embodied in them. Most specifically, as the dedication page suggests, over the years I have been greatly influenced by my uncle Dale McGinnis, who died in 1994 shortly after retiring from his career as a college professor. Dale was only two years my senior and thus we grew up together as brothers. After he was formally adopted into the Crow Nation in Montana, Dale spent many years as an anthropologist, and was greatly loved by his students. I hope this book would have made him glad.

J. H. Gill
Tucson, Arizona
July 2002

Introduction

Perspectives and Worldviews

Whenever I teach the course Native American Worldviews, I am asked "What do you mean by the term *worldview?*" It is often helpful to begin with a definition offered by Robert Redfield:

> That outlook upon the universe that is characteristic of a people . . . a worldview differs from culture, ethos, mode of thought, and national character. It is the picture the members of a society have of the properties and characters upon their stage of action. Worldview attends especially to the way a man in a particular society sees himself in relation to all else. It is the properties of existence as distinguished from and related to the self. It is in short, a man's idea of the universe.[1]

The task of charting the way through Native American worldviews is as difficult as it is rewarding, if only because it requires one to work in the area of overlap between three related yet distinct disciplines; it is never quite clear if one is doing philosophy or anthropology or religious studies. Actually, one is really doing all three, alternatively and simultaneously. This creates a certain amount of confusion. At the same time, however, the diversity and complexity add to the richness and significance of the undertaking. Thus the journey is well worth the effort, as I trust the following chapters will demonstrate.

Perhaps the first thing that should be said about this project is that it is, as the subtitle says, an *introduction* to the subject. There are many books available which explore and explain in detail various features and issues relating to specific Native American groups. There are not, however, many that provide an overview of the broad, fundamental characteristics of their views of the world. Any attempt to introduce a very complex and diverse topic will run the risk of oversimplification, since there is no such thing as *the* Native American way of thinking about and/or living in the world. Nevertheless, there are broad patterns of belief and practice which can be compared and contrasted in order to provide an initial understanding and appreciation of Native American conceptual systems and values. This is the goal of the present book.

The fulfillment of this task requires relying on the efforts and insights of a number of original researchers and Native Americans as they have been recorded in published texts, and these will be documented along the way. While I shall seek to be faithful and fair to these resources, they will not be at the forefront of this presentation, since the goal of the project is to render the findings and reflections of these primary sources accessible to the general reader. The same holds true for the categories and concepts of philosophy, anthropology, and religious studies, which will serve as the background against which the beliefs and practices under discussion will be highlighted. Although it is impossible to treat worldviews without employing such concepts and categories, they will remain but an important means to the overall end.

As has been said, the term *worldview* designates an area of overlap of the three fields of study involved in this type of exploration. Philosophers generally call such subject matter "metaphysics," for it deals with questions that pertain to the fundamental nature of reality. Anthropologists sometimes use the term *worldview* itself, or they may speak of "belief systems" and "conceptual frameworks." Scholars of religion also employ the above terms, although occasionally they may speak as well of "doctrinal systems" or "theological beliefs." Put briefly, the notion of worldview simply indicates the way a particular people or culture understands the world in which it finds itself. Once again, it is important to remember that throughout this study we shall be dealing with a plurality of worldviews. There is no *one* Native American worldview, though there are many similarities and overlappings.

To be more concrete, Native American understandings of the importance of the sun, for instance, clearly reflect a specific way of construing the world and of orienting oneself in it. Among nearly all Native American peoples the sun plays an extremely significant role in matters of belief and practice. The cruciality of light and heat in daily life and survival is quite obvious to folks living close to the earth and often at the subsistence level. Moreover, people who depend on agriculture for their way of life must pay special attention to the paths and patterns of the sun as a guide for sowing and reaping. Thus we see the prevalence of orienting one's life, both individually and collectively, toward the sunrise in the east. Very many if not most Native Americans situate their dwellings so as to face the sunrise as well.

In addition, a great many Native American peoples envision life as a *journey along a path*, a journey in which the purpose is to follow the path as faithfully as possible without straying from it into impropriety, sickness, or evil. This path is considered to be the way of wisdom, health, and beauty, and its ultimate goal is a life that culminates in the maturity and fulfillment of character embodied in old age. Various rituals are enacted whenever a person wanders or falls from the path, rituals which seek to restore the balance or harmony of a truly wholesome life. Thus the prayer and/or admonition that one will "walk in wisdom," or in health or beauty, is a common one among Native Americans.

The notion of worldview may be further delineated by comparing the two features of the Native American perspective introduced above with those of the traditional Western perspective. Generally speaking, the Judeo-Christian heritage has not given a great deal of attention to spatial orientation or to the role of the sun in its understanding of the world. Rather, it has focused on *historical* events and personages such as Moses and Jesus as the crux of reality. Moreover, the human condition is usually understood in this tradition as more a function of one's *standing* in the sight of God than as a journey along a path. Even more specifically, Jews think of their life in relation to commandments and duties, while Christians generally believe that the original human condition is one of being out of favor with God by virtue of sin. Native American worldviews, by contrast, tend to view reality as primarily spatial rather than as historical and life as good unless one's balance is disrupted.

Many of the scholars working in this field are hesitant to address themselves to the issues involved in dealing with a comprehensive concept like that of worldview. At the one extreme, it is frequently claimed by philosophers that Native Americans and other nonliterate peoples do not really have a coherent view of the world because they have not yet conceived of the possibility and/or necessity of sequential and critical thought. Anthropologists, on the other hand, tend to begin their investigations at the physical or archaeological level, then advance to the cultural and political level. Only rarely do they offer generalizations concerning a larger perspective. As social scientists they seek to explain each level of culture in terms of the ones beneath it. Scholars in the history of religions, or in what used to be called comparative religion, have backed away from providing generalized accounts of Native American thought systems in favor of detailed analyses of particular rituals and social roles.

Without seeking to minimize the legitimate concerns inherent within each of these positions, it is my contention that it is both possible and valuable to investigate the various contours and ramifications of Native American beliefs about the world and their place within it. Philosophical reflection is surely not confined to written language. Nor are a people's religious and ethical beliefs and practices simply the effect of less complex causes; often, as we shall see, they may actually be the cause of sociopolitical, and even domestic patterns. Finally, as the philosopher Alfred North Whitehead insisted, knowledge must *begin* at the general level so as to enable one to distinguish the forest from the trees.

Before proceeding further, I would like to clarify the scope of the present study. First, the primary emphasis will be traditional Native American worldviews as they were developed and lived prior to the invasion and conquest by Europeans. How Native American peoples have evolved over the past four or five hundred years, and continue to do so, will be briefly dealt with in the final chapter.

Second, the focus throughout will be exclusively on those peoples living on the North American continent. The indigenous peoples of Mexico, Central America, and South America constitute a field of study all their own, as does the study of those peoples residing in the arctic and subarctic regions.

Third, it is important to bear in mind that these explorations are meant to be representative rather than all-inclusive of Native American worldviews. There is, to be sure, a wide variety of beliefs and practices which will necessarily go unmentioned in the following investigations.

Nevertheless, there remains a great deal of value in seeking to generalize on the basis of representative characteristics. There are far more commonalities than there are differences between Native American worldviews.

The various dimensions of Native American worldviews are presented according to several different aspects, each being taken up in a different chapter. In chapter 1 Native American groups are placed within *time and space* in a general fashion, marking their arrival in and occupation of North America. Such migrations and patterns of domicile span a great many centuries and areas, and were largely the function of climate and food supply. Thus both geography and environment play an important role in understanding the background against which Native American worldviews have developed, especially since these peoples lived so closely related to the earth.

It was within the parameters of time and space that Native American cultural patterns evolved, giving concrete expression to their emerging worldviews. The degree to which a given people may value individuality and self-fulfillment, for example, is often directly though not exclusively related to their mode of domestic life. The hunting peoples of the Great Plains value these qualities very differently from the way the pueblo dwellers of the Southwest value them. Likewise, the many diverse languages that arose among Native Americans are at least partly to be understood in terms of the separation caused by vast prairies, lakes, and mountain ranges. In northern California alone there were over fifty distinct *languages*, to say nothing of dialects. Some of this linguistic diversity probably resulted as well from various waves of migration over many centuries. Today linguists can trace these developments with remarkable accuracy.

Chapter 2 takes up some of the different accounts that various peoples give concerning the formation of the world as humans know it. These tales are often called "creation myths" or "origin stories." It is very important to clarify the meanings attendant on these different designations, since our understanding of these accounts will largely depend on which terms we use. At the popular level the term *myth* is generally taken as the equivalent of "fairy tale" or "fantasy." The term *story* is perhaps the most suitable for our purposes here, because it is broader and less pejorative in its connotations. The Native American stories are parallel in function to the Judeo-Christian creation stories in the Book of Genesis.

In neither case is the primary concern with providing a scientific or historical account of the origins of the world. The major difference between the two sets of stories is that the Judeo-Christian stories were written down long ago while those of Native American peoples have been recorded only recently.

In most Native American origin stories the time frame involved is clearly not meant to be historical in nature. It is more akin to what the Mojave, like the native peoples of Australia, call "dream time," a time in which the original beings, including animals, set the world in motion and gave it its basic patterns. Perhaps the term *primordial time* will best serve our purposes here. In primordial time there is almost always a great deal of interaction between the original beings and the natural elements, especially mountains, rivers, and trees, and such animals as coyote, beavers, turtles, bears, and eagles. In addition, these stories generally involve journeys or migrations by human beings once they are on the scene.

The relationship between the world and the spatial dimension of reality is treated in chapter 3. Often the structuring of space at the cosmic level seems built into the very fabric of reality even prior to the creative activity recounted in the origin stories. Generally in Native American views it is understood that the cosmos is composed of different realms or worlds stacked upon one another and that both creation and human development involve various movements upward and downward in this vertical hierarchy of worlds. In addition, the horizontal dimension of reality is constituted by what are usually called the "Cardinal Directions," namely North, East, South, and West, as well as by upward and downward movement. Each of these directions plays an important role in the beliefs and practices of many Native Americans.

At the center of these vertical and horizontal dimensions stands the living space of the community, frequently formed into a circle, or sometimes a rectangle. Villages, whether composed of tepees, long houses, or pueblos, serve as the hub around which all of life, individual, collective, and cosmic, revolves. Moreover, the boundaries of this living space constitute the line between the ordered world of meaning, literally the "cosmos," and the outside world of "chaos," which in reality is no world at all. Thus, those who live within the community are usually called "the people," while those existing outside the community are designated in some other way, as gods, enemies, or subhumans. More specifically, each dwelling is viewed as a miniature cosmos, with its entrance often facing east and those living inside it generally arranged according to status and/or function.

In chapter 4 the focus will be on the role played by *time* in the ordering of the Native American world. Generally, Native Americans view time in terms more of cycles than of chronological progression. The repetitive passing of the yearly seasons, the paths of the heavenly bodies, and the stages of life from birth to death and to birth again all embody this cyclical pattern. Moreover, as has already been mentioned, this pattern received its initial impetus from the actions of original beings dwelling in the primordial time before human time began. Thus many of the stories and legends that are central to Native American oral tradition are more likely to focus on these "timeless" characters and heroes than on events in historical time.

Another aspect of Native American understanding of time pertains to the intricacies of kinship and clan structure. While these relationships are generally viewed as spreading out in a horizontal manner, as illustrated in various charts and diagrams, they can also be understood as a record of the temporal evolution of life within the family or wider community. As such, these clan and kinship interrelations thoroughly structure daily and yearly life by regulating rites of passage and rituals. The culmination of these cyclical patterns is, of course, death itself. Death does not represent the end or termination of life so much as it symbolizes life's fulfillment, either as the achievement of a harmonious existence or as proof of courage and loyalty in battle. Even human destiny after death is typically not portrayed as a continuation of time, but more as a non-temporal state. The pattern here remains cyclic rather than temporal.

Rituals and rites and their connection to worldviews are discussed in some detail in chapter 5. Many crucial ceremonies revolve around the harvesting of crops, in an agricultural community, or around the seasonal hunting of game, among hunters and gatherers. In either case, the ceremonies tend to follow the yearly cyclical pattern and serve as peoples' way of ensuring the *renewal* of their world and community life. Other rituals and rites, such as the Potlatch and the Sun Dance, serve to highlight or commemorate specific events or announcements by different groups or individuals.

Many of the more important ceremonies center on the life of the individual person within the family and the broader community. Both the birth of a child and its reception of its initial name are typically marked by special ritual patterns. The passage from childhood to adulthood is almost always considered an extremely important step and follows a specific ceremonial procedure. For males among the Plains Indians this rite generally takes the form of a "vision quest" in which the individual endures great hardship and encounters his guiding spirit. For females the passage to womanhood is usually less rigorous, but may involve all-night vigils, a vigorous run, the blessing ceremony of a medicine man or woman, and a ritual meal. Marriage ceremonies also play a significant part in life, with entire clans and tribes being involved. The members of the extended family are closely connected with a married couple in most Native American cultures.

Chapter 6 describes the main elements of an individual's life in relation to the notion of *balance* or harmony. Many peoples envision life as a journey along a path, as was mentioned previously. The goal of life is to maintain a balance on this path so as to achieve a full and harmonious maturity in one's later years. Life is understood as difficult; indeed, it is often depicted as a maze or labyrinth through which one must find his or her own way. There are, to be sure, traditions and the teachings of the elders to guide one along the way, as well as the help of one's own guiding spirit. When something disrupts the balance or harmony, certain rituals and medicines can be provided by a shaman in order to set things right again.

When people live in small, frequently threatened groups, a premium is placed on group loyalty and courage. Everyone must work hard and together, whether to find and process the food supply or to defend the group against the possibility of attack. Thus much of adulthood in Native American life is focused on ways to evoke and ensure these qualities in each person. The industry and faithfulness of wives and the skills and bravery of "warriors" are seen as indispensable. What the West has come to denigrate as "old age" Native Americans have generally viewed as the full realization of human life, characterized by great wisdom, peace, and "beauty." At the end of a life of harmony and balance one can expect to be at peace with all of nature, other people, and the divinities. These are the supreme virtues among the majority of groups.

The final chapter of this book is devoted to a consideration of the impact of Western European culture on that of Native America, highlighting the conflict between two quite diverse worldviews and the resulting near destruction of the latter by the former. From the initial stages of contact, whether in the Southwest or the Northeast, the sociopolitical as well as the religious values of what has come to be called the "dominant culture" have been those of conquest, exploitation, and domination. Through warfare and disease the white man's worldview has been forced upon that of the indigenous peoples of this continent. The processes of relocation and containment on reservations, together with religious "conversion," have nearly brought an end to both the world and the worldviews of Native Americans.

The choices left for Native American peoples in the face of this onslaught have, until fairly recently, been limited to eventual elimination or slow assimilation into the Euro-American culture. Life on reservations basically led nowhere and life off reservations has always been very difficult at best and impossible at worst. Within recent years, however, there has been emerging a legitimate renewal of Native American culture, a virtual renaissance of pride and growth. All over the country a great deal of energy is being put into revitalizing traditions, languages, and values. Native American schools and colleges, located on reservations and run by Indian leaders and teachers, are beginning to establish a whole new model for an integration of the two worldviews, an integration which may well ensure the survival and enhancement of the Native American way.

The final section of this volume is a collection of readings that present a cross section of early accounts of Native American peoples' basic beliefs about the origin and structure of the world and their own place in it. These readings are offered in order to provide some concrete and direct, albeit brief, documentation of the broad themes explored in the book. Inconsistencies in spelling are as they appear in the original readings. An effort has been made to include accounts which are not generally accessible in other collections.

NOTE

1. Robert Redfield, "The Primitive World View," *Proceedings of the American Philosophical Society* 96 (1952): 30–36.

Chapter One

Time and Space— An Overview

The first order of business when setting out to explore the diverse and fascinating views of reality and life exhibited by Native Americans is to get a feel for the lay of the land over time. This chapter provides a brief sketch of the history and environment that form the context for the worldviews of Native American peoples. In addition, attention is paid to the diversity of cultures and languages which have served to embody the relationship between this context and the resultant worldviews.

MIGRATIONS AND BEGINNINGS

Until quite recently the general scholarly consensus has been that the peoples who initially populated North America migrated across the Bering Strait land bridge from Siberia during the Pleistocene period before the passing of the Ice Age. This migration is thought to have taken place over a long span of time and to have consisted of several waves. The dates for these migratory waves are typically set somewhere between 10,000 and 50,000 years ago. However, as a result of recent and ongoing research there is now a tendency to push these dates further and further back. In fact, current archaeological work at Monte Verde in southern Chile seems to date that site at around 20,000 years ago. This not only raises difficulties for the Bering Strait hypothesis, but suggests that some people may have migrated by boat from the Pacific islands. In any case, the migrations of the initial human inhabitants are thought to have followed those of various large prehistoric animals throughout the Americas.

A nomadic, hunting and gathering way of life seems to have characterized most Native American peoples until about 2,000 B.C.E., except in Mexico where it appears that a general shift to simple forms of agriculture began to take place around 5,000 B.C.E. Settled village life in stable dwellings, with domesticated animals, pottery and weaving skills, and the use of the bow and arrow became the more typical pattern. As would be expected, these changes came slowly and at different times and places throughout the continent. Nevertheless, when they did occur they gave rise to the development of distinct cultural patterns in different parts of North America. These prehistoric cultures form the roots out of which the worldviews of traditional peoples arose and evolved, and thus it is important to obtain a rough understanding of their character.

In the Southwest, from the Sonora Desert, including northern Mexico, to the southern regions of Utah and Colorado encompassing Arizona and New Mexico, a number of diverse cultures arose and faded within about the same time frame, beginning around 500 B.C.E. and ending around 1200–1400 C.E. The people who settled in the area of the Mogollon mountains, on the border between southern Arizona and New Mexico, continued to rely on hunting long after they had adopted the more sedentary life associated with agriculture. Early on they lived in "pit houses," log frames over holes dug in the ground, covered with branches. Later they began to build pueblo-type houses out of large rocks and adobe plaster. A subculture known as the "Salado" arose out of the interaction between these Mogollon peoples and the "Anasazi" living to the north.

The culture that arose on the desert of southern Arizona along the converging valleys of the Gila, Santa Cruz, and Salt Rivers is usually called "Hohokam" from the word for "vanished ones" in the Pima language. The Hohokam people devised an intricate system of irrigation canals and dams, using woven mat valves and shallow ditches to bring water to their vast fields of corn, beans, squash, tobacco, and cotton. These people lived primarily in pit houses similar to those of the Mogollon, but they also built ball courts and platform mounds which seem to have been used for special occasions and suggest the influence of Mesoamerican cultures. The people of the Hohokam culture were most likely the first to devise the process of using acid to etch designs on shells obtained from the shores of the Pacific and the Sea of Cortez.

In the "Four Corners" area where northern Arizona and New Mexico meet southern Utah and Colorado, there arose a people now known as the "Anasazi," from the Navajo word for "ancient enemies." The Anasazi people were perhaps the most influential prehistoric group in the Southwest. They developed a pueblo form of housing. Many of their buildings were built into large caves in the cliffs within the many canyons of the area, such as those at Mesa Verde and Canyon de Chelly. The Anasazi also constructed extensive towns and villages of three- and four-storied houses, complete with verandahs and terraces, connected by ladders. The most extensive and well-preserved pueblo center is in Chaco Canyon, New Mexico. It consisted of at least a half dozen distinct pueblo communities joined by an extensive system of roads and trails. These people had an intricate system for conserving and using the little rainfall that came their way.

There were other, smaller cultures in the Southwest, such as the Patayan in the desert along the Colorado River, the Sinagua in the Verde Valley of central Arizona, and the Salado in the Salt River Valley. These, along with the major groups just discussed, all passed away, perhaps primarily because of the twenty-five-year drought between 1275 and 1300 C.E., although recent scholarship seems to indicate there may well have been political or religious causes as well.

Most probably these people evolved into the Pueblo peoples of the Rio Grande area and the Hopi, as well as the "Pima" and "Papago" peoples of the Arizona desert. Although we know very little about these ancient cultures' worldviews, it is safe to say that since they were primarily farmers they understood the life-giving forces of the earth and paid attention to the cycles of the seasons and to the patterns of the heavenly bodies.

In southeastern and midwestern North America there arose what today are popularly known as the "Mound Builder" cultures of the Adena and Hopewell peoples. These groups developed extensive agricultural communities along the Ohio River Valley and down the Mississippi River Valley. They were characterized by the various mounds they built, which seem to have been central to their political and religious life. The Adena culture was centered in Ohio and existed from about 1000 B.C.E.

to 200 C.E., while the Hopewell culture was more extensive, stretching more than a thousand miles from east to west and from north to south. It spanned the period from about 300 B.C.E. to 700 C.E. There is no consensus as to where the forerunners of these mound building cultures came from, nor as to why these cultures faded out. It is clear that they were succeeded by the Mississippian culture which probably used its larger mounds as temples.

The Mississippian culture was essentially similar to that of the Adena and Hopewell, but there seems to have been a far more extensive Mesoamerican influence, especially with respect to the size and significance of the temple mounds around which the people structured their lives. They were master farmers and traders, and the extent and complexity of their economic achievement would seem to indicate an equally sophisticated and complex sociopolitical system. The largest and most famous temple mound site is Cahokia, near St. Louis. This city stretched over six miles along the Illinois River, contained 85 temple and burial mounds, and sustained a population of about 75,000 people. The largest mound covered sixteen acres at its base and stood over 100 feet high. The mounds were all made of dirt and were rectangular in shape. Many are still standing today.

The Mississippian culture lasted until just before contact with European culture in the seventeenth century. Some anthropologists have suggested that the Natchez people of the lower Mississippi valley, who interacted with French traders when the latter were exploring the Southeast region, are direct descendants of the Mississippian culture. The French traders, whose presence contributed to the demise of the Natchez through the transmission of diseases, nevertheless managed to record many of their beliefs and practices. The Natchez seem to have had a preoccupation with death, which linked them both to the mound building cultures before them, by virtue of their many burial mounds and artifacts, as well as to Mesoamerican cultures, such as those of the Mayans and Aztecs. We shall return in later chapters to the implications of these characteristics for an understanding of the worldviews involved.

The foregoing account of these prehistoric cultures is made possible by the significant archaeological record left by the structures these people built. Not only are the remains still standing, because of their size and the cooperation of the climate, but they frequently contain well-preserved and articulate artifacts. These factors and conditions do not obtain, unfortunately, in the other areas of the continent, such as the frozen North and tropical South. In addition to the Southwest and Southeast, the main cultural locales of Native American peoples are the Northeast, the High Plateau and the Great Basin between the Rocky and Cascade mountain ranges of the west, the Northwest coastal strip from British Columbia down through the states of Washington and Oregon, the California coast, and the Great Plains.

It is possible that the peoples just mentioned represent a second wave of nomadic migration across the Bering Strait. A third wave may well have consisted of the Inuit and Aleut peoples who now inhabit the Arctic regions of Alaska and Canada, as well as the Athapascan peoples who dwell in the subarctic regions. It is virtually impossible to say much about the beginnings of the cultures of these latter peoples because of the restrictions imposed by the climate and resultant lifestyle. On the basis of genetic and linguistic data it is clear that they came out of Siberia quite recently, perhaps around 5,000 years ago, and did so by boat and/or on ice floes. In addition to possessing different physical characteristics, the Inuit and Aleut peoples speak a language quite distinct from the Athapascan spoken by those living in the subarctic area.

In considering those groups comprising the second migratory wave, it is helpful to follow the counterclockwise course already established in the discussion of the cultures of the Southwest and the Southeast. The peoples of the Northeast lived in the forests and low mountain ranges which stretch from the Atlantic coast to the Great Lakes and down to the Carolina Piedmont. Most congregated along the shores of bodies of water, including rivers, and thus were fishers as well as hunters and farmers. Because these people did not build large structures and because the climatic conditions were not conducive to long-term preservation, there is less prehistoric material from which to construct cultural hypotheses than in other areas.

The climate of the Pacific Northwest coastal region is not nearly as harsh as that of the Northeast, but the extreme dampness makes it almost as difficult to find ancient artifacts on which to base any sound conclusions about prehistoric life. One significant exception is the discovery of a village that had been buried in a huge mud slide near Ozette on the coast of the Olympic Peninsula in Washington State. Here entire cedar longhouses, 80 feet in length, together with thousands of significant artifacts, have been uncovered and are now on permanent display in the Cultural Center of the Makah Indians in Neah Bay, Washington. In addition to reed sandals and rain hats, sleeping mats, baskets, and ropes, these people made elaborate wooden boxes and fishhooks. It is estimated that the village was covered by the mud slide around 1600 C.E.

The peoples who initially populated the Great Basin and High Plateau region of the inland western states, Idaho, Utah, Nevada, and western Colorado, also remain a mystery to us. Although the hot, arid climatic conditions are much more favorable to the survival of artifacts, fewer people lived in this region and they were essentially nomadic hunters and gatherers, so they have left a limited archaeological record. There is evidence of ancient habitation in numerous dry cave sites, however, where various types of rock art have been found. It was not until after contact with Europeans that the peoples of these areas, whom we know today as the Utes, the Shoshoni, and the Paiutes, acquired the horse and developed more extensive and complex cultures.

The coastal area of California, including the low-lying mountain ranges of the north, as well as the inland valleys, was heavily populated for many centuries prior to the arrival of European explorers and missionaries in the sixteenth century. Because of the mountainous terrain, the many different groups were relatively isolated from one another and thus developed distinctive cultural patterns. Food throughout this area was plentiful, and these peoples were able to thrive without recourse to agriculture. Nuts, berries, fish, and small game provided ample sustenance for those who lived here, clustering along the shores of the Pacific Ocean and the many rivers and lakes. The relative isolation of these peoples from one another would seem to be the chief reason for the density and diversity of languages spoken in this region.

The Great Plains area of North America is the final one to be mentioned in our survey because it was the last one to be populated by Native American peoples. This vast region, stretching from central Canada to Texas and from the Rocky Mountains to the Mississippi River, was initially inhabited by wandering bands of hunters who left vast numbers of what today are known as Clovis and Folsom spearheads used in the hunting of the numerous buffalo (bison) roaming the region. Some of the early, more culturally complex inhabitants of the plains were the Mandans and the Hidatsas. There was little farming in this region due to the scarcity of water, and it was not easy to hunt buffalo on foot. After people in these areas had acquired horses, as well as guns, from the Spanish *conquistadores*, however, the Great Plains became an important center of Native American life and culture. Indeed, it is these people that others think of when picturing Native Americans, riding horses and wearing long flowing headresses.

GEOGRAPHY AND ENVIRONMENT

It is now possible to turn to the actual geological and ecological charac-teristics of the North American regions in order to understand better the particular qualities of the cultures that emerged within them. Geological and ecological characteristics not only affect the specific elements of a given culture's adaptation to an area, but they have significant bearing on the shape of its worldview as well. For the concepts of space and earth, as well as the character of animal life, play a central role in people's understanding of reality and their place in it.

As a glance at a relief map of North America reveals, there is a very wide variety of geological formations and resultant climatic conditions on this continent. Moreover, west of the continental divide these forma-tions and conditions change quite dramatically within a short distance. Thus, for instance, in the Pacific Northwest the Cascade Mountains sep-arate the damp, densely forested coastal strip from the arid plains of the inland plateau. The total temperature range on the coast fluctuates roughly between 30 and 85 degrees Fahrenheit, while on the eastern side of the mountains it varies between −20 and 110, yet the actual distance from one to the other is only about 50 miles. The same situation obtains in California, where one can drive from the coastal plain over mountains to the desert in a few hours.

The variation in vegetation and wildlife that accompanies these wide geological differences obviously strongly impacts cultural patterns, since to a great degree these patterns reflect the ways in which people manage to subsist in relation to their environment. In many cases the availability

FIG. 1.1. MAP OF MAIN NORTH AMERICAN GEOLOGICAL REGIONS

and nature of a water supply directly determine what can be eaten and/or grown. In addition, these factors all play an important role in the formation of a people's worldview, in their understanding of the character of reality and how they are related to it. People who are primarily hunters and gatherers develop different views than horticulturalists do.

On the eastern side of the Great Divide, however, the changes in geology and climate, together with those in vegetation and wildlife, are not nearly so dramatic. The Great Plains of the Midwest flow almost imperceptibly into the low mountain ranges which separate them from the eastern seaboard. The temperature variation between the area around the Great Lakes and the area of the Gulf Coast, for instance, while significant, is gradual. Along the Atlantic coast, as on the West Coast, there are dense forests, extending into the mountain ranges, while to the west of these mountains there are mostly grasslands.

One other major contrast is that between the low-lying nature of the vast region stretching from the Rocky Mountains across the great river valleys of the Ohio, Missouri, and Mississippi to the Appalachians, including the Smokies, and the high altitude of the desert plateau situated between the Cascades along the Pacific coast and the Rockies. Although both of these areas are relatively flat, the extreme difference in elevation between them produces an extreme difference in lifestyles. The food sources are quite distinct, and this strongly affects population size, movement, and cultural characteristics. One major contrast in worldviews pertains to the role played by the sun in religions and ways of life.

Beginning again with the *Southwest* region, a brief survey of the specific environmental characteristics of the major geological and cultural areas will facilitate a better understanding of the diverse paths of life exhibited by North American Indian peoples. The aridity of the entire *Southwest* is its most consistent environmental feature. The annual rainfall ranges from 20 inches in some places to around 4 inches in others. Average altitude ranges between 2,500 and 10,000 feet above sea level. Thus, in addition to vast stretches of desert, the area contains numerous rolling mountain ridges, steep-walled canyons, and mountain ranges. The deserts are full of cactus, mesquite, Joshua, and palm trees, while the higher elevations support large forests of pine and fir trees, as well as many pinyon and juniper trees.

While there is not much edible wildlife in the desert, apart from rabbits, coyote, birds, snakes, and javelina, the mountains are populated with a variety of deer, mountain lions, and bears. Thus during the wintertime people lived in the warmer desert, near rivers, engaging in horticulture and making use of the various ways in which cactus, agave, and yucca plants

FIG. 1.2. MAP OF MAJOR NATIVE AMERICAN CULTURAL AREAS

can be rendered edible. In the summertime they moved into the cooler mountains and hunted game, engaged in some farming, and gathered pinyon nuts and berries. Others, in the more northerly regions, remained stationary, dwelling in pueblo communities and doing subsistence farming.

The *Southeast*, by contrast, is characterized by a nearly uniform geological and environmental landscape. Although there are rolling mountains and hills, there is also a great deal of flat, arable land and there are vast areas of grassland. This area is bordered by many miles of coastal waters fed by numerous rivers and marshes. Much of the land is heavily forested and contains a great deal of animal life, berries, and nuts. Thus it was possible for people in this area to hunt, gather, and farm, as well as fish in both fresh and salt water. The climate of the Southeast is mostly mild, with short winters and warm, humid summers. There is ample rainfall and rich soil, especially near the Mississippi Delta. It is not surprising that this region was able to support the large population and complex culture of the people known as the Mound Builders.

There is some reason to believe that the culture that emerged in this region was strongly influenced by those of Mesoamerica, for example, that of the Yucatan Mayans. The most obvious point of likely influence is the emphasis placed on the construction of large, multilevel temples or mounds to serve as the center of political and religious life. The use of enhanced elevation as both a literal and a symbolic way of delineating superiority reflects a distinctive approach to the expression of a culture's worldview. The understanding of vertical space as an indication of hierarchical values is a concept to which we shall return later. It is perhaps to be seen as more appropriate to those living in an area of low elevation, such as the builders of the Mayan pyramids in the Yucatan.

The *Northeast* region, from the Great Lakes to the Atlantic coast in the east and to the Smoky Mountains in the south, contains mountains, valleys, rivers, lakes, and ocean shores. Throughout this vast area there is an abundance of woodlands and deep forests, composed of both deciduous and coniferous trees. The wood from these trees provided shelter, fuel, and tools, as well as a great many animals as the primary food source. So, while they did a good deal of gathering, fishing, and farming, the Native Americans of the Northeast were mainly hunters of deer, bear, and very many smaller animals. The climate of the region includes warm, humid summers and cold, snowy winters, necessitating a variety of eating and living styles.

In the northern part of this region, in and around the Great Lakes, people often traveled by canoe, engaged in extensive trapping, and traded with one another. It was through this type of enterprise that these Native Americans first came into contact with Europeans, namely, French explorers and trappers. While there was a great similarity of cultures among the people of the Northeast, there were differences as well. Perhaps the most significant and influential grouping in this area was the Iroquois Confederacy of what is now northern and western New York State. Here five, later six, distinct peoples joined together in order to stabilize their area through peaceful cooperation and united defense. This produced a common worldview and value system.

The *Northwest coastal region* is characterized by an amazing number of inlets, bays, and fiords, tucked in between dense, extensive forests. This extremely narrow corridor, lying between the Cascades and the Pacific Ocean, stretches nearly 2,000 miles from southern Alaska to northern California. Because of the high mountains, the numerous coastal inlets, and the dense woodlands, travel in this area was almost entirely by canoe, kayak, or longboat. While in the mountains there is considerable snow in the winter, along the coast the climate is extremely temperate, with the temperature varying only a few degrees each day, whatever the season. The rainfall is prodigious, the coast is warmed by the Japanese current, and the many rivers are full of salmon.

In addition to fishing, the inhabitants of this region gathered the many nuts and berries growing in the forest and hunted deer, bear, seal, and sea lion. The availability of cedar wood for fashioning fishhooks, harpoons, and bows and arrows, as well as huge long houses and longboats, made it possible for the people here to survive with some ease. Not only is it relatively easy to split cedar into long, straight planks which can be roped together to make walls, but cedar is quite easy to carve and resists rot and insect infestation. Some of those living in this area also engaged in whaling, paddling their longboats far out to sea. The whale, as well as the bear and the salmon, played a significant role in the traditions and rituals of many groups.

Along the coast of Oregon and California the terrain and climate remain very much the same as in the Northwest until one reaches the area just north of San Francisco Bay. The rest of the *California coastal region* divides up into three quite distinct geological and climatic locales. The coast itself is characterized by beaches and rolling hills, while the inland area alternates between arable river valleys and deserts. These two contrasting zones are separated by a high mountain range, the Sierra Nevada, which is a continuation of the Cascades. The coastal weather is mild all year round, except in the most southerly parts extending to the Baja Peninsula, which can be extremely hot in the summer. Even the inland river valleys become very hot during the growing season, receiving rain only in the winter. The mountains of California are thickly wooded and are inhabited by a great variety of wildlife. They receive a large amount of snow in the winter.

Because of its mountainous terrain, travel along the northern coast of California, as in the Pacific Northwest, is quite difficult on foot, so people moved about by boat. A great deal of fishing was done in the many rivers, while the mountains yielded plenty of game. The people of southern California, however, were very active on the ocean, fishing, and even farming on the many islands that dot the coastline. Indeed, fish was almost the only food source in the entire Baja area. Those people who dwelt in the fertile river valleys of California depended on subsistence farming and hunting in the mountains for their livelihood.

Even though the peoples of the *Great Basin* and *High Plateau* regions lived near those on the coast, the mountains that separated the Great Basin and High Plateau dwellers from the people to the west, as well as from the Plains Indians to the east, created a totally distinct geological and climatic environment. This area is cradled between two nearly inaccessible mountain ranges and is over a mile high. The air is thin and dry, the weather is hot in the summer and cold in the winter, and except for ponderosa pine forests in the mountains, there is almost no vegetation. Since there are no river outlets to the ocean from the Great Basin in the south, the salt content of both land and water in this area is high; hence the Great Salt Lake in Utah. The plateau to the north, extending well into Canada, on the other hand, is the home of a vast river system, the best-known of its rivers being the Columbia and the Fraser.

Although the peoples of the plateau area were primarily fishers like those of the Northwest, they engaged more in nomadic hunting than in either gathering or farming. Thus they were somewhat similar to the plains peoples in lifestyle. Actually, passing through the Rocky Mountains, especially by way of what is now Montana, was far easier than trying to cross over the Cascades to the west. For this reason there was far more contact between the plateau peoples and those of the plains, both before and after contact with Europeans. This was the area traversed by the Lewis and Clark expedition, as well as by Chief Joseph's Nez Perce when fleeing from the U.S. Army. As both groups discovered, the winters here can be brutal.

Finally we turn again to the *Great Plains* region. As anyone who has driven across, or even flown over, this vast area will remember, it is a seemingly endless expanse of treeless grasslands crisscrossed by numerous rivers, around which cluster small gatherings of cottonwood and willow trees. It is a land of prairies and plains, of grazing bison, of powerful winds, dust storms, dry bitter winters, and hot humid summers. Not many people lived here on a permanent basis prior to being able to hunt bison on horseback. None of the usual sources of food, like nuts and berries, fish, and crops such as corn and squash, were available in any abundance. In addition to bison, there were, to be sure, many other forms of game, both large and small, from rabbits to deer. Those who lived near the few major rivers, such as the Platte, the Missouri, and the Mississippi, were able to develop simple irrigation techniques for growing some basic crops and thus established more lasting and extensive cultures.

On the basis of this brief survey of the geography and environments of North America, it is easy to see why different groups of Native Americans living in distinct locales developed diverse cultural patterns. Where and how a group of people live greatly affects the way they come to conceive of themselves and of the nature of reality. It is also true, however, that there are many commonalities among Native American groups, as the overview of their cultures provided in the remaining pages of this chapter makes clear. The succeeding chapters will pinpoint these differences and similarities.

CULTURES AND LANGUAGES

Within the context provided by the preceding sections of this chapter, it is now possible to reflect on the different, specific cultural patterns which arose among various Native American peoples. Since the primary means

of cultural transmission is always a people's native language, it is necessary to examine the diversity and character of Native American language
families when discussing cultural patterns. Some linguists argue that language shapes culture as much as it transmits it, so a consideration of this
relationship is also in order.

Every individual is born into a culture which not only shapes his or
her basic thought patterns, practices, and values but largely shapes the
individual's very identity as well. Thus a person may be thought of as a
relational reality constituted by the symbolic and behavioral interaction
between his or her individual qualities, be they genetic or acquired, and
the characteristics of the society within which the person is raised. Even
self-understanding is mediated in and through one's status and role
within the culture into which one is born and in which one is raised. Different cultures, and even different subgroups within cultures, define
status and roles, as well as the dynamics among them, in diverse and specific ways. In exploring the cultural patterns of Native Americans it is
necessary to pay attention to the ways in which these different factors
play themselves out within the diverse traditions.

One important distinction that can be made is that between cultures
which emphasize *ascribed* status and those which stress *achieved* status. In
the former, one's position or rank at birth is taken to be the crucial deter-
minant of one's character, role, and destiny, while in the latter there is
much more flexibility with regard to these. Another significant issue is the
amount of emphasis placed on *individuality*, on the one hand, and *social
conformity*, on the other. In some cultures there is considerable room for a
person to develop his or her own belief system, while in others everyone is
expected to blend into the group, to be as much like others as possible.

Among Native American peoples there seems to have been a full
range of patterns between each of these extremes. In precontact times
the hunting and gathering cultures seem to have had a less complex
mode of social organization, with only minor differentiation among the
roles and identities available to their individual members. Conformity to
the needs and practices of the group received the greatest approval. At
the same time, however, since there was little elaborate political structure in such societies, this conformity was not imposed from above, but
was largely a function of the practical needs and decisions of community

life. Thus, in a sense, the contrast between individuality and social conformity would not even have arisen in such cultures, the primary emphasis being on cooperation and custom. The peoples of the Northwest may well have been an exception to this pattern, as we shall see.

When it comes to cultures organized around agriculture, the picture is quite different. Here the need for a corresponding form of hierarchical sociopolitical organization by means of which to administer large-scale planting and harvesting, as well as to construct irrigation systems and oversee food distribution, gave rise to more complex and diverse patterns of both individual and societal identity. The Mound Builders of the Southeast and the Pueblo peoples of the Southwest were both characterized by a complex, formalized social structure and a diversity of roles and statuses. Here again it is possible to hypothesize about the possible influence of Mesoamerican cultures, for example the culture of the Aztecs, who were roughly contemporaries of both the Mound Builders and the Pueblo peoples.

Many of the peoples of the Northwest, while not essentially agricultural in nature, also developed complex sociopolitical systems. Perhaps this was because their food supply of fish, berries, and wildlife was stationary and abundant. Thus the economy had to be planned and administered rather than strenuously pursued, as the Kwakiutl Potlatch reveals.

Another way to think of these issues is in terms of broad patterns of social identity and organization. Some peoples were organized in what may be called "bands," as with simple foragers, while others were grouped together into what may be termed "tribes," which hunted and gathered across a wider area and may have engaged in farming as well. Within some groups there arose subgroups such as "clans," and these frequently factored into marriage and kinship customs. Finally, there were overarching groupings, including the Iroquois Confederacy and the chiefdoms of the Northwest coast.

There are other categories by means of which to examine the contours of various cultures. Often, variations in type of residence from one group to another or even within the same society serve to indicate a significant aspect of a culture's character. Nomadic groups, for instance, generally reside in movable dwellings, such as tepees, which serve as single-family housing units. On the other hand, the long houses of the

Northwest and Northeast reflect a sedentary lifestyle in which larger groups, such as clans, live together cooperatively. Again, the temple mounds of the Southeast suggest special dwellings for religious and/or political leaders, while the pueblo village's "apartment"-like pattern clustered people tightly together in individual family units set around a common plaza and/or ceremonial center known as a *kiva*.

Age and gender also account for a significant degree of social patterning within a culture. Some groups put children into a common group and raise them cooperatively, while others confine them to their immediate natal family. In nearly all Native American groups, elderly folk are treated with special respect as wise and experienced leaders. Even the dead are generally regarded as having achieved a superior position in relation to the group. In parallel fashion, it is safe to say that most Native American people have made a strong distinction between males and females, with the former generally seen as providers and protectors and the latter as householders and nurturers. We shall return to the question of political leadership shortly.

Native American cultures are often divided into different societies for men and women; they have frequently been organized according to other criteria as well. Sometimes it is simply a matter of clan or national identity, as with the Iroquois, for example, and occasionally an entire culture or clan will be grouped and stratified into two or more halves or "moieties," as are the Tewa Pueblo people of the Rio Grande Valley in New Mexico. Most of the time such groupings are assigned and not a matter of choice, but occasionally it is possible for an individual to switch to a different group later in life. Generally this is accomplished by means of an established adoption process. Nearly all Native American groups have procedures for such adjustments.

Perhaps the most important feature of any culture, but especially of Native American cultures, is *kinship*. Some anthropologists say that when one understands the kinship patterns of a people one holds the key that unlocks the remaining dynamics of the culture. In addition to the obvious implications of biological kinship within any family, there are sociocultural kinship patterns that not only reach far beyond the immediate family, but may override biological kinship. Both the behavioral and the terminological aspects of this broader form of kinship are important. The former governs how various persons may and may not relate to one another in everyday life, while the latter governs the designations that delineate these relationships. A few concrete examples will serve to illustrate these points.

Crow Indians call their mother's sister by the same term they use for their mother, and they call their father's brother by the same term they use for their father. Thus a Crow's behavior toward the mother's sister and the father's brother is very similar to that toward the mother and father. Moreover, the biological father's role toward his children is one of affection and support, while the role of his wife's brother, whom we would call the uncle, toward the same children is that of disciplinarian. Some years ago a new teacher at the school on the Crow Reservation found that he was unable to get any help with an unruly student by appealing to the student's father. When he eventually spoke with the mother's brother about the student he got immediate results. When this same teacher seated male and female cousins together in a double school desk, they did not return to school. Only later did he discover that cousins are called and considered to be brothers and sisters among the Crow, and that this seating arrangement was experienced by the students as a form of incest.

In like manner, when a Crow couple have their first child, its grandmothers, on either the mother's or the father's side, may raise it themselves if they feel that the parents are too immature for the job. Thus even the biological kinship relationship may be overridden by cultural kinship patterns. Biological parents who have not yet exhibited behavior appropriate to the achieved status of "parenthood" are sometimes not allowed to raise their own child among the Crow. One reason often given for this practice is that in a society in which many die young, the practice eliminates the possibility of children becoming orphans.

The phenomenon of kinship relations also exerts a powerful influence on politics. Although chiefs and elders are nearly always male throughout North America, people frequently trace lineage and inheritance through the female. Thus not only are property rights passed down through the females of the society, but married males usually go and live with the wife's family. Moreover, it is the general rule that males must choose wives outside of the family, clan, or tribe within which they have been raised. Frequently, men do the public negotiating, but the real power of decision making lies with women. Thus matrilineality sometimes actually results in matriarchy. It may also lead to levirate marriages. Among the Crow and the Iroquois the brother of a woman's husband must marry her if her husband dies, thus minimizing the difficulties faced by widows.

Generally speaking the less complex the lifestyle and subsistence pattern of a people, the more horizontal or egalitarian, the more shared, is the political power. Often in a more complex and populous group, power is arranged vertically or hierarchically. Even here, however, there is a tendency for power to be in the hands of one ruler or "big man," though sometimes it seems that a group of priestly "holy men" may hold nearly all of the clout. The peoples of the Great Plains, for instance, clearly illustrate the former pattern, while the Pueblo peoples embody both, since they have both religious and secular political structures.

As mentioned earlier, there is a fundamental sense in which language may be said to be the most crucial aspect of any culture, since it is by means of speech that a people enculturates its children into the community. Not only are the traditions and practices of a given group transmitted by storytelling and oral instructions, but it is by being drawn into speech through conversations, games, songs, and the like that infants actually become members not only of their own society but of the human race in general. Language is not an optional aspect of what we know as human culture; it is the key vehicle and focal lens through which it must be understood. Thus a brief account of Native American language patterns will enhance our exploration of the worldviews which language mediates.

At the time of first contact with European culture, there were enormous numbers of languages in North America. Linguistic scholars estimate that there may have been as many as 2,000 different *languages*, not dialects, spoken in the Americas prior to the coming of Europeans. Although most of these tongues are no longer in use today, for a variety of reasons, at least 200 languages are still spoken by North American Indians. More distinct languages are spoken in northern California alone than in all of Europe. This incredible linguistic diversity continues to be one of the greatest and most intriguing mysteries for anthropologists and linguists. A strenuous and increasingly successful effort is being made all across the country by Native Americans to sustain and revive their languages within their own communities.

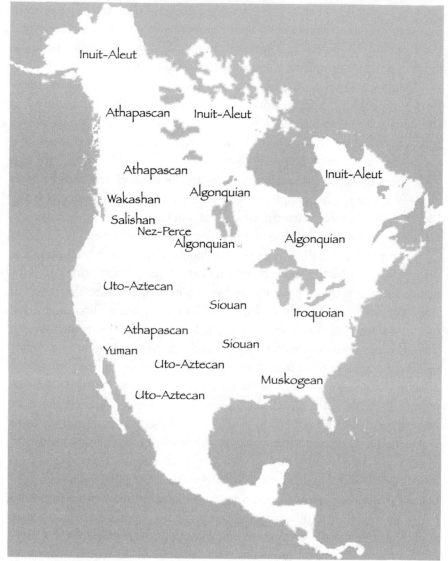

FIG. 1.3. MAP SHOWING LANGUAGE FAMILIES FOUND IN NORTH AMERICA

This linguistic multiplicity is related to questions of origin and migration. The distinctive character of the numerous tongues suggests that their speakers have been separated from one another for a very long period, thus implying an extremely early arrival at their locations at the time of first contact with Europeans. This, in turn, raises difficult questions as to the number and dates of their initial migrations into the continent and their population of it. Some studies have estimated that the degree of linguistic diffusion and evolution involved here requires at least 50,000 years in which to develop. Recent work in the field of genetics, using DNA samples, tends to substantiate the possibility of an early arrival.

As the map showing the distribution of the major language families indicates, there are at least twelve distinct language families, which correspond to the major cultural areas and group locations already introduced. Along with the amazing diversity of languages in the California coastal region, another interesting puzzle is the presence of Athapascan-speaking peoples, the Navajo and Apache, in the midst of an area dominated by Uto-Aztecan and other speakers. Most scholars agree that the Navajo and Apache came to this region from northwest Canada within the last five hundred years or so. The speakers of the Uto-Aztecan languages, on the other hand, most likely came to this region from Mesoamerica over a thousand years ago. The East Coast of North America has always been dominated by Algonquian speakers, except for the speakers of Iroquoian languages in what is now upper New York State.

While this is not the place to launch into a full-scale examination of Native American languages, a few specific points should be made. It is impossible to generalize about all the different tongues, since they are as diverse as they are numerous. It can be said, however, that many of them bear very little if any similarity to Indo-European languages. One rather prevalent pattern differentiation between these two groups of language families is that while Indo-European tongues tend to focus on *nouns* as the names for entities and qualities, Native American speech patterns often emphasize *verbs* and events as the nexus of meaning.

In a number of Native American languages, up to ten parts or units may be required in order to make the verb complete and give meaning to a sentence. In addition to the verb stem, which has no meaning by itself, there may be a whole host of prefixes and suffixes, indicating who or what is acting and being acted upon, from which direction, for what purpose, in what mode, and so on. Until all the required pre- or postpositions are filled in, nothing can really be said. Thus it is the subtleties of the verb that serve as the "parts of speech," rather than nouns, particles, or clauses. This is what lies behind the misleading notion that the Inuit have many words for snow; the verb for snowing has a myriad of facets and patterns. This feature of Native American language is called "polysynthetic" and renders it highly complex.

An interesting example of the verb-centered quality of Native American tongues can be found in the Hopi language. Whereas in Indo-European languages architectural space and locations are designated by means of nouns or names, in Hopi this is done by indicating the activity taking place, using a specific verb form. The ceremonial space in which the Hopi engage in ritual activity has been given the name *kiva* by anthropologists, but in Hopi speech the stem of this locution is used as a verb and can also serve to indicate other activities which take place within this space, such as weaving, relaxing, and holding meetings. Similar features include the Hopi concern with *aspect* rather than tense in verb formulations, and with a dual form of nouns as well as with singular and plural forms.

A parallel example can be found in the Navajo tongue, even though the Hopi and Navajo are members of quite distinct language families. In the Navajo expression "He picks something up," the action designated cannot be expressed merely by uttering the stem of the verb; one must specify what is being picked up, by whom, and how through the use of the different suffixes required to fill the post-positions of the verb. Many of the differentiations used pertain to very specific differences among sizes, shapes, textures, and colors. Thus the language patterns of a people will strongly influence the manner in which they perceive, construe, and interact with the world around them. In short, these patterns will help shape their worldview. In the following chapters the general contours of these worldviews will be our central focus.

Chapter Two

Origin Stories

It is often difficult for those of us who have grown up in what Marshall McLuhan has called the "Gutenberg Galaxy" to understand the important role played by oral discourse in cultures that do not convey their traditions, beliefs, and values by means of written language. Although it is more direct and forceful, oral language is also far more precarious than its written counterpart because it is more easily forgotten and/or altered. Moreover, the absence of just one generation may result in the complete loss of a culture's customs and worldview. Speech in oral cultures functions specifically to transfer and reinforce the traditional beliefs and values by means of which a people maintains and sustains itself. In many cases these traditional beliefs and values are embodied in the stories that are told of a people's origin.

STORIES AND MYTHS

We should begin our consideration of the nature and function of Native American origin stories with a brief discussion of the difference between the popular and the reflective uses of the term *myth*. In popular usage, myth is synonymous with the notion of "fairy tale" or untruth. Thus we speak, for example, of the myth of Zeus, or of the myth that hard work is always rewarded, and so on. The reflective or more specialized meaning of the term, however, denotes a story which embodies a timeless and profound truth about a given people's view of the world and of their place in it. Thus literary scholars speak of the myth of Zeus in a way that is quite different from the way historians speak of it, since literary scholars see it as conveying a conceptual and valuational pattern central to the classical Greeks' understanding of life and the powers that existed.

Anthropologists and scholars of religion, as well as many philosophers, use the term *myth* in this more specialized sense to designate those forms of oral discourse that seek to express cultural worldviews. However, because of the confusion and negative connotations surrounding the term *myth*, it is preferable to use the term *story* when discussing this particular function of oral language. This allows for a consideration of the content and significance of the origin stories told by Native American peoples without becoming involved in questions of scientific and historical reliability. This approach does not imply that the stories are unreliable; it simply suggests that our primary concern is with the worldview inherent within them.

A related issue concerns the reliability of the stories handed down by oral tradition. Those who dwell in the world of the written word naturally assume that oral transmission of the beliefs and values of a culture must be subject to systematic error and alteration. We may think, for instance, of the party game where one person whispers something to another, and so on around the circle, until the message comes back to the sender in almost unrecognizable form. However, in cultures where the life of the community depends exclusively on oral communication, the margin of error is far less than in cultures that have learned to rely on the written record. It is not uncommon to encounter people in the Arab world who have memorized the entire Qur'an word for word.

Many oral cultures have designated storytellers whose responsibility it is to retain the culture's crucial stories and relate them on demand. In addition, the elders of any group are generally reliable sources of the stories that embody their society's understanding of the world and their people's place in it. These designated individuals function in much the same way as sacred books in a literate society. The keepers of the traditions, of the wisdom and commitments of a culture, may even be said to serve as the "scripture" of that culture. Of course, this does not eliminate the need for specific interpretations and applications of the teachings conveyed by the sacred stories.

Native Americans, as well as many other oral peoples, pay a great deal of attention to the powerful link between speech and the world. Names indicate the character and nature of what they name, and ritualized verbal formulas and songs are used to invoke and sustain certain realities in a way that signifies the essentially interrelated character of speech and reality. There is an "Orphic" or "performative" thrust to a great deal of Native American speech; reality is thought to be created and shaped by language.

One of the more frequent elements found in Native American origin stories is the presence of speech in the creation of the world. Sam Gill makes this point:

> In several Pueblo stories of creation, the first figure to exist—who, in a sense, has always existed—was Thought Woman. The world was literally formed as she thought what form it should take. Her partners in creation followed her act of creative thinking by naming those things given form by Thought Woman. Thus her acts of creation became humanly meaningful through language; names gave distinction and identity to the forms created.[1]

Another expression of the creative function of language in Native American thought is found in the work of N. Scott Momaday, a Kiowa Indian. In his essay, "The Man Made of Words," he responds to the question, "What is an Indian?"

> I hope to indicate something about the nature of the relationship between language and experience. It seems to me that in a certain sense we are all made of words; that our most essential being consists in language. It is the element in which we think and dream and act, in which we live our daily lives. There is no way we can exist apart from the morality of a verbal dimension.[2]

PRIMORDIAL TIME

The origin stories of Native Americans recount events which "establish" time and history rather than actually take place within them. They are best understood not as scientific accounts but as tales that mark the boundaries and internal structures of a culture. We may speak of these stories in terms of "primordial time" for they tell of the period from and within which the reality of their world was originally established. This primordial time is conceived of as both the time in the far distant past when everything began *and* the system of order that flows therefrom.[3]

Most Native American origin stories just *begin* with certain creative activities performed by specific supernatural and/or divine beings without providing any explanation of how this primordial reality came to be. If we try to put these events into a temporal framework, we must continue to ask what preceded them, *ad infinitum*. If, however, we think of them as stories that mark the parameters of experienced reality and not its chronological order, then we may appreciate them as revealing cultural patterns and values.

Shifting the scene to a different part of the country, here is one version of the Iroquois tale of the creation of the world:

> Before this world came to be, there lived in the Sky-World an ancient chief. In the center of his land grew a beautiful tree which had four white roots stretching to each of the four directions: North, South, East, and West. From that beautiful tree, all good things grew.
>
> Then it came to be that the beautiful tree was uprooted and through the hole it made in the Sky-World fell the youthful wife of the ancient chief, a handful of seeds, which she grabbed from the tree as she fell, clutched in her hand. Far below there were only water and water creatures who looked up as they swam.
>
> "Someone comes," said the duck. "We must make room for her." The great turtle swam up from his place in the depths. "There is room on my back," the great turtle said. "But there must be earth where she can stand," said the duck, and so he dove beneath the waters but he could not reach the bottom. "I shall bring up the earth," the loon then said and he dove, too, but could not reach the bottom. "I shall try," said the beaver and he too dove but could not reach the bottom.
>
> Finally the muskrat tried. He dove as deeply as he could, swimming until his lungs almost burst. With one paw he touched the bottom, and came up with a tiny speck of earth clutched in his paw. "Place the earth on my back," the great turtle said, and as they spread the tiny speck of earth it grew larger and larger and larger until it became the whole world.

Then two swans flew up and between their wings they caught the woman who fell from the sky. They brought her gently down to the earth where she dropped her handful of seeds from the Sky-World. Then it was that the first plants grew and life on this new earth began.[4]

Perhaps the most obvious thing about this story of the origin of the world is that many of the entities which we think of as comprising the world are already present when the story begins. Not only is there a previously existing world, the Sky-World, which contains a tree, a chief, his wife, and many "good things," such as seeds, but there are creatures and features of nature such as a duck, a turtle, a beaver, a loon, a dove, and a muskrat, and even water and mud. No effort is made to explain the origin of these entities and aspects of the world. Although numerous versions of this story are told, none seek to explain the origin of every major feature or character with which the world's story begins.

In this story, the animals not only talk to one another, but they engage in deliberate efforts to protect and sustain the falling woman. Thus the world is construed as being founded on what seems like an accident or malevolent action, while the creatures of the field and forest are seen not only as friendly toward other beings, even supernatural ones, but as on equal terms with them. The overturning of the tree, like the presence of the serpent in the Garden of Eden story, remains unexplained but nature and wildlife are deemed friendly kin from the start. This positive attitude toward the earth and its creatures, relating to them essentially as mother and siblings, respectively, is quite different from that of the Western, Judeo-Christian worldview. The latter construes nature and animal life as created and thus as separate from and completely dependent on the divinity that created them. Humans are superior to the natural world.

It is characteristic of Native American cultures to see all the entities in the world as interdependent, as the Iroquois creation story clearly demonstrates. Even personages who fall from the Sky-World must rely on the good will of the tiny animals of the primeval world for their well-being, and the plant world is also dependent on both the animals and the seeds brought from the upper world by the person who fell from there. This way of looking at reality is often referred to as "naturalism" because it does not make a strong division between the natural and supernatural realms and it endows the animal world with human qualities. It is also frequently termed "animism," since it understands the whole of nature to be animated by personality and spiritual energy.

There is a distinctively "ecological" flavor to the Native American way of portraying the world and the place of humans within it. In the Iroquois origin story, as in many others, the whole of creation is seen as a mutually interdependent ecosystem in which all the participants are symbiotically related to one another. The falling woman brings seeds for plant life, while the animals provide the soil necessary for its growth and guide the woman to a safe place. Human life takes root in a balanced and harmonious garden.

The origin story of the Crow in Montana goes as follows:

> According to the legend, before there was a complete world, there was only water. At that time First-maker, an indolent deity who made strong medicine, ordered a duck to dive to the bottom of the water and bring up a bill full of mud. From this mud, First-maker created the world. He next made the rivers, trees, plants, and mountains. Before he created animals, he heard a coyote howl and remarked to himself, "That is a power of itself. He will always be. . . ." First-maker then created men. . . .[5]

Clearly there are several important similarities between this account and that of the Iroquois. The previous existence of a cosmic body of water, the existence of animals, such as ducks and the coyote, and the use of mud from which to fashion nature, other animals, and humans strike one immediately. There are also some parallels between these accounts and the Book of Genesis, where formless water and mud are both involved in the creation process. Moreover, in the account given in the first chapter of Genesis, which differs from that given in the second chapter, the order of creation is roughly the same as in the Crow story, namely the earth, plant life, animal life, and finally human life. The primordial character of the coyote, however, is unique to the Native American worldview, at least for those west of the Mississippi River. As we shall see, the role of the coyote in Native American stories turns out to be as complex as it is crucial.

The origin story of the Pueblo people, unlike those already discussed, portrays humankind as emerging into the present world from a world or worlds beneath the earth. Thus, rather than being characterized by a downward movement, the peoples of the Rio Grande Valley in New Mexico, as well as the Hopi in Arizona, view the creative order as arising from an upward movement. We shall return to a consideration of the overall significance of such vertical "migrations" in chapter 3. For the present I want to focus on the specifics of the Tewa version of the Pueblo emergence story as told by Alfonso Ortiz, a renowned Tewa anthropologist:

> The Tewa were living in *Sipofene* beneath Sandy Place Lake far to the north. The world under the lake was like this one, but it was dark. Supernaturals, men, and animals lived together at this time and death was unknown. Among the supernaturals were the first mothers of all the Tewa, known as "Blue Corn Woman, near to summer," or the Summer mother, and "White Corn Maiden, near to ice," the Winter mother. . . . After many difficulties and false starts the Tewa eventually climbed up into the present world and began their trek south toward the Rio Grande River. At this time they divided themselves into two groups, the Summer and Winter people, with the former following their chief along the west side of the river and the latter following theirs down the east side. Although they rejoined each other at their present location, the migratory division has remained as perhaps the most distinctive feature of Pueblo sociopolitical life.[6]

The Iroquois origin story subsequently involves the birth of twin boys who set out to create much of the world as we know it. One of these twins personifies good, while the other personifies evil. This dualistic pattern of twin boys explaining good and evil in the world is present in a great many Native American origin stories. The Seneca version of the character and activity of the twins is typical of this dualism:

> When the twins grew to manhood, they set out on their tasks. The Good Spirit made the form of human beings, male and female, in the dust and breathed life into them. He created the good and useful plants and animals of the world. He created the rivers and lakes. He even made the current run both ways in the streams to make travel easy. Meanwhile, the Bad Spirit busied himself with the creation of annoying and monstrous animals, pests, plant blight, and diseases for human beings.

He introduced death. He turned the currents in the streams so they would run only one way. Once he even stole the sun. The Good Spirit tried to reverse these things, but he was not able to reverse them all.[7]

In the origin stories of nearly all peoples and cultures, in North America and around the world, we find such efforts to explain the struggle between good and evil that lies at the heart of so much of human experience. Generally speaking, these efforts seek only to *place* this struggle in relation to the rest of the world without actually trying to explain *why* the struggle is necessary in the overall plan of things. In the Judeo-Christian story, for instance, the serpent just "turns up" in the Garden of Eden without any account of why it is there or who put it there. As in the stories of the twins, the sources of good and evil are incorporated into the worldview without our being told the why and wherefore. The world simply *is* structured in this dualistic format.

The Navajo story of the world's origin serves as a further example of origin stories. Like the Pueblo story, the Navajo account of the origin of the world begins with a series of previous worlds located beneath the present one, worlds which various beings have traversed in their efforts to find a peaceful and harmonious existence. These efforts have repeatedly been thwarted by conflicts, generally between males and females, which seem to have been irresolvable. At last First Man and First Woman emerge onto the earth and human life as we know it begins.

In this story, a new phase of the creation process begins when the original people emerge from a previous world onto the earth's surface. The opening through which they emerge is at the center of Navajo sacred geography and sacred history. This new world is quite different from their earlier worlds. It is covered with water and the winds from the four cardinal directions are invoked to dry up the earth. The landscape is flat and uniform, and here First Man and First Woman talk about what the new world should be like. They open their sacred medicine bundle and use the objects it contains to form spiritual objects or personages, holy figures in human form. Finally, First Man and First Woman build a ceremonial house, a hogan, within which they create what comes to be the Navajo world.

The benevolent creator of the Navajo people is Changing Woman.

She is born into the world previously created by First Man and First Woman in the original house. When Changing Woman reaches maturity she gains possession of the crucial medicine bundle and uses its powers to create corn. By performing ritual acts with epidermal waste, which she rubs on her body and mingles with cornmeal, Changing Woman creates the first Navajo people.[8]

The role of a special creator, such as Changing Woman in the Navajo story, who is the originator of a specific group of people, is repeated in many Native American origin stories. This personage is usually referred to by anthropologists as the "culture hero," since he or she is the one credited with initiating the common life or culture of the people in question. In the origin stories of many peoples of the Northwest coast, for instance, this role is filled by one called the "transformer," a serious-minded culture-bringer who does not engage in unpredictable activity like its paradoxical counterpart the "trickster," sometimes designated "Coyote," who can behave in either malevolent or benevolent ways.[9]

ORIGINAL BEINGS

The beings involved at the origin of the world in the majority of Native American stories are often already on the scene when the story begins. While many other beings are created by and through these original ones, no account is usually given of how the original beings came to be. Perhaps they are thought to have always existed. In any case, a number of creators and creator helpers are often on hand at the outset.

There is nearly always some sort of Supreme Being or High God, who is frequently referred to as the "Great Spirit." The Lakota Sioux call this being *Wakan Tonka*. There has been a great deal of controversy about the relationship between the Supreme Being among Native Americans and the theistic God of the Western theological tradition. There are significant similarities between them, sufficient to warrant at least an exploratory comparison. While both notions entail the essential spiritual reality of the original creator, in contrast to the Western tradition the High God or Great Spirit of Native American belief tends to reside in the distant background of the universe rather than taking a dominant role in its formation and ordering. This is akin to what in the West has been called a "deistic" view, as contrasted to the more traditional Western "theistic" view of God's relation to the world.

The relationship of the Great Spirit to various other creative personages in Native American origin stories is well described by Åke Hultkrantz:

> We have seen that the Supreme Being is at times regarded as a creator. Although he is discernible in mythology and his appearance there is one of individual substance and dramatic action to a greater extent than in religion proper, he is not a typical mythological personage. On the contrary, in mythology he withdraws in favor of other beings who are more closely connected than he to the very beginning of existence: the culture hero, the twin gods, the tribal ancestor. These beings are grouped together in the most diverse combinations in accordance with their historical context.[10]

Against the background of the original primal sea or world ocean, which represents the primordial chaos out of which the world order was created, are found a fairly consistent group of cosmic players who together or in sequence orchestrate the formation of the earth and its inhabitants. Very frequently there is an "Earth Diver," commonly a duck or muskrat, who brings up land from the primal waters. Often, too, there is a spider figure who seems to spin the world into existence out of its own being. Then there are "Father Sky" and "Mother Earth," from whose sexual union proceeds the whole of the natural world, including plants and animals. In Native American thought the entire creative process is complex and naturalistic.

The transition from this general pattern of fixing the world order to the shaping of the particular features of a given people's identity is frequently managed by the "culture hero." This figure is said to be the one responsible for bestowing on a given people their material and spiritual heritage. This hero is not thought of as a god or other religious being but as a cosmic force or personage that brings special gifts to the community and exercises control over its relation to animals, of which it is the master. The raven is the culture hero of the peoples of the Northwest coastal region, while in much of western North America the coyote serves in this capacity. In the Northeast the "Great Hare" is commonly the story of his life and vision with an account of the Sioux worldview, an account that clearly portrays the major characters who were active in the creation of the world in which the Plains Indians lived. Black Elk begins his story in this way:

> It is the story of all life that is holy and is good to tell, and of us two-leggeds sharing in it with the four-leggeds and the wings of the air and all green things; for these are children of one mother and their father is one Spirit. . . . See, I fill this sacred pipe with the bark of the red willow; but before we smoke it, you must see how it is made and what it means. These four ribbons hanging here on the stem are the four quarters of the universe. The black one is for the west where the thunder beings live to send us rain; the white one for the north, whence comes the great white cleansing wind; the red one for the east, whence springs the light and where the morning star lives to give men wisdom; the yellow for the south, whence comes the summer and the power to grow.
>
> But these four spirits are only one Spirit after all, and this eagle feather here is for that One, which is like a father, and also it is for the thoughts of men that rise high as eagles do. Is not the sky a father and the earth a mother, and are not all living things with feet or wings or roots their children?[12]

In Black Elk's account, all living creatures come from the same source and are thus in a real sense brothers and sisters. We shall come back to this theme later on when we consider the place of wildlife in the Native American worldview, especially in relation to the distinction between theistic and pantheistic philosophies. It is sufficient here to note the kinship between humans and plant and animal life.

The common source for all forms of life is, according to Black Elk, the union of the "Father Sky God" and the "Mother Earth God." It is not exactly clear how this notion of a holy cosmic couple as the progenitors of all life on earth is to be coordinated with that of the "One Great Spirit" of which Black Elk also speaks. Further on in his story he refers to the Great Spirit as "Grandfather." This way of speaking seems to have been common among Plains Indians across the Midwest and the West. Perhaps they considered the sky and earth gods as the "children" of the Great Spirit, rather as others think of First Man and First Woman. Or

thought of as the bestower of all cultural values and patterns. Among th
Navajo, "Spider Woman" is said to have brought them the arts in gen
eral and the craft of weaving in particular.

In a great many origin stories a cosmic struggle takes place betwee
the Great Spirit and the culture hero. While the latter generally assist
the former in the basic aspects of creation, it may also seek to alter and/o
steal certain powers in order to make them available to humans. Thi
relationship is reminiscent of that between Prometheus and the gods in
Greek mythology; the gods punished Prometheus for stealing fire and
giving it to humans. The dual nature of the culture hero prompts some
to suggest that it is the same being as the "trickster," which bedevils both
divine beings and humans with its capricious and at times evil acts.[11]

Other important players in many Native American origin stories
include the twins. Sometimes the culture hero is the parent of the twins,
and they represent the two-sided character of the hero, one for good and
the other for evil. At other times, as with the sons of "Changing Woman"
in the Navajo tradition, the twins both work for the well-being of
humanity by destroying the monsters which dwelt in the earth prior to
the creation of people. On the whole, however, it seems that the concept
of the twins is designed to focus and personify the forces of good and evil
as encountered within human experience. This is reminiscent of the
struggle between good and evil found in the religions of the Near East,
especially Persia. In Zoroastrianism, for example, a fundamental dualism
exists between the forces for good and evil, thus giving rise to an eternal
battle into which humans are cast.

Primal parents also frequently take part in the creative enterprise.
These may either be represented as sky and earth, respectively, or as First
Man and First Woman. Generally the peoples and often the creatures of
the world are said to be the result of the sexual union of this primordial
couple. Here, again, we see possible comparisons with the Book of Genesis. Adam and Eve are portrayed as the father and mother of all humankind, and their first offspring are two boys who behave like some of the
twins in the Native American stories. Dualism is characteristic of many
worldviews.

Many of the aforementioned figures are operative in the opening
chapter of *Black Elk Speaks*. The famous Oglala Sioux holy man begins

perhaps sky and earth are simply diverse manifestations of the same Great Spirit.

In Black Elk's account, both the directional patterns and the seasonal cycles of the earth are seen as established by the original creators of the world. Traditional peoples everywhere pay a great deal of attention to such patterns and cycles, since their survival very largely depends on doing so. Native Americans are no exception. We also see that specific colors are associated with the Cardinal Directions and the eagle with the Great Spirit. Other birds and animals also play a significant role.

Further on in his story, Black Elk tells of the coming of the sacred woman, the one who originally gave the sacred pipe to the Sioux people. She came wearing a beautiful white buckskin dress and as she gave the sacred pipe to the chief of the tribe she said:

> Behold! With this you shall multiply and be a good nation. Nothing but good shall come from it. Only the hands of the good shall take care of it and the bad shall not even see it.

As she departed from the midst of the people, she was transformed into a white buffalo.[13] This personage is the culture hero of the Sioux, the "White Buffalo Calf Woman" who brought them their cultural identity and the symbolism around which they focused their political and religious life. Indeed, as Black Elk indicates in his story, it was White Buffalo Calf Woman who taught them to organize their tepees in a circle with one in the center to symbolize her presence among them.[14]

In many Native American origin stories, female characters play an extremely important role. Not only are women at the center of many accounts of the creation process, like First Woman of the Navajo and the Iroquois woman who fell from the sky, but sometimes the culture hero is a woman as well. White Buffalo Calf Woman is a case in point, as is the Spider Woman of the Hopi. The crucial part played by females is reflected in the social and political dimension of Native American life wherever women function as the political power center for their people in choosing male chiefs and serving as the vehicle of family inheritance.

The significance of White Buffalo Calf Woman among the Sioux points the way toward a fuller understanding of the role of animals, birds, and fish in the cultural life of Native American peoples. Not only is the essential character of the food chain discernible wherever one looks, but since the buffalo became the primary, if not almost exclusive source of food for those living on the Plains, it would naturally become the center of their cultural life as well. Add to this the fact that the buffalo was also the source of nearly every other aspect of the material culture of these people, from clothing to weaponry, and its pivotal symbolic role becomes even clearer.

Black Elk also mentions the eagle as the symbol of the Great Spirit, a symbol shared by nearly all Native American cultures. We see the significance of eagles' feathers in a great many rituals and customs, especially those involving special costumes and dances. As Black Elk says, the fourlegged and the winged creatures of the forest, field, and air are regarded as kinfolk, primarily because they are both fellow denizens of the earth and a source of food. When these "brothers and sisters of the earth" are killed for food, proper respect, and even at times apologies, must be offered in order to acknowledge this kinship. Respect for these creatures involves making sure that nothing is wasted in the food procuring and preserving processes. The natural connection between the practical and the spiritual in Native American thought and practice is here made extremely clear.

The question of whether or not the Native American worldview is fundamentally pantheistic deserves to be addressed, if only briefly. Pantheism is the belief that "all is God and God is all," that the universe is essentially one holistic, divine reality composed of what appear to be individual parts but are in fact only aspects or modes of one reality. In contrast, traditional Western theism is the belief that God exists as an independent, all-powerful spiritual reality which creates the material world as a separate and dependent entity. Materialism, or naturalism as it is sometimes called, is the belief that this natural or material world is the only reality there is and that there is no real need to think of it as divine or supernatural.

In light of the fact that Native American worldviews emphasize the reality and activity of spiritual beings in the original ordering of the natural world, it seems best to conclude that they reveal a mixture or synthesis of the types of belief defined above. They are not straightforwardly theistic, because the progenitors of the world do not seem to create it "out of nothing" as in the traditional Judeo-Christian view. At the same time, they are not basically pantheistic either, since they speak as if the Great Spirit and/or other original beings actually shape the world, as if it is a reality at least partially distinct from them. Some Native American origin stories, such as those of the Navajo and the Mojave, speak of the original beings actually creating the cosmos out of nothing other than pure thought and/or speech.

One final example of Native American origin stories is that of the Skagit peoples living at the southern end of the Northwest coastal cultural area, along the shores of present-day Washington State. Here we are presented with an account of the ordering of the world which seems to imply that the basic "stuff" of the world is already present when the creative process begins. In addition we see that various members of the animal world are active participants in the dialogical process of deciding how things will be. One version of the story goes like this:

> In the beginning, Raven and Mink and Coyote helped the Creator plan the world. They were in on all the arguments. They helped the Creator decide to have all the rivers flow only one way. . . . They decided that there should be bends in the rivers, so that there could be eddies where the fish could stop and rest. They decided that beasts should be placed in the forests. Human beings would have to keep out of their way.
>
> Human beings will not live on this earth forever, agreed Raven, Mink, Coyote, and Old Creator. They will stay only for a short time. Then the body will go back to the earth and the spirit back to the spirit world. All living things, they said, will be male and female—animals and plants, fish and birds. And everything will get its food from the earth, the soil.
>
> The creator gave four names for the earth. . . . One of the names is for the sun . . . another is for the rivers, streams, and salt water. . . . The third is for the soil. . . . The fourth is for the forest.[15]

JOURNEYS

Another important motif found in many Native American origin stories is the primal journey or pilgrimage undertaken by one or more of the supernatural beings or heroes involved in the formation of the world. It is likely that these journeys were incorporated into the origin stories as a result of the many centuries of migration that were embedded in the cultural memory of the people. Generally speaking, the journeys in the origin stories revolve around the efforts of the traveler to find his or her way to the world in which the people now dwell.

Crucial to such journeys is the overcoming of various obstacles and hostile forces along the way. These trials symbolize the struggles and courage of the persons or cultures involved and serve to inspire those who seek to live by them in the present. The conquering of environmental barriers, enemies, monsters, and mysterious powers not only displays the courage and wisdom of a people's ancestors, but it also provides hope, insight, and strength for the trials which the people may face now and in the future. A look at several stories in which such journeys are paramount will demonstrate their significance. Although the journey motif is common in world mythology, it is important to acknowledge the differences among such stories as well as the similarities. Primal ways of relating to reality cannot be reduced to a single category in this instance or in any other.

Consider the primal journey involved in the Skagit origin story introduced at the close of the previous section. After Old Creator, Raven, Mink, and Coyote had set the world in motion there was a great flood. A small group of people survived the flood in a large canoe and a child named Doquebuth was born to one of the surviving couples. When he was sent out to acquire his spirit power, in the manner generally called a "vision quest," he failed to take his task seriously and was deserted by his family.

> When he found that his family had deserted him, he realized that he had done wrong. So he began to swim and to fast. For many, many days he swam and fasted. No one can get spirit power unless he is clean and unless his stomach is empty.[16]

By means of a series of dreams in which he was visited by Old Creator, Doquebuth was instructed and enabled to create a new race of people from the dry bones of those who had died in the flood. Unlike the original people who spoke only the Skagit language, the new people were created speaking many different tongues.

In his dream, Old Creator told him to step over the big island, from ocean to ocean, and blow the people back where they belonged. . . . So Doquebuth blew them back. . . . Some he placed in the buffalo country, some by the salt water, some by the fresh water, some in the forests. That is why the people in the different places speak different languages.[17]

The fact that Doquebuth accomplished all this by swimming suggests that he was in fact a salmon, since the Northwest coastal peoples sometimes claim to be descendants of the "salmon people."

To shift to the Southwest region, the Zuni origin story, like that of the Navajo, begins with an account of the people's travels through various other worlds beneath the present one until they finally arrived on the surface of the earth. After their arrival they turned from a vertical journey to a horizontal one in search of their new home.

The instructions given to the Zuni people were to embark upon a journey in search of the "middle place of the world." For many years the Zuni people traveled here and there, searching for this middle place. As they traveled in distinct groups, the deities instructed them to take names to identify themselves. This was the origin of the Zuni clans and clan affiliations. Each time the Zuni settled, some disaster destroyed their village and forced them to move on, showing them that they had not yet ended their quest for the "middle place." Finally the Zuni came upon an old man who was a rain priest and who possessed a very sacred object. Their own rain priest prayed with this man, and together they caused much rain to fall. This signaled to the people that they had found the "middle place," and their anxiety was further allayed when a water strider came along, spread out its legs and declared that the middle of the world be directly beneath its heart. The Zuni villages were built here; one at the place beneath the heart and one at each place marked by the six feet of the water strider. . . . The Zuni conceive of their world as a large island of earth surrounded by oceans. Lakes and springs on the island open to an underground water system that interconnects the oceans.[18]

The concern manifested in this account, and many others like it, with the task of finding the center of the whole world, or at least the center of the world of a particular group of people, is a common theme. In the

Skagit story, for instance, the original site in the region of the Skagit River from which the people were scattered was taken to be the pivotal point of creation. Also, in the tale of the origin of the Tewa peoples presented earlier, the initial emergence from the lower worlds was said to have taken place at what Pueblo cultures call the *Sipapu* (Hopi) or *Sipofene* (Tewa). It is not uncommon and quite understandable that a people will think of its own culture and domain as the axis of the entire world.

Another quite different journey involves First Man, First Woman, and Changing Woman (or White Shell Woman), who serve as progenitors and culture heroes in the Navajo origin story. When the primal couple first emerge from the underworld they discover that they have forgotten to bring the sacred medicine bundle by means of which they eventually fashion the world. After the bundle is retrieved, they give birth to Changing Woman who is the personification of good. Changing Woman later enters into a struggle with First Man over the medicine bundle and eventually steals it from him. It is at this point that she takes the bundle to the West and proceeds to share its power with the Navajo people. In a way, this is the journey of the medicine bundle rather than the journey of any particular personage.[19]

In the Northeast, the travels of the two legendary heroes of the Iroquois, Hayonwhatha (Hiawatha) and Dekanawida, serve as a pivotal feature of the Iroquois origin story. Both of these personages have become discouraged and disgusted by the continual preoccupation with warfare demonstrated by the peoples living in the region between the Great Lakes and the corridor formed by the Hudson River. Together they wander from tribe to tribe preaching a message of peace and seeking to join the diverse peoples into a common community.

What they propose is a confederation or family of nations. Each tribe accepting the message of peace will be a nation within the confederation. As a group they will be known as the "League of Five Nations." In designing the government of the confederation the leaders make use of the structures with which they are already familiar. They become a kind of extended family, based on the local kinship groups known as "clans."[20]

Dekanawida, who becomes "the Peacemaker," chooses as a symbol of the League of Five Nations the pine tree, which becomes known as "the Great Tree of Peace." When he and Hayonwhatha first meet,

Dekanawida cures Hayonwhatha's sorrows by means of "the Three Words" of the condolence ceremony. The first opens his eyes, the second his ears, and the third his mouth. It is this ritual that empowers Hayonwhatha to preach the peace; this is the turning point in the primal journey of these two culture heroes. It serves as a symbol of the cleansing and forgiveness required for the preservation of the peace.

Generally, Native American origin stories project an initial period or ordering of the cosmos which does not so much exist *in* time as it posits the parameters of both time and space, as well as those of cultural value for the world in which the people live. The events in this primordial time establish and honor the people's basic beliefs and practices, while at the same time inspiring them to continue to embody these beliefs and teach them to their children. The significance and fate of each group depends on the telling of these stories to the next generation, preferably in the native tongue.

The actions portrayed in these origin stories are performed by a rather standard set of original beings, some of whom are supernatural in character, while others are human beings or animals. These primordial personages constitute an authoritative source of insight, courage, and skill by which peoples can order their own lives. Not only do these personages set the boundaries and patterns for both nature and humans, but they also engage in struggles and journeys which exemplify the spiritual qualities and aspirations that serve to unite the community seeking to live by and for them. These personages are realistically presented; they are almost never all good or all bad, and they often learn from their mistakes.

NOTES

1. Sam Gill, *Native American Religions: An Introduction* (Belmont, Calif.: Wadsworth, 1982), p. 39.

2. N. Scott Momaday, "The Man Made of Words," in Convocation of American Indian Scholars, 1st, Princeton University, *Indian Voices* (San Francisco: Indian Historian Press, 1970), p. 49.

3. K. M. Stewart, "Mohave," in *Handbook of North American Indians*, ed. Alfonso Ortiz, vol. 10 (Washington, D.C.: Smithsonian Institution, 1983) pp. 557–70.

4. Joseph Bruchac, *Iroquois Stories: Heroes and Heroines, Monsters and Magic* (Trumansburg, N.Y.: Crossing Press, 1985), pp. 15–17.

5. Dale McGinnis and Floyd W. Sharrock, *The Crow People* (Phoenix, Ariz.: Indian Tribal Series, 1972), p. 26.

6. Alfonso Ortiz, *The Tewa World: Space, Time, Being and Becoming in a Pueblo Society* (Chicago: University of Chicago Press, 1969), pp. 13–16.

7. A. F. C. Wallace, *The Death and Rebirth of the Seneca* (New York: Vantage Press, 1969), p. 88.

8. Sam Gill, "Navajo Views of Their Religion," in *Handbook of North American Indians*, ed. Ortiz, vol. 10, pp. 502–505.

9. Del Hymes, "Mythology," in *Handbook of North American Indians*, ed. Wayne Suttles, vol. 7 (Washington, D.C.: Smithsonian Institution, 1990), p. 594.

10. Åke Hultkrantz, *The Religions of the American Indians* (Berkeley: University of California Press, 1979), p. 30.

11. Ibid., p. 33.

12. Black Elk, *Black Elk Speaks: Being the Life Story of a Holy Man of the Oglala Sioux*, as told through John G. Neihardt (Lincoln: University of Nebraska Press, 1979), pp. 1–2. A number of scholars have raised objections to taking Neihardt's account of Black Elk's memories as an objective presentation of Black Elk's worldview or that of the Oglala Sioux. There is a tendency for those who record traditional people's interpretations of their own views of things to understand and represent these in terms of the recorders' own cultural and conceptual categories. However, Neihardt's version of Black Elk's worldview is the one we have, and it has been well received by many Native American thinkers, including Vine Deloria Jr. in his introduction to Neihardt's book. For further discussion of this issue see *Black Elk's Story: Distinguishing Its Lakota Purpose*, by Julian Rice (Albuquerque: University of New Mexico Press, 1991).

13. *Black Elk Speaks*, pp. 3–5.

14. Ibid., p. 6.

15. Wayne Suttles, "A Skagit Belief about the Origin of the World," in *Major Problems in American Indian History*, ed. A. Hurtado and P. Iverson (Lexington, Mass.: D. C. Heath, 1994), pp. 15–16.

16. Ibid., p. 16.

17. Ibid., p. 17.

18. Gill, *Native American Religions*, p. 17.

19. John Farella, *The Main Stalk: A Synthesis of Navajo Philosophy* (Tucson: University of Arizona Press, 1984), pp. 87–90.

20. Barbara Graymont, *The Iroquois* (New York: Chelsea House, 1988), p. 26.

Chapter Three

Space and Cosmos

Chapters 1 and 2 provide the canvas on which Native American worldviews may now be sketched. The geographic and historical background along with the cultural and linguistic character of Native American peoples form the time, space, and depth coordinates for understanding the major themes and patterns of their way of being in the world, of their view of reality and human existence. It is now possible to fill in the colors and textures of these patterns by considering certain specific beliefs and practices which characterize a good many cultures. The first of these has to do with the way people see themselves situated in what might be called "cosmic space."

In chapter 1 the term *space* was used in a geographical sense, and in chapter 2 the term *time* was used in a historical sense. In the present chapter and the next we shall use these terms in a much broader, more philosophical sense, in connection with one's understanding of one's place in the universe in relation to both meaning and destiny. This sense of these terms is often called their "cosmic" significance. The present chapter, then, focuses on the notion of space in this sense, on the meaning of human placement in the world both "vertically" and "horizontally" in a spiritual or philosophical sense. Chapter 4 pursues a similar approach to the notion of time.

ABOVE AND BELOW

Many Native Americans structure their origin stories around journeys through various worlds located beneath the earth, finally emerging into the present world. In spite of the fact that the previous worlds were full of difficulties, dangers, and failures, most Native American peoples think of them as in some way sacred. Not only were they the place of origin for their progenitors, but they were also the home of the supernatural beings who created their world and continue to interact with the people while on earth. Thus for many peoples the ground beneath them and the earth in general are viewed as holy and as a continual source of wisdom and power.

Belief in the sanctity of the earth beneath this world probably played a significant role in the evolution of the dwellings and sacred places that archaeologists trace among the peoples of the Southwest. The prehistoric peoples of the desert, for example, initially constructed pit houses for their dwellings. After digging rectangular pits a few feet into the ground, they covered them with domed roofs made of tree limbs and brush. Often these pit houses contained, in addition to small firepits, other small pits which seem to have served as places to store valued objects. It is possible that these latter pits actually functioned as shrines around which the people patterned their religious life. Later on the people of the Hohokam culture also built adobe houses above ground, along with ball courts, platform mounds, and extensive canal systems.[1]

Another prehistoric group of people who dwelt in the Southwest, the Anasazi, lived at higher elevations amidst the canyons of northern Arizona and New Mexico. They built their homes in the shallow caves of the canyon cliffs using stone, logs, and mortar, while farming along the stream beds below. In their living space the Anasazi also constructed circular and square rooms which were essentially underground and which were used as centers of religious activity. Archaeologists call these rooms *kivas*, after the Hopi's name for their ceremonial centers. They seem to have been put below the ground for a specific reason, probably because the people felt a close tie with the earth and the underworld as their source of spiritual strength. A parallel version of the Anasazi culture was located in the shallow canyons of New Mexico, in Chaco Canyon, where the people built large pueblo-type village complexes with many *kivas* of different sizes and at different levels.[2]

The placement of dwellings and especially worship centers beneath the ground goes hand in hand with the common belief that human beings initially arrived on the surface of the earth by emerging from worlds located beneath it. The origin story of most Pueblo peoples, who center their spiritual activity around the *kiva*, thus finds its natural expression in this ritual practice involving an underground sacred space. Indeed, at the center of Pueblo *kivas* one can usually find a small hole which symbolizes the point of connection with the sacred world below.[3]

This concern with the lower range of the vertical dimension of reality is matched among many other groups by an equal if not even stronger interest in the higher range. The Iroquois origin story has its beginning in the sky-world above this earth. Moreover, in nearly every Native American culture great attention is paid to the patterns and characteristics of heavenly bodies, since they are believed to carry special significance. Before exploring the role of astronomical considerations in Native American cultures, however, we shall expand the discussion of the structural forms by means of which people gave expression to their vertical interpretation of the world around them.

Mention has been made of the Hohokam platform mounds as most likely serving as centers of sacred activity. If a group of people are convinced that the sacred realm is located in a world above this earth, then it is reasonable to expect them to build their religious structures in such a way as to get nearer to this higher world. This is generally the rationale, for example, behind the building of steeples and cathedrals in Western Christendom. These constructions, along with those of the Mound Builders in the Southeast, probably represent people's efforts to be closer to the heavenly spiritual reality during their religious ceremonies. This interpretation is reinforced by the conclusion of many archaeologists that the building of mounds by North American peoples suggests the direct influence of Mesoamerican pyramid-building cultures.

The tendency to build upward so as to get closer to the realm of the gods and/or sacred spirits is paralleled by the reverence for mountains as holy places. Nearly all Native American peoples in the West designate the boundaries of their world in terms of a set of mountains within which they dwell and which they revere as sacred. Even the people living on the Plains, where there are no real mountains, pay special attention and tribute to certain high places and/or rock formations within their territories. Devil's Tower, near the Black Hills, is one example. In the Northwest, along the range dividing the coast from the High Plateau, there are numerous sacred mountains, including those known today as Mt. Baker, Mt. Rainier, Mt. Hood, and Mt. Shasta.

An interesting example of the intersection of the building of religious structures as close as possible to the world above and the perception of mountains as having special spiritual significance is the giant medicine wheel located at the 10,000-foot level in the Bighorn Mountains near the Wyoming/Montana border. Many large boulders and stones have been laid out so as to form a large circle some twenty-five yards wide with spoke-like lines of stones radiating out from the center. This formation dates from between 1200 and 1700 C.E. and is only accessible during the summer. Some of these stone "spoke" lines seem to have been designed to mark the summer solstice and the yearly first appearance of several constellations of stars. The full significance of the wheel remains a mystery, but its high placement and symbolic pattern are surely not accidental.[4]

The Iroquois origin story began in the sky-world, and at the center of that world stood a large and beautiful tree. When this tree was uprooted, the sky chief's wife fell to the earth through the hole created by the tree's uprooting. The symbolism of the tree standing at the center of the world is duplicated in many Native American traditions, especially those of the Northeast and the Great Plains, where a "sacred pole" is placed at the center of the lodge house or tepee. The Iroquois story of the Peacemaker concludes with the establishment of the Great Tree of Peace as the central symbol of Iroquois cultural life. We shall focus on the centrality of the sacred tree or pole in the next section. It is the vertical significance of this symbol that is our concern at the moment.

The sacred tree or pole not only serves as the link between this world and the one above, as the means of passage for the superior spirits interacting with the people on earth, but also as a means for shamans or "medicine men" to contact the spirit world during ritual activity and/or healing ceremonies.[5] The totem poles of Northwest coastal peoples and the fact that Pueblo *kivas* are entered by ladder from the roof suggest the importance of the higher span of the vertical dimension. The sacred tree or pole unites the spirit world above with the underworld below and in so doing passes directly through this world of human experience. In some pictures of the cosmos, it is the sacred pole that holds these worlds in place.[6]

One of the most dramatic and well-known instances of the use of the sacred tree as a ritual center is in the Sun Dance ceremony of the Oglala Sioux. Performed primarily as a ritual of thanksgiving or rededication, this ceremony is initiated by a single individual but involves the individual's entire family, and eventually almost the whole village. A special tree is selected and brought to the village where it is erected in relation to the orbit of the sun. Then a ritual lodge, within which the ceremony will take place, is constructed. The tree establishes the vertical connection with the sun at the center of both the natural and the spiritual worlds. A Native American's description of a Lakota Sioux Sun Dance ceremony was recorded by James Walker:

> Well now the place where the sacred pole is has been made *wakan*; no one goes near the place. Now again the holy man goes there and commands them to bring the offerings. The wakan tree is forked. The top of the tree is towards where the sun goes down. . . . Now they carefully push upright the wakan tree, the forked tree. Now they place it erect and the people all shout excitedly. Then all the women sing. . . . Well now, the sun is at the meridian, so they will now mark the Sun Dancers. So they first take two braided thongs and approach the wakan tree and then tie them to the wakan tree so that they will hang suspended from it. And now when the sun is at the meridian the holy man again sings.[7]

CARDINAL DIRECTIONS

The vertical dimension of human experience within the worldviews of Native Americans is complemented by the equally significant horizontal dimension. Up and down, above and below, higher and lower do not exhaust the conceptual categories within which both individuals and cultures live. Left and right, near and far, in and out, and especially East, West, North, and South also reflect the parameters of human experience as embodied and spatially situated. In Native American cultures many if not most of these parameters and categories revolve around what are generally referred to as the "Cardinal Directions" of the compass: East, West, North, and South.

For most of us living among the complex collection of intellectual constructs and technological artifacts we call "Western civilization," the prospect of orienting ourselves by means of the directions of the compass would be confusing at best. We have become accustomed to finding our way in terms of signposts, tall buildings, and arterial highways, and hardly ever actually see a full sunset or sunrise. For those who live close to the land, however, paying attention to where the sun rises and sets, and the patterns according to which it does so, is as common as it is crucial for nearly every aspect of life. We now explore some of the features of this horizontal dimension in the beliefs and customs of a number of groups, beginning with those that emphasize the various cycles and seasons of the sun, moon, planets, and stars.

The cyclical patterns of the sun may well be the most basic and universal natural phenomena known to the human race. The alternating sequence of night and day has always and everywhere served to structure human existence, and the rising and setting of the sun marks the arrival and departure of each period. Peoples around the globe have seen these two events, and especially the sunrise, as highly significant, both literally and symbolically, in their everyday existence. Nomadic hunters and gatherers, as well as farmers, though for different reasons, must pay a great deal of attention to when and where the sun comes up, goes down, and casts its shadow, and how high in the sky it rises. Deciding everything from when to plant and harvest to when to break or return to camp depends on knowing all this.

Native Americans are no exception. Their understanding of daily and yearly life and thus their views of the nature and structure of reality are organized around the positions of the sun and other heavenly bodies. Moreover, the positions relative to the horizon are taken to be especially important, for it is in relation to the landmarks along the horizon that one can determine the progress of the day and/or the year. In addition, it is in relation to the familiar landmarks of the horizon that we can locate ourselves in relation to our destinations and other points of interest. Native

American peoples are also accustomed to judging the time of day and the season of the year by the varying lengths of the shadows of familiar objects. To those enculturated to orient themselves by means of the sun, life is more like living on the surface of a compass than living on a city map.

Two of the more common features of Native American life reflecting attention to the role of the sun are the practice of situating the entrances to dwellings toward the East and of marking the point on the horizon where the sun rises on the longest day of the year. The former practice is characteristic of a great many cultures, especially those of the Southwest, where the sun has the potential for bringing both life and death in dramatic fashion. Nearly all Hohokam pit houses, Navajo hogans, and Pueblo homes are arranged to face the sunrise. Even the Anasazi, who built their cliff dwellings so as to capture as much of the southern exposure to the sun as possible, often seem to have been oriented more toward the southeast than toward the southwest. The Mound Builders of the Southeast region also situated the entrances of their structures so as to face the rising sun.

The practice of marking the summer solstice is one that Native Americans have shared with many cultures around the world. In addition to the practical importance of knowing when the sun's cycle begins and ends in relation to the timing of crops and treks, there clearly is something intriguing about the way the sun slows down and stops its daily journey along the horizon at different places as the year progresses and then begins to travel in the opposite direction. Thus most Native American and other traditional peoples have developed a good deal of symbolism in connection with this pivotal natural event that regulates their life.

In the Zuni Nation's calendar, we can clearly see the role played by the progressing positions of the sunrise along the horizon:

> [The year] is divided into two parts by the solstices, and each part is further divided into six months. The months for each half of the year bear the same names; hence both December and June, the months of the solstices, are called *'I kopu*, which means "turning and looking back," referring to the action of the sun reaching its farthest most [sic] point and turning back. During these winter and summer solstice months, there is a 20-day period designated as *itowana*. These middle places in the year are significant times for the celebration and ceremonial creation of a new phase of the year.[8]

In Black Elk's account of the Sioux origin story the sacred pipe has four ribbons hanging from the stem, one for each of the Cardinal Directions. The color of each of these ribbons corresponds to the color associated with the direction it represents. Thus black symbolizes the West, where the thunderclouds gather, white stands for the North, from whence comes the winter snow, red signifies the eastern sunrise, and yellow represents the full summer sun of the South. As a matter of fact, nearly all Native American cultures have established traditional associations between the Cardinal Directions and specific colors, though the particular associations vary a great deal from culture to culture. Among the Tewa Pueblo people, for instance, the summer colors are green, yellow, and black, while the winter colors are red and white.[9]

A parallel practice is that of locating the Cardinal Directions in relation to significant landmarks on the horizon, especially sacred mountains. Nearly all peoples living close to the land orient themselves spatially in relation to such landmarks, and they also orient themselves with respect to the journeys of the sun along the horizon in relation to these landmarks. Thus tall and sacred mountains have come to fulfill a crucial function in the worldview of Native Americans, since they frequently also serve as the boundary markers of their known world. A correlation of the two orienting patterns can be seen in the following description of the Navajo sacred mountains. The description was recorded by Father Berard Haile, a Franciscan missionary who spent over fifty years living and working among the Navajo.

> Sisnajini mountain already stood there, here on the east side. On the south side stood Mt. Taylor, on the west side San Francisco Peak, on the north side La Plata range, it was found. This (thing) that arose as a white column in the east time and again, is the inner form of sisnajini by which it breathes and this we know as the dawn. In the west (the rising column) is the inner form of San Francisco Peak by means of which this breathes. This, we see, is the evening twilight. . . . The column from the south, the inner form of Mt. Taylor by which it breathes is, we know, the sky blue. The one from the north, the inner form of Perrin's Peak by which it breathes, is really the darkness, they say. . . . Here towards the south stood a mountain yellow in color, and right opposite, towards the east there was a dark mountain.[10]

Given this employment of the Cardinal Directions within the beliefs and practices of Native Americans, it is not surprising that the number four is involved in a great many traditions and rituals. As there are four Cardinal Directions, so there are often three underworlds through which the people have traveled in order to reach this earth, their fourth world, as well as the four directions according to which some groups claim to have migrated across the surface of North America, and the four sacred mountains that demarcate a given people's territory. As has been noted, the horizontal dimension of Native American experience is often structured in terms of the progressive patterns of the sun and other heavenly bodies in relation to the horizon in fourfold divisions.

While there is evidence that nearly all Native American peoples have oriented themselves and their communal life according to the patterns and principles described above, it is possible that none have done so more extensively than the Pueblo peoples living in the Southwest. The Hopi, Zuni, and Rio Grande Pueblo peoples all depend on their tracking of the sun's progress for determining the proper times for planting, harvesting, and performing the yearly ritual cycle. The importance of such horizontal orientation to a group's physical and cultural life is dramatically expressed in the ruins left by the ancient Pueblo peoples of Chaco Canyon in New Mexico. Here we can see the crucial role played by the delineation of the cycles of the sun in the survival and worldview of the Native Americans in the Southwest.

The "Chaco Phenomenon," as it is sometimes called, consisted of at least six or seven Pueblo settlements within a shallow canyon in the San Juan River basin between 1100 and 1300 C.E. It seems to have been the focal point for a broad Anasazi trading network, with outlying settlements in the same architectural style as far as 150 miles away, connected by an elaborate system of roads. In addition to numerous sun symbol pictographs located at various sites throughout the Chaco Valley, there are two especially significant locations that suggest serious sun-tracking on the part of the people who lived here. One of these is Fajada Butte and the other is Casa Rinconada, each embodying a different mode of orientation.

On a ledge near the top of Fajada Butte a pectoglyph of a spiral is found on the face of the cliff behind three upright sandstone slabs that lean against the side of the cliff. On the summer solstice a ray of light shines between two of the slabs, forming a dagger-shaped figure on the spiral, not at sunrise but at noon. A second dagger of light appears and cuts across a smaller spiral for a few days before and after the solstice, but this seems not to be present on the solstice day itself. This second ray of light is formed by the narrow space between the second and third sandstone slabs.

> This site also works to define the equinoxes and the winter solstice. By the autumnal equinox, the second dagger of light has worked its way across the small spiral to bisect it, while the first dagger has moved right to cut across the outer rings of the large spiral. By the winter solstice, the two patterns of light frame the side of the large spiral.[11]

At ground level the only major structure situated on the western side of the canyon is Casa Rinconada, a circular *kiva* 63 feet across which may have served as a ceremonial center for all the Chaco settlements. Although each of the individual pueblo settlements, such as Pueblo Bonito, had its own *kiva* or ceremonial center, none are as grand or as complex as that at Casa Rinconada. In addition, although some of the windows and doors at Bonito are aligned with the solstices and equinoxes, the layout at Rinconada is far more exact and elaborate in this regard. Not only is it aligned perfectly with celestial North, but it also contains a hidden stairway beneath another set of stairs at the north entrance. An opening in the northeastern wall and a niche on the *kiva's* western side are aligned in such a way as to fill the niche with sunlight at sunrise on the summer solstice.[12]

The Navajo people seem to pay more attention to the patterns of certain star constellations in relation to the horizon than they do to the patterns of the sun:

> When Pleiades first reappears in the early morning sky to the northeast, after an absence of several months from the night sky, the Navajo know that it is now too late to plant any longer and still be able to harvest before the first frost. . . . When they see it in the northeast in the early evening, it tells them that the first autumn frost is not far off. This occurs in late September . . . when at about ten o'clock at night, the constellation can be seen just rising in the northeast.[13]

Perhaps one of the reasons that some groups, such as the Navajo, seem to be more attuned to the patterns of movement among the stars is that they are more nomadic, at least between summer and winter, moving their large herds of sheep from one place to another. This suggestion is even more relevant when applied to the tribes living on the Great Plains, who essentially followed the grazing migrations of the buffalo. Also the relative lack of large landmarks visible at a great distance would encourage the tendency to track the stars' rather than the sun's relation to the horizon. The Native Americans who came to live on the Plains, while they did not construct stone or adobe houses or ceremonial centers, did build a large number of "medicine wheels."

The Bighorn Medicine Wheel is laid out in such a way as to mark the arrival of the summer solstice, much like Stonehenge. Moreover, this particular wheel has 28 spokes, a number that suggests the possibility of marking the lunar months. Another such wheel, laid out in a parallel manner, is located in southeastern Saskatchewan and called the "Moose Mountain Medicine Wheel." Again, the correspondence between many of this site's features and the celestial bodies in relation to the horizon is highly significant. The sheer number of these wheel-like structures spread across the continent makes it clear that the Plains Indians were aware of and tied to the patterns of the heavenly bodies.[14]

The Pawnee of the Great Plains developed an elaborate system for charting star patterns. Their worldview revolved around the comings and goings of the morning star and the evening star in relation both to the horizon and to the yearly calendar. The Pawnee are reported to have held a ceremony every few years in which they sacrificed a young woman, captured from a neighboring tribe, to the morning star, which they regarded as God. "It is striking that the sun assumes a relatively minor role in the Pawnee conception of the cosmos and in its relationship to Pawnee ritual. This stance makes the Pawnee nearly unique among native North Americans. Even as these agriculturists appreciated the warming power of the sun, they attributed his power either to Morning Star, or to Evening Star."[15]

Even among the Mississippian Mound Builder cultures a great deal of attention was paid to orienting the world and community life according to the power and patterned movements of the sun along the horizon. An extraordinary example of this is to be found in the mounds of Cahokia, near East St. Louis. In addition to the platform mounds, which have ramifications for the vertical dimension of existence already discussed, the orientational pattern among the mounds not only lines up extremely well on a north-south axis, but serves as well to indicate the summer and winter solstices. Orientations such as these have also been found in Florida and Vermont.[16]

DWELLING AT THE CENTER

So far the focus has been on the vertical and horizontal dimensions of human existence as interpreted by various Native American peoples. When these two dimensions are brought together, the intersection between them forms the dwelling place or native territory of any given group. This intersection marks the center of a people's known reality, and it serves as the very axis of their history, traditions, beliefs, customs, and ceremonies. It acts as the fulcrum of their worldview. In the following discussion of the way this center displays itself within several diverse cultures, many features will be seen as simply the mirror image of those noted in the discussion of the vertical and horizontal dimensions. In both cases the coordinates of any worldview make sense only in relation to a center around which they revolve.

In a number of origin stories, this present world, earth, stands at the midpoint between the world above and the worlds below. Indeed, more than a few peoples refer to this earth as the "middle place." In like manner, the incorporation of the four Cardinal Directions into the worldview and cultural practice of so many peoples virtually always places each of the peoples right in the center of the cosmos as they experience it. The territory of a given group, whether it be a village or a vast plain, is invariably seen as the axis around which all else orbits. This territory constitutes a large circle at the center of which a given people dwells.

Nearly every Native American group demarcated its territorial living space by means of bodies of water and/or sacred mountains. The Great Lakes, as well as the Atlantic and Pacific Oceans, formed stable boundaries for those living on or near them, while large rivers functioned as the main sources of sustenance and transportation for inland peoples. The outlying spatial parameters for the Native Americans of the Plains and the Southwest were formed by sizable, conspicuous mountains. Within such boundaries existed the ordered world, while beyond them there was no cosmos, only chaos. It is generally the case that people view their world in this way, with themselves and the area within which they live taken as the axis of reality. This is not to say that Native American peoples did not travel and explore geographic regions outside their own, but they generally did so with great caution.

At the very center of such territorial areas lies the home village or pueblo, which constitutes the actual hub of the wider circles of reality. The Tewa Pueblo people devised an elaborate and encompassing interpretation of their own physical and social existence in the Rio Grande Valley. The symbolic and iconic character of the layout of the courtyards and dwellings and that of the surrounding mountains combine to form a tight, intricate pattern of spiritual and cultural life. The following diagram and its explanation are provided by Alfonso Ortiz, a native of the Tewa Pueblo and a well-known anthropologist, in his seminal work, *The Tewa World*.

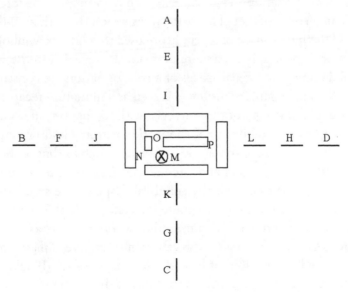

FIG. 3.1. WORLD OF THE TEWA

Taking the outermost tetrad first, the world of the Tewa is bounded by four sacred mountains, the same mountains which were seen by the first four pairs of sibling deities as they were sent out to explore the world in the origin myth. . . . The next tetrad (E, F, G, H) represents the sacred *Tsin* or flat-topped hills created by the *Towa e'* of the directions. . . . The third tetrad (I, J, K, L) represents the principal shrines of the directions. . . . The final tetrad (M, N, O, P) represents the *bu pingeh* or dance plazas within the village. . . . Point X on figure 2 represents the *Nan echu kwi nan sipu pingeh* or "Earth mother navel middle place." This is the sacred center of the village, and it is located on the south plaza. Ritual dances and other performances must continue to be initiated here, as the Tewa explain it, because this is the true center of the village. I might go a little further and say that this is the center of centers, or the navel of navels.[17]

In the majority of Native American groups the village not only stands at the axis of the world, as the "middle place" of reality, but functions as a model or metaphor of that reality. The layout of many villages and pueblos is meant to mirror the structural relations that characterize the world around the central living area. The long houses of the Northeast, the lodges of the coastal Northwest, and the tepee villages of many of the Plains Indians are set up to face the East and to symbolize the forces that hold the universe together. This pattern, in which the format and architecture of the living space of a people are used to model or symbolize the structure of the world, is even more dramatically revealed in the way the personal dwellings and ritual spaces of a tribe or nation are constructed.

The Navajo hogan, for instance, is seen as a miniature recapitulation of the overall framework of the universe, with its support pillars actually contributing to the stabilizing of the world's patterns and principles. In like manner, the architecture of the sweatlodge, such as that of the Plains Indians, with its domed roof and circular shape, is taken to represent the curved ceiling of the sky and the spherical shape of the sun. Moreover, within certain of these structures there is a center pole that serves to signify the pivot or fulcrum of the surrounding world, the very axis of reality.

Here is an account, taken directly from a Native American informant's detailed description, of how the formation of the Blackfoot Sun Dance lodge embodies and focuses this idea of the center of the world as located at the center of tribal life and belief:

The architecture of the Sun Dance lodge, like that of the hundred willow sweat house, was a material form that symbolized the final power in the Blackfoot universe. Its circular shape, its opening toward the east, and its center pole were complex and interconnected material forms that evoked specific horizons of transcendent meaning in the experience of the people. It is, however, the center pole which will receive the most attention in this context. While the Sun pole may have associations with the World Tree of other religious traditions, for the Blackfeet it also seems to symbolize the concentrated Sun power which flowed from its source above, through the pole, and horizontally out into the social and natural worlds. This flowing of Sun power into the world is coextensive with the renewal of the world and the people.[18]

It is largely on the basis of the rituals that take place within or around these central spaces that they acquire their special powers. The sacred lodge and the *kiva* both symbolize and function as the axis of the world. This axis is located precisely at the intersection of the vertical and horizontal dimensions of human existence and experience.[19]

Alfonso Ortiz quotes a Tewa informant who summed up the three-dimensional dynamics involved:

An earth navel is like an airport. . . . Airplanes, no matter where they go, always have to return to an airport. In the same way all things . . . always return to the earth navel.[20]

THE CIRCLE

A further aspect of Native American ways of interpreting their experience within the framework of spatial boundaries and patterns deserves special mention. Once the center or axis of a people's physical and cultural existence has been established, this not only determines the point of intersection between their vertical and horizontal dimensions but also delineates a boundary between what is inside the center or circle of meaning and what is outside it. In a way, this directional phenomenon is an inevitable result of embodied existence in a physical environment. When one turns to face in any direction, one must turn one's back on another direction. If we face toward the center we must at the same time face away from whatever and whoever is at the periphery of the circle.

Another aspect of living within the circle circumscribed by one's geographic and cultural center is related to the reality of the horizon. Just as one cannot see beyond the limits set by one's visual horizon, so it is difficult at best to understand what lies beyond one's cultural horizon. Only by advancing toward such limits can one alter and expand them. As we extend our horizons by changing our position in relation to them, the circle within which we live also shifts its center. Thus although our horizon seems to confine us, it also places and centers us within the fabric of everyday life. This circular character of human existence was a profound though often unarticulated feature of Native American worldviews, as the following examples reveal.

The symbolism of the circle or sacred hoop is a well-known feature of the worldview of the Plains Indians. It is, for instance, introduced by Black Elk in his account of the vision he received as a Sioux youth:

> Then when the many little voices ceased, the great Voice said: 'Behold the circle of the nation's hoop, for it is holy, being endless, and thus all powers shall be one power in the people without end.' . . . And I saw that the sacred hoop of my people was one of many hoops that made one circle, wide as daylight and as starlight, and in the center grew one mighty flowering tree to shelter all children of one mother and one father. And I saw that it was holy.[21]

While the seminomadic sheep-herding Navajo do not arrange their dwellings in a circular fashion, many if not most other Native American peoples do so. The Pueblo peoples often operate within a rectangular pattern of houses and *kivas*, as do some of the peoples of both the Northwest and Northeast coasts. Nonetheless, even these rectangular patterns create a shape which has an inside and an outside, a center around which the common life of the people is organized and flows. In addition to the obvious advantages of such an arrangement for purposes of safety, it also provides both a natural and a symbolic embodiment of the meaning of community life. Whenever people turn toward one another for protection and social relationships, they create an axis that holds them together, a circle or communal hoop that identifies and sustains them.

An interesting aspect of this circle motif is the notion of the broken circle within Navajo aesthetics. Among the Navajo, while the symbolism of the circle is well established in the architecture of the hogan and the weave of the basketry, the phenomenon of the broken circle is also frequently encountered. It is generally understood that the broken circle signifies an acknowledgment that the world, including human artifacts, is never complete or perfect. There is, however, another interpretation that can shed light on this symbol. A broken circle provides a point of connection between the inside and the outside of the circle, a way of encouraging exploration beyond the confines of one's traditional world and of allowing outside influences into that world. Sam Gill offers the following explanation:

> The broken circle nonetheless constitutes a boundary. It sets off a space and gives it significance. The break or opening that is the most distinctive aspect of the motif serves in a pragmatic sense as an orientation device. That position is the one to be aligned with the east or to define the direction east. . . . But at another level, we find that the Navajo people consider the break or opening as a pathway leading out of the enclosed space. It is always seen as the "road out" and this road is the road of life. Navajos say that to draw a closed circle around someone's house would cause sickness, perhaps even death. It would be a symbolic obstruction of the life road going out.[22]

Despite the fact that the North American continent was far from overcrowded, most Indian peoples engaged in numerous conflicts with those around them, those whom for one reason or another they thought of as outsiders. Although these conflicts can hardly be considered "wars" in the usual sense of the word, they were predicated on the distinction between those who dwelt within the sacred circle and those who did not. Thus the invasion by European *conquistadores*, of whatever nationality, was experienced as a violation of the inner, sacred space. The distinction between insider and outsider need not be seen as involving inherent hostility toward outsiders, although this sometimes became necessary when groups were required to defend themselves against those who were busy "winning the West." Rather, it should be read as the basic marker between the familiar and the unfamiliar, a marker that signifies both curiosity and caution.

One way in which the insider/outsider phenomenon expresses itself among Native Americans is in the names which many of them have acquired but which do not correspond to their own names for themselves. Many of these names, such as "Navajo," "Sioux," "Apache," and "Iroquois," were given to these groups either by their neighbors or by foreigners such as the French and Spanish. Often these names were terms of derision or even hostility in the name-giver's language. Sometimes the name is the result of sloppy pronunciation on the part of a non-native speaker. Generally speaking a group's name for itself simply means "the people" in its native language. Thus these designations, given by "the people" or by others, clearly reflect the insider/outsider motif.

Two ways in which the distinction between inside and outside the sacred circle was altered were migrations and intergroup trade. Around five hundred years ago the peoples who eventually became the Navajo and Apache migrated from the Athapascan-speaking region of western Canada to their present home in the Southwest. Along the way they assimilated some of the cultural beliefs and practices of other peoples, such as those of the Pueblos and the Plains. The Navajo acquired the skills of weaving and sheep herding from the Hopi, while the Apache learned horsemanship from the tribes that had acquired horses from the Spanish and hunted bison on the Plains.

Many of the Plains peoples had themselves been forced to move around a good deal, some merging with peoples of different languages and cultural patterns. The Crow did not become a separate people until after they separated from the Hidatsas, who themselves had migrated from the Great Lakes region to the Missouri River Valley. The people who became the Crow moved west into the Montana area and later subdivided into two relatively distinct tribes, the River Crow and the Mountain Crow. Even some of the Tewa Pueblo people moved west to join the Hopi in Arizona. This sort of migration inevitably led to a merging of genetic stock and cultural worldviews among a great many Native Americans. In each case the result was a widening of the sacred circle. Even raiding contributed to intermarriage and cultural adaptation.[23]

In addition to the extensive trade and ensuing cultural influences between the peoples of the Southwest, and even the Southeast, and the large, sophisticated cultures of Mesoamerica, there is evidence that for many centuries there was considerable trade between the peoples of the Southwest and those on the Great Plains and in the Great Basin to the Northwest. Here again, inroads were created that helped to soften the line of demarcation between those on the inside and those on the outside of various cultural spheres. The material artifacts that were exchanged certainly carried with them cultural connections and implications. Some of these artifacts clearly originated in areas far distant from the people who eventually received them. The sacred circle was not as insular as it might at first seem.[24]

Even within similar cultural regions, such as the Northwest coast or the Eastern seaboard, there was always a large-scale exchange of goods, customs, and even marriage partners. The Iroquois Confederation is perhaps the most obvious example, since through participation in this union each group was challenged to overcome differences and to include others within an ever-widening circle. Dennis Tedlock pinpoints some of the ways in which local exchange in the Southwest served to unify rather than separate the cultural circles:

> Inter-Indian exchange was a complex of interactions among kinsmen, neighbors, formal friends, and distant strangers. The social and ceremonial fabric encouraged outside contacts, thus assuring that all had equal information about rates of exchange and access to goods. All groups provided some special resource or craft or functioned as middlemen for some commodities. However, a network of alternative sources for every good prohibited monopolistic and exclusionary practices. . . . Exchange as a social aspect of foreign relations made friends of potential enemies. Each gift made a foreigner a quasi-kinsman. Kinsmen could not bargain and could defer payment; strangers bartered and paid immediately. A kinsman or trade partner was protected and provisioned; a stranger was feared as a potential enemy. . . . Traditional Southwestern exchange was a splendid example of multiple means for moving goods within an open communication network to insure the adequate provisioning of politically independent, egalitarian communities.[25]

All this brings us back to the words of Black Elk:

And I saw that the sacred hoop of my people was one of many hoops that made one circle, wide as daylight and as starlight, and in the center grew one mighty flowering tree to shelter all children of one mother and one father.[26]

This vision of inclusiveness was not unique to the Sioux or any other people; many if not most Native American worldviews provide for the gradual acceptance of outside influences and the eventual merging of different belief systems and cultural practices. The well-known Blessingway of the Navajo, for instance, contains clear-cut references to the eventual merging of diverse worldviews, as do the Iroquoian vision of the Peacemaker and the message of Handsome Lake, a more recent Iroquois religious leader.

A negative result of this willingness to broaden the sacred hoop or circle was, of course, the almost total destruction of Native American peoples and cultures by European warriors, traders, missionaries, and settlers through diseases, wars, forced schooling, and treaties which almost seem to have been made in order to be broken. Native American readiness to trust the intentions and promises of those outside the sacred circle was rewarded with overwhelming evidence that such trustfulness was often not the best choice to make.

A positive result of willingness to broaden the circle or sacred hoop, however, has been the recent and ongoing renaissance of Native American cultural life which is often called the "Pan-Indian" movement. Over the past twenty-five years, great strides have been made toward recovering the lands, artifacts, languages, and rights which once belonged to Native Americans, and they have accomplished this largely by uniting to protect and revive their common cultural heritage. At the same time, many individuals and groups have incorporated Euro-American cultural ways into their own ethnic style and vision. Perhaps the circle may eventually widen to include those who sought to destroy it.

NOTES

1. George J. Gumerman and Emil W. Haury, "Prehistory: Hohokam," in *Handbook of North American Indians*, ed. Alfonso Ortiz, vol. 9 (Washington, D.C.: Smithsonian Institution, 1979), pp. 75–90.

2. Ibid., pp. 131–51.

3. Ibid., pp. 577–80.

4. Ray Williamson, *Living the Sky: The Cosmos of the American Indian* (Norman: University of Oklahoma Press, 1984), p. 1.

5. Åke Hultkrantz, *The Religions of the American Indians* (Berkeley: University of California Press, 1979), pp. 109–10.

6. Ibid., p. 77.

7. James R. Walker, *Lakota Belief and Ritual* (Lincoln: University of Nebraska Press, 1980), pp. 179–80.

8. Sam Gill, *Native American Religions: An Introduction* (Belmont, Calif.: Wadsworth, 1982), p. 19.

9. Alfonso Ortiz, *The Tewa World: Space, Time, Being, and Becoming in a Pueblo Society* (Chicago: University of Chicago Press, 1969), p. 40.

10. Quoted in John Farella, *The Main Stalk: A Synthesis of Navajo Philosophy* (Tucson: University of Arizona Press, 1984), pp. 104–105.

11. Williamson, *Living the Sky*, p. 107.

12. Michele Strutin, *Chaco: A Cultural Legacy* (Tucson, Ariz.: Southwest Parks and Monuments Association, 1994), pp. 27–28.

13. Williamson, *Living the Sky*, p. 165.

14. Ibid., pp. 199–217.

15. Ibid., p. 228.

16. Ibid., pp. 240–68.

17. Ortiz, *The Tewa World*, pp. 19–21.

18. Howard Harrod, *Renewing the World* (Tucson: University of Arizona Press, 1992), p. 133.

19. Hultkrantz, *The Religions of the American Indians*, pp. 110–11.

20. Ortiz, *The Tewa World*, p. 24.

21. Black Elk, *Black Elk Speaks: Being the Life Story of a Holy Man of the Oglala Sioux*, as told through John G. Neihardt (Lincoln: University of Nebraska Press, 1979), pp. 35 and 40.

22. Gill, *Native American Religions*, p. 34.

23. Howard Harrod, *Becoming and Remaining a People: Native American Religions on the Northern Plains* (Tucson: University of Arizona Press, 1987), pp. 13–30.

24. Charles Lange, "Relations of the Southwest with the Plains and Great Basin," *Handbook of North American Indians*, ed. Ortiz, vol. 9, pp. 201–205.

25. Richard Ford, "Inter-Indian Exchange in the Southwest," *Handbook of North American Indians*, ed. Alfonso Ortiz, vol. 10 (Washington, D.C.: Smithsonian Institution, 1983), p. 722.

26. Black Elk, *Black Elk Speaks*, p. 43.

Chapter Four

Time and Cosmos

T ime, like space, not only serves as a useful means of organizing everyday life within a given culture but also functions as a basic structuring factor for every society. Time and space, as thinkers such as Edward Hall and Mircea Eliade have pointed out, are the warp and weft out of which the fabric of any worldview is woven. As Hall puts it, "The Pueblo Indians . . . who live in the Southwest have a sense of time which is at complete variance with the clock-bound habits of the ordinary American citizen. For the Pueblos events begin when the time is ripe and no sooner."[1] This chapter explores aspects of the temporal dimension of human existence within various Native American worldviews.

CYCLES OF SEASONS AND LIFE

It is frequently said that Westerners regard time as linear, with a specific beginning in the past and a specific end in the future. The cultures of the East, on the other hand, regard time as following a cyclical pattern in which all things and events continuously repeat themselves. Although this may well be an oversimplification of a very complex issue, an important truth is contained in this statement. Time is thought of differently in the Orient and the Occident, and noting such differences can lead to greater understanding. This applies to understanding Native American worldviews as well.

The common idea of time in the Euro-American worldview does seem to imply a linear construct that results in our notions of history, progress, and even in some sort of final judgment. As Eliade says, according to this Western understanding, "The End of the World will reveal the religious value of human acts, and men will be judged by their acts. . . . The chosen, the good, will be saved by their loyalty to a Sacred History."[2] It is this view of time that has contributed to America's interpretation of history, including the use of such terms as "Manifest Destiny" and "The war to end all wars." In the West the future is almost invariably seen as better than the past, whereas in the traditional culture of China, for example, it was generally seen as a steady process of degeneration.

In general the Native American way of thinking about time is more like that of Eastern cultures. For central to the Native American understanding of time is the concept of continuous renewal or regeneration. This idea plays a key role both in community life and in individual lives. In the former the notion of renewal is connected to the cycle of the seasons, while in the latter it turns on the stages and passages of a person's development as a man or a woman. In both cases there is an implicit understanding that within the set of cycles a deeper, more fundamental pattern of cosmic renewal is expressing itself. So, while every yearly cycle is somewhat different from those already completed, in a profound sense each is also the same. Similarly, though each person is a unique individual, the regenerative pattern of a given life partakes of the ongoing life of the world.

In a sense, construing the temporal dimension of human experience as essentially cyclical can be seen as a natural progression from the concept of cosmic space as a vast circle. As Ray Williamson explains,

> This notion of cyclical time was crucial to the Pawnee and to other Native Americans as well. For them, sacred events occur again and again in a pattern that repeats the cycles of the celestial sphere. Thus time does not progress along a linear path but moves in a cyclical manner so as to provide an enclosure or total setting in which events occur. Past, present, and future all exist together because the cycles turn continually upon themselves.[3]

This connection between the cyclical character of time and the cosmic shape of reality is evident in Black Elk's account of his nation's sacred hoop.

The generative pattern of nature is one of the more obvious characteristics of the world in which we all live. In addition to earth, sky, mountains, and bodies of water, there is plant and animal life, involving birth, growth, decay, and death. Moreover, much of this overall pattern is tied directly to the cyclical paths of the celestial bodies, especially the sun. Peoples of all times and places have found it practical not only to pay attention to the seasonal cycles but to tie their social and religious life to them as well. Even in the West we often think of life in this way, as Vivaldi's *The Four Seasons* reveals.

The sun's cycles have often been at the center of the human effort to structure cultural life in relation to the natural world. Each day begins with the sunrise and closes with the sunset. Not only does this continuously repeated cycle provide the basic structure for the specifics of daily life, such as work schedules, meals, and sleep, but it also serves as a metaphor for the life cycle itself. Dawn symbolizes birth, noon the zenith of life, and dusk the completion of life. In addition, the position of the sun in relation to the horizon at any given time of the day and/or year affects how and where dwellings are built, crops are planted, and journeys are planned. Both hunting and gathering societies, on the one hand, and agricultural societies, on the other, organize the day as well as the year around the varying positions of the sun in the sky throughout its seasonal, cyclical pattern.

As we have seen, one way people around the world have charted the sun's seasons is the use of some sort of celestial calendar and/or astronomical "observatory." The Pueblo peoples of the Southwest, both historic and prehistoric, built devices for recording and predicting the course of the sun into the very architecture of their dwellings. Sometimes they even constructed special edifices for this purpose, as in the case of the "Big House" at Casa Grande, Arizona, or the pectoglyphs on Fajada Butte in Chaco Canyon. The Plains Indians used medicine wheels to accomplish this same task. The cultural and economic life of the people largely depended on knowing and abiding by the sun's cycles.

The spatial patterns discussed in chapter 3 dovetail with the temporal ones under consideration here. The Cardinal Directions, for instance, not only serve to establish the boundaries and the center of community life, but they function as markers of the sun's progress through the sky, on both a daily and a yearly basis. These markers, in turn, are employed as signs or signals of the best times to plant and harvest, to hunt, or to gather berries. Even the migrations of the buffalo can be charted in relation to the cycles of the seasons, as the Plains Indians knew.

If one thinks of the sky as a vast celestial clock, with the sun and moon functioning much like the big and little hands against the domed background, it is possible to think of the planets and constellations as the second hand of the clock. For the patterns of these bodies provide a detailed account of the cycles of the seasons, as the astronomical corre-lations of the Big Horn Medicine Wheel, along with those of numerous sites throughout the Southwest, reveal.[4] Especially for those who migrate frequently, herding sheep or following bison, the constellations provide a far better mode of detailed orientation than do the sun or moon, since the latter require a stable horizon for the purpose. The early sailors of the Pacific navigated thousands of miles of open ocean using star patterns.

In chapter 5 we shall see how by means of regular ceremonial prac-tices Native Americans seek to renew and regenerate those powers and processes that constitute their social and physical realities. In the present chapter we are primarily concerned with understanding how time itself, as an aspect of human experience, is construed within various Native American worldviews. As we have seen, it is as if time and space were part of the skeleton upon which hangs the body of a given culture's belief system and cultural practices. Space forms another vital part of this skeleton. In later chapters we shall explore the body or external expres-sion of this conceptual skeleton as it is embodied in ceremonies, rituals, and other traditional customs.

It has often been noted that non-Western peoples do not think of "history" in the way that the West does. If divided up at all, time is gen-erally seen as having five phases: beginnings, or "primordial time," the legendary past, the recent past, the present, and times yet to come. This last phase usually refers to what comes after death, when the whole cycle of life will once again begin to repeat itself. Sometimes, however, it refers to the culmination of humanity's sojourn on earth. It is possible to think of the Native American interpretation of time as a spiral rather than as a line or a simple circle. Each time the cycle repeats itself it circles back to incorporate what has gone before into what is happening now, and

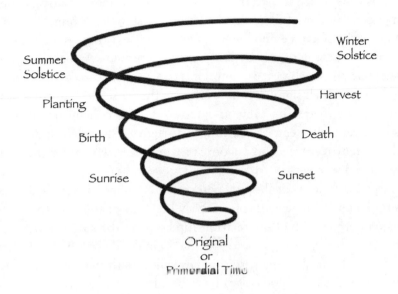

Winter Solstice

Summer Solstice

Harvest

Planting

Birth

Death

Sunrise

Sunset

Original
or
Primordial Time

FIG. 4.1. CYCLICAL, SPIRALING NATURE OF TIME

both of these cyclings will in turn be incorporated into what happens in the future.

As an example of this cyclical pattern, even among a people living in an environment that provides them with an abundance of food sources, consider the following account of the yearly cycle among the Kwakiutl in the Northwest coastal region, based on Native Americans' descriptions:

> The Kwakiutl year is divided into two periods. Summer, called *basux*, is the time for extensive hunting and fishing activities. The people live in small groups, often separated by some distance. This is a time of limited ceremonial activity. Winter is called *tsetsega*. The villages are occupied once again, and this is the ceremonial time of the year. The Kwakiutl see these seasons almost as opposites, yet as interdependent. During the winter the entire order of human existence is reversed. . . . The winter is actually not a time at all, in the sense of a succession of new moments, but rather a reenactment of that timeless era before and during which creation took place.[5]

This general spiral pattern is also displayed in many Native American understandings of the individual human life cycle. A human birth is often thought of as an embodiment of an already existing divine being or as a reembodiment of a previously existing person. As each stage of development is reached it is common for a person to receive an additional name, which signifies a new phase of the person's character but in no any way negates the previous phases. At the conclusion of life a person is generally seen as fulfilling a pattern or completing an open circle, thereby reentering an ongoing progression in which life grows out of death and vice versa.

Aspects of the cyclical, spiral perception of temporal experience pertain to the practical patterns of everyday life. One example of this is the Navajo interpretation of the relationship between the stages of the sun's progression through the sky and specific symbolic colors. White is associated with dawn, sky blue with midday, yellow with twilight, and black with darkness. Thus these colors have become the symbols of the Cardinal Directions. As John Farella explains,

> Certain times of the day . . . are appropriate for certain types of activities. This has two aspects. On the one hand, it is "natural" to behave or to feel certain ways at certain times. On the other hand, the cardinal phenomena and their inner forms instruct earth-surface creatures by transmitting certain thoughts and feelings to them.[6]

According to Navajo belief, it is important to rise with the sun at dawn if one wishes to be "healthy, wealthy, and wise." Likewise, it is expected that one will carry out tasks and pursue goals in the daylight hours, that one will, as our expression has it, "make hay while the sun shines." Twilight is the time for reuniting with others, resting, and reflecting on the accomplishments of the day. The darkness of night is to ensure inactivity, since what transpires during this time is generally thought to be evil.[7] Here we see again the merging of the spatial and temporal dimensions to provide the framework or loom on which a Native American worldview takes shape.

There is an ongoing debate among anthropologists over whether or not different worldviews really entail conflicting understandings of time. Benjamin Lee Whorf claimed, for example, that the Hopi language essentially has no notion of time as an abstract entity in the way that

Indo-European languages do. It is true that Hopi puts more stress on what Whorf called "aspect" than on tense in its verb patterns, but it is unclear what this implies. What is clear, however, is that in Hopi it is possible, by means of verb aspect patterns and suffix "post-positions," to make subtle distinctions that require the use of a number of adjectives and adverbs in Indo-European languages. At the very least it can be said that the languages in which different worldviews are expressed contain formulations uniquely compatible with the special features of those views.[8]

On a universal level it is easy to see that all human experience arises within a space-time context which provides the arena for both consciousness and action. All peoples have some way of conceptualizing these aspects, or axes, of human meaning and behavior, and they can be traced by examining the ways people speak and order their common life together. As we have seen, Native American worldviews clearly exemplify the significance of space and time. Although neither space nor time can be experienced directly by sensory observation, both are inextricably intertwined within nearly every facet of individual or corporate life.

LEGENDS AND HEROES

As has been noted, there are roughly five phases of time inherent within many Native American worldviews: primordial time, long-ago time, recent time, the present, and the time yet to come. The world-structuring acts of the original beings in the primordial phase have already been discussed. The details of the present and future phases will be considered later. The long-ago, legendary past of the Native American time frame is more complicated to discuss because it is difficult to discern where the primordial phase ends and the legendary phase begins. Put slightly differently, the difficulty has to do with determining which characters in the stories are original beings and which have some basis in the relatively ancient experience of a specific people.

In general, the crucial dividing line or pivotal point in our understanding of Native American culture and experience is the occasion of contact with European explorers and culture. Although there is good reason to believe that there may have been incidental contact with

Viking explorers around a thousand years ago, the first significant encounter was in the Southeast and Southwest with the Spanish invasion in the 1500s. In the 1600s many European countries sought to colonize large sections of the Atlantic coastal region, as well as parts of the Pacific coast. These initial encounters inaugurated a three-hundred-year period of open conflict that was finally brought to an end in the 1880s. Over the last hundred years we have seen numerous abortive attempts alternatively to extinguish Native American Indian cultures or to completely assimilate them into Euro-American society.

This history, which pertains to the near end of the temporal continuum introduced above, is fairly clear and familiar. It is the other end of the continuum that is more difficult to sort out, since the line of demarcation between the primordial phase of origins and what might be considered the "historical period" of Native Americans prior to contact with European cultures is hazy at best. Nevertheless, there is a difference between those events and characters involved in the ordering of the world, as set forth in stories of origin, and those that have more to do with what transpired in the life of the people between their origination and their more recent memories. This "in-between" phase is the period of legends and heroes which is now under discussion.

These crucial differences are illustrated by the contrast between the twins, "Good Spirit" and "Bad Spirit," on the one hand, and the Peacemaker and Handsome Lake (a religious leader) in Iroquois traditions on the other. The former are clearly nonhistorical, spiritual beings who played a crucial role in the ordering of the cosmos at the inception of the world as we know it. The Peacemaker, however, seems to have been a person with a historical anchorage in the more recent cultural life of the Iroquois. In this way he functions more as legendary hero than as original spiritual being. Furthermore, there is every reason to conclude that Handsome Lake was a historical person, especially since there is good evidence that his message was at least partially influenced by Christian teachings, which puts him within the postcontact period.

Thus in considering traditions it is crucial to distinguish between personages who belong more properly to the original ordering of the world and those who play an important role thereafter. There seems to be a significant difference between them simply because such interaction places these personages in a category different from both original beings, on the one hand, and legendary heroes on the other. It seems best to classify beings such as Trickster and/or Coyote, who play an important role in nearly every Native American worldview, and who continue to be active in the lives of many cultural groups, as spiritual beings in their own right, rather than as legendary or heroic characters.

The culture hero, on the other hand, while generally not regarded as an original being who helped establish the order of things in the natural world, is usually not thought of as a straightforwardly historical figure either. Rather, he or she is seen as the one who established the quality and shape of a given people's cultural heritage and destiny at the outset. This sort of activity and role would seem to place such beings in a category of their own between original beings and historical figures. A useful parallel here is the relationship between the Titans and the gods of ancient Greek mythology. The former were already on the scene when the gods began to be conceived, while both were said to exist prior to the arrival of human beings. Thus the Greek gods were not gods in the sense that we in the West have come to use the term. In a way they were more akin to Native American culture heroes than to divine beings. A consideration of some specific culture heroes will prove helpful here.

In the Navajo stories of their own beginnings as a people, Changing Woman plays the crucial role. Not only was she responsible for many of the qualities and contours of the natural environment, but she gave the Navajo people corn and sheep as their traditional means of livelihood. It is interesting to speculate about when and how the stories of Changing Woman were put together, since corn and sheep became part of the Navajo culture after their arrival in the Southwest some five hundred years ago. At this point the accounts of the Navajo and those of anthropologists part company and thus fail to provide an answer. Changing Woman would seem to be both an original being and a legendary figure, since she both participated in aspects of natural creation and established the character of Navajo culture.

Perhaps this in-between status of Changing Woman is the result of the fact that in the Navajo origin stories she is not only born of two original beings, First Man and First Woman, but she eventually entered into direct conflict with the former over the sacred medicine bundle from which she was able to establish and structure the Navajo world. Thus she seems to function both as a divine being and as a culture hero. In other traditions the culture hero is turned into the trickster as a result of a conflict between it and the original Creator Spirit. The trickster, often identified as a coyote, continuously bedevils both divine beings and humans by turning things upside down and doing things backwards, sometimes in jest and sometimes in earnest. In a sense, then, this figure can be said to function as an antihero in many cultures.

The following passage, based on Native American accounts, summarizes the positive role of the culture hero as one who operates in the hazy temporal phase between original creation and the present:

> In his serious function the culture hero is primarily originator of the present conditions in nature and culture and of human fate. He is, as has been mentioned, an assistant creator or transformer of the world. . . . He is spoken of as the wandering magician who changes the shape of the landscape and divides living beings into animals and humans. The period previous to this is often specified as the age when animals acted as people and could speak. Numerous myths . . . describe how the culture hero steals fire, daylight (or the sun), and water from the "other" world, how he releases the water . . . and sets free the game which has been enclosed in some place like a cave inaccessible to humans. In several myths the culture hero is the great monster slayer. . . . Then there are a great number of instances concerning the culture hero as inventor of arts and crafts and as founder of laws and ceremonies. . . . Finally, the culture hero is responsible for human fate. According to a myth found throughout western North America, the culture hero and another being, generally the Supreme Being, dispute or discuss the future of mankind. The culture hero is for death, the other for life, either continued or renewed. The culture hero wins either because of his aggressiveness in getting the last word or through divination. Here is clearly detectable the same opposition between the culture hero and the Supreme Being as that so often expressed in creation myths.[9]

There are interesting parallels between the character and function of Changing Woman in the Navajo stories and those of White Buffalo Calf Woman in Black Elk's story of how the sacred pipe first came to the

Oglala Sioux. These personages both serve as the culture heroes for their respective peoples, providing the concepts and materials that are crucial for their identity and survival. White Buffalo Calf Woman might be regarded as more of a legendary character than Changing Woman, since the Sioux are already in existence when she first appears to them. Thus she does not participate in the formation of the natural environment as does Changing Woman.

In addition, Changing Woman is frequently referred to as "White Shell Woman," perhaps because of her early association with the American West and its coastal waters. Thus both of these culture heroes incorporate the color white into their image and character. There seems to be a positive symbolism connected with the color white, since it is often related to the dawn, and therefore to the East as a Cardinal Direction. Unlike Changing Woman, however, White Buffalo Calf Woman functions in full harmony with the "Great Grandfather Spirit," rather than in any way conflicting with him. It is also clear that White Buffalo Calf Woman played a significant role in the cultural heritage and ritual practice of other Plains peoples, such as the Hidatsas and the Mandans.[10] Here again her role is more that of a legendary hero than that of either an original being or a culture hero. However, the line between these three categories is never absolute.

Nearly everyone is familiar with the historical Native American heroes who lived and guided their people during the many conflicts with the European invaders over the past few centuries. Chief Seattle, Sitting Bull, Crazy Horse, Chief Joseph, Red Cloud, Cochise, and Geronimo are all famous for their courage and skill in the many battles with their conquerers. Not so familiar are Metacom, or "King Philip" as the colonists called him, Popé, Pontiac, Joseph Bryant, Tecumseh, Black Hawk, White Cloud, Osceola, and Quanah Parker. These figures led their people in uprisings against, respectively, the English colonists in New England, the Spanish *conquistadores* in New Mexico, the French in the Great Lakes region, the American revolutionaries, America in the War of 1812, American domination in the Great Lakes area, and American expansionists in Florida and the southern Great Plains.

There are also many Native Americans who are famous within Euro-American culture in the United States for the wisdom and courage they exhibited in cooperation with various American endeavors. These include Pocahontas, Sacajawea, and Sequoyah. These people, however, are not properly to be counted among heroes who are the stuff of legend among Native Americans. A great deal of work remains to be done in uncovering Native American stories that tell of the contributions of the heroes who lived in the period between the founding of the various groups and their first contact with Europeans. Unfortunately, time is not on the side of those engaged in this quest since the few Native Americans who remember such stories become fewer every day.

CLANS AND KINSHIP

An equally helpful way to think about the temporal dimension of human existence is in terms of social and family connections. In various times and places peoples have divided themselves into subgroups so as to facilitate sociopolitical interaction and economic exchange. Also, people naturally join together according to family lineage as a means of survival and procreation. Native American peoples have most frequently organized themselves in clans and have always kept very careful track of family relationships in terms of kinship. Both of these cultural patterns extend through time, from generation to generation, as well as across the culture in any given period, and are thus to be understood as aspects of the temporal dimension of community life.

Although the central idea behind the clan structure is that of kinship and lineage, Native American peoples construe clan membership somewhat differently depending on the circumstances in which they find themselves. Both strangers and orphans may be adopted into clans when it seems appropriate, and clans themselves may be reorganized when it becomes necessary. Sometimes clan membership and lineage have been determined on the basis of male descent, from father to son, and so on. Quite often, however, Native American groups have been organized according to a matrilineal pattern whereby kinship and inheritance are determined by descent from mother to daughter. We shall return to kinship after clan patterns have been discussed.

Iroquois clan patterns are typical of those found throughout the

Northeast region. The most fundamental unit has been a group of relatives that traces its descent from a single woman. In the Mohawk language, for instance, this group is called the *ohwachira*, with two or more of
the eldest women and their descendants making up a clan. The Iroquois
trace this matrilineal pattern back to the fact that the first person to
accept the message of Great Peace was a woman whom Dekanawida, the
Peacemaker, named "Mother of Nations, the Great Peace Woman" and
appointed as the custodian of the message. In this way Iroquois women
became the main line of connection for the various groups and lineages.[11]

While they are matrilineal in social structure, the Iroquois are patriarchal in political structure, since they are governed by male chiefs.
Nonetheless, since the female elders appoint males as chiefs, and can
remove them if it is determined that they are behaving inappropriately,
the matrilineal social reality of Iroquois culture actually controls the
political reality. Thus while the male chiefs carry on the formal business
of the group, they are accountable to the female leaders in the long run,
from generation to generation. This same general pattern of matrilineal
governance controlling patriarchal politics can also be found among the
Crow, where all decisions about land are referred back to women elders,
even though they do not appoint the chiefs.[12]

A person is born into one of the Iroquois clans and inherits clan affiliation and material wealth from his or her mother. In addition, every
member of a clan considers every other member a relative and thereby
acquires membership in a very large family structure. Because of this,
marriage to someone in the same clan is forbidden, since this would be a
form of incest. The requirement that a person marry outside of the clan
is almost universal in Native American cultures. Being a member of a
very large, extended family through clan affiliation ensures that a person
always has relatives to turn to in times of difficulty or loss of immediate
family members. Since Native Americans often lived short and relatively
dangerous lives, this pattern proved useful in maintaining social conti-
nuity and enhancing survival possibilities.

The inner dynamics of the development of the clan system and especially of the emergence of the matrilineal inheritance pattern are difficult to trace. There is reason to think that they are connected to the
change from a hunting and gathering economy to a horticultural one,

which in turn played a large role in determining where a family would live. If it lived near the husband's family it would be termed "patrilocal," while if it took up residence near the wife's family it would be "matrilocal." This latter arrangement often led to a matrilineal pattern of clan membership and inheritance. Here is how one researcher describes the process:

> The Iroquoian matrilocal residence pattern seems to have evolved after a new division of labor resulted in men being away from their communities, performing a variety of different tasks in small scattered groups, for much of the year, while women remained in their home communities in daily face-to-face contact. Under these circumstances it became desirable for several generations of related women to live together and to help each other and for men, when they came home, to live with their wives' families. . . . Matrilocal residence also encouraged the development of matrilocal descent groups and matrilineal inheritance of clan membership and clan offices.[13]

Generally speaking, each clan within a tribe identifies itself with and by an affiliation with a prominent form of wildlife, such as the turtle, wolf, bear, eagle, heron, or hawk, in its locality and in its oral tradition. It is within clan relationships that Iroquoian peoples "live and move and have their being" socially speaking. Among the peoples of the Great Plains, however, there is generally no clan system. Here people generally

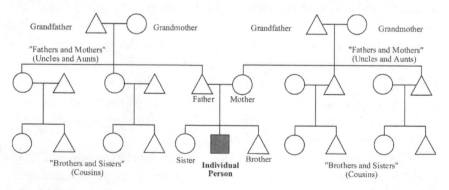

FIG. 4.2. IROQUOIS KINSHIP PATTERN, INDICATING RELATIONSHIP
OF AN INDIVIDUAL WITH UNCLES, AUNTS, AND COUSINS

trace their kinship to everyone to whom they are biologically related, whether through the mother or the father. There are few delineated lineages among the majority of Plains groups, since the inheritance of land was rarely an important consideration. Also, Plains Indians usually traveled and camped in collections of more or less closely related kindred groups who were accustomed to functioning together, a pattern well suited to a people on the move.[14]

A basic characteristic of Tewa Pueblo society is its division into halves, or what anthropologists call "moieties," a word derived from the French. This dualistic pattern is fairly common around the world, but Alfonso Ortiz claims it has unique aspects among the Tewa. The Tewa origin story tells of how the people were divided into two groups as they traveled down the two sides of the Rio Grande River to their present home. Eventually this division became the basis for dividing the Tewa into two major groups, the Summer People and the Winter People. The many, complex ritual and ceremonial responsibilities of the Tewa yearly calendar are divided between these two groups, and the stratified social structure of clans and political leaders is contained within this dualistic pattern.

Membership in the two Tewa moieties is not strictly a matter of kinship or clanship, but remains flexible since it incorporates various adoption and transfer of membership processes. Moreover, the different responsibilities of those in charge during each half of the calendar year sometimes override moieties altogether.[15] Unlike other Pueblo people, the Tewa are free to marry members of their own moiety. Alfonso Ortiz, a Tewa himself, thinks that Tewa marriage rites have been influenced by Catholic practices here. He says, "There is no clear post-marital residence rule, and the only restriction on the selection of a spouse is that he or she not be closer than a fourth cousin. This, of course, is also the rule of the Catholic Church."[16]

Another aspect of any people's worldview as it is related to the temporal dimension of human experience is that of kinship. It is, after all, through kinship relations that the various generations are connected to one another. A wide range of kinship patterns exists among the Native Americans of North America, and anthropologists have devoted a great deal of energy to tracing these patterns in order to be able to chart the various sociopolitical duties and rights encoded therein.

One of the more important features of many kinship patterns is the merging of what Western tradition sees as distinct relationships. Thus, among both the Iroquois and the Crow, for instance, the sisters and brothers of a person's parents are called parents and regarded as parents. Cousins are called by the same term as siblings and are related to as such. Among the Crow and some Plains tribes, such as the Omaha, this pattern is limited to the relatives of one parent. These patterns are involved in the temporal dimension of Native American worldviews because they serve to track lineage through successive generations.[17]

DEATH AND DESTINY

The origin stories of many Native American cultures are clear about how and why death, as the end of the temporal dimension of human existence, became a fact of life. The Supreme Being and the culture hero had a disagreement as to the fate of humankind, with the one wanting humans to live forever and the other insisting that human life be limited in time so as not to overcrowd the earth. In the end the culture hero usually saw to it that this latter view prevailed and thus all humans must die. This fate in no way hinged on anything humans did or did not do, in contrast to the Judeo-Christian story in Genesis where death was the result of disobedience to God.

In general, Native Americans' attitude toward death also differs markedly from that of people who live within Western culture. In the latter there exists a puzzling dilemma. For, on the one hand, human life is traditionally viewed as a temporary and preparatory existence in which one looks forward to a life after death, while at the same time Westerners clearly regard this present life as their major concern and resent and fear death. By contrast, Native American worldviews usually regard death in old age as the culmination and fulfillment of a life well lived. Thus this present life is indeed the primary mode of existence, yet death itself is in no way feared or resented. If one has lived a life that is faithful to the Native American way, old age and death are welcomed as the final phase of life in which its meaning and purpose are realized. Rather than something to be feared or resented, the end of life is viewed as a crowning achievement.

The fundamental reason for this attitude toward old age and death concerns the correlation between living well and acquiring of knowledge that is inherent in the worldview of most Native Americans. Since knowledge is basic to becoming wise, and wisdom is seen as the highest of human achievements, it follows that the knowledge gained through living a long and faithful life is a necessary condition to such an achievement. Death itself can be looked forward to or at least welcomed as the capstone of a truly meaningful life. This way of looking at the world and at life leads naturally to increased honor and respect for those who have lived long and faithful lives and are thereby the epitome of wisdom and goodness. Thus those who have achieved death in old age are revered after they have died.[18]

In the majority of Native American worldviews, death at an earlier age is generally regarded as unfortunate but to be accepted as natural. Indeed, to die defending one's people was frequently counted as one of the highest honors one could achieve. This was especially true of the Plains Indians, but in nearly all cultures it was customary to award extremely high honors to those who gave their life for their people. Moreover, all cultures develop patterns for paying homage to and honoring everyone who dies, irrespective of their age or position in life. Native American peoples are no exception in this regard.

Generally, death is regarded as the last event of this life and the first of a life to come, whatever form this future life might take. As such, death is treated as the final stage of this life or the final passageway through which a person must pass on this earth. Thus most Native American peoples incorporate death into their cultural practice with a ceremony that assists the person making the transition from this life to the next. Burial rituals and procedures vary a great deal from one culture to another, but nearly all involve practices that prepare the dead person for the journey that lies ahead, including special clothes and/or personal items which will provide comfort or help along the way. Most cultures also make provision for enabling those who remain behind to deal with their loss. This usually involves rituals of purification and reincorporation into community life.

Alfonso Ortiz describes these rituals among the Tewa:

Some days after the releasing rite, just before the next festive occasion in the village, the two moiety chiefs go together to the home of the recently deceased. They ask those within to "leave all sadness behind, for he whom you miss so much is now at the place of endless cicada singing." They are invited to join in the festivities or the ritual now near at hand. This is the "rite of reintegration" . . . of the survivors back into the society. . . . The releasing rite is repeated for the deceased exactly one year after death. . . . On each of these occasions, however, the sadness and uneasiness is gone and the festive aspects are emphasized.[19]

The "releasing rite" is performed in many Native American cultures because it is believed that the soul or spiritual aspect of the dead person may have difficulty leaving its natural surroundings and loved ones. At the same time, those still living are often uncomfortable with the thought of the deceased's presence among them. Thus a special ceremony releases the dead ones or empowers them to move on to the next stage of human destiny, for their own good as well as for the good of those remaining behind. Sometimes it is even thought that the dead may harm those still living if they are not shown the proper respect and/or appeased with gifts, and so on.[20]

Among the Tewa, however, fear of the dead has more to do with the possibility that a dead one may be lonely and return to take one of the living for companionship. The releasing rite launches the deceased into the next world and assuages the discomfort of the living.[21]

As to the question of what becomes of the individual self after death, there is a great variety of beliefs. Some people, like the Navajo, believe that the individual person "will return to the Dawn and become part of the undifferentiated pool of *nilch'i* (life) that will animate future living things."[22] Others, like the Crow, believe that the person first acquires a spirit or a soul at death and then "enters an ethereal realm where all other Crows who have died are camped."[23] Still others, such as the Hopi, believe that the dead continue to interact with this world as Kachina cloud spirits who bring rain.[24]

The broader question of the destiny of Native American peoples as a whole is even more complex and the answers more diverse than those pertaining to the question of the fate of individuals. In general, within the traditional worldviews of most if not all Native American cultures the inherent assumption is that the cyclical pattern of time will continue forever just as it has in the past. It is true that from time to time one encounters a foreboding undertone in the stories, which suggests that the world as it is presently structured will eventually come to an end. For instance,

> There is some talk at Zuni about the death of the world itself. At the beginning the earth was soft and wet; the fathers and grandfathers of the present-day elders began to wonder whether it was getting old and dry. They prophesied a famine. . . . At the end, they said, all man-made things would rise against us and a hot rain would fall.[25]

For the most part such pessimistic visions of the future of the world may have crept into Native American worldviews as a result of the devastating consequences of conquest by white invaders. The unrelenting pressure of conflict and eventual domination made nearly all Native Americans susceptible to an apocalyptic interpretation of their immediate as well as long-range destiny. The "doomsday" tone and content of many beliefs and practices shortly after the full onslaught of the European invasion were frequently accompanied, however, by a final vision of the return of the original world picture and way of life.

Hultkrantz summarizes these final visions:

> In many places prophets proclaimed visions of clearsightedness, in which the old culture and the ancestral religion were again restored in purified form. The perspective was clearly eschatological and what is called "nativistic": there was a desire for a renaissance of the more vigorous and significant spiritual values within the inherited culture and an elimination of foreign influence. Elements of messianism, a goal-oriented ethics, an eschatological message, all seem to bear witness to a Christian background for these movements.[26]

The best-known example of this phenomenon was the Ghost Dance movement which swept across the Great Basin and the Plains in 1889–90. Its founder was a Paiute named Wovoka and its message was that by participating in continuous round dances Native Americans could bring about the fulfillment of the revivalist vision. On the Plains the movement took on a strong anti-white emphasis and brought about a crucial confrontation with the U.S. military which had been dispatched to put an end to the movement. The result was the murder of Chief Sitting Bull and the ensuing massacre of hundreds of Sioux camped at Wounded Knee in South Dakota in 1890. This atrocity essentially marked the conclusion of the wars between the Native Americans and the U.S. government. There were other visionary movements at this time, such as the Shaker Church in the Northwest and the Peyote Cult in the Southwest, but these will be discussed later, since they represent attempts to accommodate Native American worldviews to European culture.

The massacre at Wounded Knee brought a deep feeling of doom to many Native Americans regarding their worldview. To Black Elk, who actually witnessed the conclusion of the slaughter of women and children it symbolized the end of his people's dream: "You see me now a pitiful old man who has done nothing, for the nation's hoop is broken and scattered. There is no center any longer, and the sacred tree is dead."[27]

Shortly before his death, however, Black Elk stood at the spot where he had first received his vision as a young boy and prayed these words: "In sorrow I am sending a feeble voice, O Six Powers of the World. Hear me in my sorrow, for I may never call again. O make my people live!"[28] At that point in time it seemed as though the traditional Native American way of life was fast coming to an end, but Black Elk and other leaders still hoped for its revival.

The temporal dimension of Native American worldviews can be seen to flesh itself out in relation to the various aspects of human existence and culture. The basic cyclical pattern of the seasons of nature and the phases of life extends from the time of origins through the legendary past and the weave of clan and kinship to death and beyond, both for the individual and for the culture. The focus on death and destiny can be incorporated into Figure 4.1 by inserting a vectorial line running from the point of origin at the bottom up through the center of the spiral and pointing ever upward. The lifeline of both a person and a culture progresses within the cyclical orbits of the sun through time.

NOTES

1. Edward Hall, *The Silent Language* (Garden City, N.Y.: Doubleday, 1959), p. 21.

2. Mircea Eliade, *Myth and Reality* (New York: Harper and Row, 1963), p. 65.

3. Ray Williamson, *Living the Sky: The Cosmos of the American Indian* (Norman: University of Oklahoma Press, 1984), p. 313.

4. Ibid., pp. 201–17.

5. Sam Gill, *Native American Religions: An Introduction* (Belmont, Calif.: Wadsworth, 1982), p. 125.

6. John Farella, *The Main Stalk: A Synthesis of Navajo Philosophy* (Tucson: University of Arizona Press, 1984), p. 108.

7. Ibid., pp. 109–11

8. C. F. and F. M. Voegelin, "Hopi Semantics," in *Handbook of North American Indians*, ed. Alfonso Ortiz, vol. 10 (Washington, D.C.: Smithsonian Institution, 1983), pp. 581–86.

9. Åke Hultkrantz, *The Religions of the American Indians* (Berkeley: University of California Press, 1979), pp. 135–36.

10. Howard Harrod, *Becoming and Remaining a People: Native American Religions on the Northern Plains* (Tucson: University of Arizona Press, 1995), pp. 70–76.

11. Barbara Graymont, *The Iroquois* (New York: Chelsea House, 1988), pp. 24–26.

12. Dale McGinnis and Floyd W. Sharrock, *The Crow People* (Phoenix, Ariz.: Indian Tribal Series, 1972) p. 13.

13. Bruce Trigger, *The Huron: Farmers of the North* (Fort Worth, Tex.: Holt, Rinehart, and Winston, 1990), p. 67.

14. E. Adamson Hoebel, *The Cheyennes* (New York: Harcourt Brace, 1988), pp. 36–37.

15. Alfonso Ortiz, *The Tewa World: Space, Time, Being, and Becoming in a Pueblo Society* (Chicago: University of Chicago Press, 1969), pp. 43–45.

16. Ibid., p. 46.

17. Linda Amy Kimball, Dale McGinnis, and Shawna Craig, *Anthropological World: An Introduction to Cultural Anthropology* (Dubuque, Iowa: Kendall/Hunt, 1986), pp. 96–100.

18. Farella, *The Main Stalk*, pp. 29–30.

19. Ortiz, *The Tewa World*, p. 55.

20. Hultkrantz, *Religions of the American Indians*, pp. 129–30.

21. Ortiz, *The Tewa World*, pp. 53–54.

22. Farella, *The Main Stalk*, p. 179.

23. McGinnis, *The Crow People*, p. 28.

24. Lewis A. Hieb, "Hopi World View," in *Handbook of North American Indians*, ed. Alfonso Ortiz, vol. 9 (Washington, D.C.: Smithsonian Institution, 1979), p. 577.

25. Dennis Tedlock, "Zuni Religion and World View," in *Handbook of North American Indians*, ed. Ortiz, vol. 9, p. 508.

26. Hultkrantz, *Religions of the American Indians*, p. 151.

27. Black Elk, *Black Elk Speaks: Being the Life Story of a Holy Man of the Oglala Sioux*, as told through John G. Neihardt (Lincoln: University of Nebraska Press, 1979), p. 270.

28. Ibid., p. 274.

Chapter Five

Ceremonies and Customs

M uch of the Native American interest in locating and tracking the course of the sun, moon, and stars has to do with a concern to renew or reinforce the patterns and processes by which the cosmos is structured. Because their survival and well-being depended almost entirely on being able to predict and trace the natural course of events in the world around them, it generally became imperative to devise ways to participate in these patterns and processes through regular rituals and ceremonies which helped ensure that events continued to follow their established course. Other ceremonies and rituals inevitably evolved for marking and celebrating other regular occurrences in the life of the community, such as birth, coming of age, marriage, and death. All these practices factor into the warp and weft of any Native American worldview, as well as into its concept of time.

THE HARVEST AND THE HUNT

> Central among religious ceremonies for most Indians, hunters and gatherers as well as cultivators, are the annual rites denoting the beginning or the climax of the hunting season or the crop year. . . . These ceremonies are often under the auspices of the Supreme Being. Their main purpose is to renew the world and life itself with the aid of the powers, in particular by replenishing the supply of food.[1]

Here we see how such ceremonies and rituals can directly express the worldview of a people.

One of the more elaborate ceremonial cycles is that of the Rio Grande Pueblo peoples, especially among the Tewa. Alfonso Ortiz indicates that the entire Tewa ritual year can be understood as consisting of three levels or layers. The Tewa year is divided into four parts by the solstices and equinoxes, with each half of any given year being the responsibility of one of the two moieties, the winter and summer societies. Each of these moieties is in turn subdivided into eight separate groups to carry out the required, appropriate rituals. The first layer of the annual Tewa cycle is composed of nine "works" or rituals, nearly all of which pertain to the various phases of the yearly planting and harvesting seasons. Each "work" takes thirty-two days to complete, which means that 288 days of every year are given over to fulfilling some aspect of this ceremonial cycle.

When discussing the precise timing of these different works, Ortiz remarks that "each of the first four works in the traditional cycle actually comes about a month before the phenomenon it is supposed to bring about."[2] Pointing out that this pattern is quite different from those of western Pueblo peoples, such as the Hopi, he hypothesizes that a major reason for this difference may well be the influence of the Catholic Church's year, especially between Advent and Easter. Unlike the Hopi, the Rio Grande Pueblo peoples celebrate both their traditional religious festivals and those of Catholicism, in parallel fashion through the year.

In Ortiz' words,

[The] entire cycle of works is tied to nature's basic rhythm and to the Tewa's attempts to influence that rhythm for his well-being. In this sense it is the structure of structures in Tewa life. The one basic division in this cycle is that between the agricultural and the nonagricultural series of works.[3]

This latter remark leads him on to an account of the two nonagricultural layers of the Tewa ritual cycle, each of which seeks to coordinate the sociopolitical life of the people with the fundamental agricultural ritual pattern. The subsistence cycle aims at incorporating the nonagricultural aspects of Tewa economic life into the ceremonial practices. The hunting and gathering activities of the people take place almost exclusively in the late fall and winter, and thus do not conflict with the agricultural activities.

The third layer, the cultural ritual cycle, involves such things as transference of authority from one moiety to the other, special "retreats" set aside for prayer and meditation, and elaborate relay races between the two moieties. When one superimposes these latter two layers of ceremonial practice onto the basic agricultural ritual pattern, it becomes clear that the Tewa ritual year is as dense as it is significant. It seems as if ceremonial activities are held on every day of the year, and that all cultural life, from economics through social relations to politics, is tied to the yearly seasons. The density is accentuated when one remembers that each pueblo has but a few hundred people, nearly all of whom must participate in these rituals.

When we shift our attention to Native American cultures in regions which have different climates and different varieties of food sources than do the peoples of the desert and plateaus, we find that the ceremonial patterns are correspondingly different as well. Among the peoples of the Great Lakes and Northeast regions, for instance, the winters are long and hard and thus become the primary period during which the more significant ritual activities take place. The main food supply is obtained from fishing, from hunting, and to a lesser extent from what anthropologists term *horticulture*. Thus here the ceremonial patterns conform more to hunting and fishing seasons than to planting and harvesting. Also, the sacred aspect of these ceremonies is more tied to animals indigenous to the area than to the cycles of earth and sky.

Among the Iroquois, however, the yearly rituals tend to focus on the planting and harvesting of the "Three Sisters," corn, beans, and squash, which were given to them by the Creator as the sustainers of life. At the same time, however, a number of ceremonies are also devoted to various aspects of the "Great Peace" commemoration during the winter months between harvesting and planting. In addition, many rituals pertain to hunting, especially of bears, which are greatly feared and prized. The Iroquois regularly tell stories of bear hunts, and point to the bowl of the Big Dipper as the "Great Bear" in the sky. The stars forming the dipper's handle are said to be the hunters chasing the bear across the sky; when the constellation turns upside down in the fall, the hunters are said to have been successful. The bear rises again in the spring and the chase is renewed.[4]

As with the Tewa Pueblo peoples, the Kwakiutl of the Pacific Northwest divide their year into two parts corresponding to summer and winter.

The four main aspects of the world, humans, animals, vegetable life, and supernatural beings, are thought of as mutually interdependent, with the relationship between humans and animals playing an especially crucial role, since these forms of life were originally identical. The winter rituals generally revolve around a reenactment of the hunting activities of the summer, thus seeking to reverse and yet reinforce the relationship between humans and their prey. Sam Gill describes this ceremonial pattern:

> Throughout the summer portion of the year, the relationship between human beings and animals is that of hunter and hunted. The hunter kills and eats the flesh of the animals. Eating of the animal flesh causes the animals to become one with the human beings but in human form. It is during the long, elaborate Winter Ceremonial that this relationship is reversed, in order to regain the primordial identity of human and animal in animal form. Human beings take up the masks of animals in ceremonial dances, thus becoming the animals. They return to the original conditions so as to engender the supernatural powers of creation that may benefit the community.[5]

The ritual employment of animal-like masks in dances to imitate and invoke the presence and power of different forms of animal life is common to many Native American peoples who revere such animals even while depending upon them as their main food source.

Groups such as the Northwest coastal peoples who rely mostly on salmon and the Plains Indians who follow the bison do not practice their renewal rituals with quite the same degree of regularity as groups that rely largely on agriculture. The salmon and the bison do, to be sure, run according to seasonal patterns, but these vary far more than do those of planting and harvesting. Nevertheless, those who depend upon these animal food sources do engage in ceremonies aimed at ensuring the continuation and the increase of these sources' appearance. Some anthropologists suggest that the Plains cultures place more emphasis on individual experience and achievement than most other groups, and thus they have fewer ceremonies that involve the entire community.

Among fishing and hunting peoples a good deal of attention is frequently paid to what are called "bone rites." These are rituals that involve the rearrangement of the skeleton of the eaten fish or animal so as to encourage a continued supply. This ritual is practiced both individually and collectively, as Hultkrantz makes clear:

> [T]he separate rites are sometimes repeated for each felled animal, regardless of when it is hunted (for example, for the bear and the whale), whereas the bone rites in the collective seasonal festivals are always initial rites linked to the beginning of the hunting season. It is possible that . . . the salmon rites of the Northwest Coast . . . have undergone a secondary development into seasonal rites under the influence of "first-fruits" ceremonies with fruits and berries.[6]

There is considerable scholarly debate as to the origin and purpose of the Sun Dance ceremony among the people of the Plains. Some interpreters maintain that it was originally a thank-offering to the Great Spirit for sending the buffalo, and a number of rituals do involve dances in which buffalo skins are used as costumes, even as far west as the Rio Grande pueblos.

Other accounts of the Sun Dance see it as a nonregular, individually initiated ceremony which seeks to honor a recently departed person or to mark an important crisis or decision in the life of the individual who sponsors it. In this latter case, the individual must procure the consent and support of other members of his or her family and/or clan, since the preparations for and the performance of the week-long Sun Dance ceremony are complex and arduous.

In general the Sun Dance ceremony was held during the long summer encampment when smaller units gathered together to recount familiar stories, share traditional rituals and customs, arrange marriages, and most important of all, to participate in the great buffalo hunt. This was the time when nearly all the food for the next winter had to be procured and preserved, and the buffalo was the primary food source as well as the main source of hides for clothing and bone for tools. The culminating event of this crucial time of renewal was frequently the Sun Dance, and this association in time and space suggests a connection in symbolism as well.[7]

The Cheyenne culture of the Great Plains varies some from others in that in addition to celebrating the Sun Dance ceremony and other rituals, it also practices the "Sacred Arrows" or "Medicine Arrow" renewal rite. This rite is said to renew the Cheyenne people as a nation, while the Sun Dance is said to renew the whole world, although neither is performed according to a strict annual schedule. Both of these ceremonies are initiated by an individual who pledges to accomplish a great task but they both usually involve the entire community. The Sacred Arrows ritual lasts four days, during which time women are confined to their tepees, and it revolves around a bundle of sacred arrows that has been handed down from one generation to the next.

The arrows are said to have been originally given to the Cheyenne by their culture hero Sweet Medicine, who in turn received them from the Great Spirit. The bundle consists of four arrows, two of which have power over buffalo and two of which have power over human beings.

> When the buffalo arrows are ritually pointed toward animals, they become confused and helpless, are easily surrounded and killed. When the arrows are carried against an enemy tribe on the rare occasions when the Cheyenne go on the warpath with all the tribe along, the man arrows are ritually pointed at the enemy before the attack. The foe becomes blinded and befuddled. Thus, the arrows are the Cheyennes' greatest resource against their most besetting manifest anxieties: Failure of the food supply and extermination by enemies.[8]

I conclude this section with two general observations. First, while the Euro-American culture does celebrate the beginning of the new year and the seasonal patterns, it does so in a rather passive manner. That is to say, for Euro-Americans these cycles occur on their own according to impersonal laws of nature and are more or less acknowledged and observed as such. For Native Americans, however, these events take place as the result of interaction between nature, spiritual forces, and human beings. In other words, within Native American worldviews, the yearly and seasonal cycles are as much instigated by the actions of humans as they are observed and obeyed by humans. All of reality is viewed as interdependent and life-giving patterns must be participated in rather than merely followed.

Second, by and large the rituals and ceremonies practiced by Native Americans do not so much serve to bribe or control the forces behind the natural processes and cycles as to provide a way for the people to *participate* in bringing these processes and cycles about. There is a significant difference between trying to appease or cajole superior forces and making one-self a means of their fulfillment in the cyclical patterns of the world. Native Americans do not so much fear or worship such forces as they seek to understand, respect, and cooperate with them. Hopi Kachina dancers, for instance, do not engage in their rain dances until it is the normal time for the seasonal rains to begin; nor are planting and harvesting ceremonies held in the winter or buffalo rituals enacted in the fall, even though people might well wish to obtain their food sources at these times.

BIRTH, NAMING, AND COMING OF AGE

In addition to ceremonies that serve to mark and renew the various life-giving forces of the community and the world, nearly all Native American peoples also practice rituals which focus and celebrate the important events and stages of each individual's life. These rituals have always been part and parcel of any culture's ceremonial life, since such recognition is vital to any person's growth and sense of well-being. Here we concentrate on those rituals that relate to a person's childhood years, from birth to entrance into full membership in the community.

A fascinating approach to birth and selfhood is found within the Navajo worldview. Among the central notions of the Navajo view of the self is that of "Holy Wind." Even in the Navajo origin story the crucial role of wind is evident, as Father Berard Haile's recording of it indicates:

> When the winds appeared and entered life they passed through the bodies of men and creatures and made the lines on the fingers, toes, and heads of human beings, and on the bodies of the different animals. The wind has given men and creatures strength ever since, for at the beginning they were shrunken and flabby until it inflated them, and the wind was creation's first food, and put motion and change into nature giving life to everything, even to the mountains and water.[9]

Thus Holy Wind plays an essential part in the maintenance of the structure and processes that sustain reality. There are parallels between this understanding of wind and that inherent in the Judeo-Christian scriptures. In both ancient Hebrew and classical Greek the word for wind is also the word for breath and for spirit; the three realities are treated as one. In the opening chapter of Genesis the wind or spirit (*ruach*) of God is said to have been "moving over the face of the waters" at the creation of the world. In like manner, in the second chapter God is said to have "breathed" into the nostrils of the first human in order to impart life. Similarly, in the New Testament the Holy Spirit is identified with wind (*pneuma*) in such instances as Jesus' discussion of spiritual birth in the second chapter of John's Gospel and the account of the early church's experience of Pentecost in the second chapter of the Acts of the Apostles.

In Navajo thought, the birth of each person is understood as a function of the interaction among the winds of the Cardinal Directions at the moment of conception. The resultant individual wind or soul is at the deepest level still one with the supreme Holy Wind as a concrete manifestation of it.

> This unity of Wind as a single entity and deity requires repeated emphasis in view of the Navajo practice of naming its various aspects. The basic concept to be appreciated is that the Holy Ones identified with the cardinal directions send wind to the individual at birth and provide the means of life and guidance all throughout the individual's life.[10]

Although the Navajo have no particular ritual for birth as such, the Blessingway rite, used on all momentous occasions, is employed at this time as well. At future stages of a person's development and experience additional winds become active in his or her personality. These occasions are also marked with the Blessingway ritual.

In a great many Native American cultures the "Naming Ceremony" is closely associated with birth, just as it is within Western society. The naming practices of the Tewa people and those of the Plains Indians are especially interesting.

The Tewa peoples have an extremely elaborate ceremony by which a newly born child receives its name. This takes place on the fourth day after birth. A specifically appointed "Naming Mother" makes the necessary preparations for the ceremony involving two perfect ears of corn and various artifacts that have been endowed with spiritual value. Well before dawn she performs several ritual acts with these items to induce rainfall, since rain is regarded as a sign that the spirit world is pleased with the child. Then she takes the child out to meet the dawn, utters a traditional prayer, and names the child by invoking the presence of Blue Corn Woman and White Corn Maiden.

> The name itself is selected from some natural phenomenon appropriate to the season, or some unusual occurrence of the particular morning, or the name of some distinguished ancestor is revived, in hopes that the child will later manifest some of the same good qualities. This is the name by which the child is known to the village in everyday discourse for the rest of its life.[11]

At some point during the first year of a Tewa child's life it is incorporated into its appropriate moiety by means of the "Water Giving" ceremony. In this ritual a child receives another name, one that is only used if the individual actually comes in later life to embody the qualities of the spirits to which the name corresponds in the moiety. A third ceremony, the "Water Pouring," takes place when a child is between six and ten years old, but no new name is given at this time.[12]

A parallel yet distinctive account of the naming process is given by Pretty-Shield, a Crow "medicine woman" who told her life story to Frank Linderman:

> Little-boy-strikes-with-a-lance, my father's father, gave me my name . . . on the fourth day of my life, according to our custom. My grandfather's shield was handsome; and it was big medicine. It was half red and half blue. This warshield always hung on his backrest at night. In the daytime it nearly always hung on a tripod back of his lodge, which of course faced the east. No, a woman's name was never changed unless, when she was very young, she did not grow strong. If she was weak, and her parents were afraid that they might lose her they sometimes asked one of her grandfathers to change her name to help her. Do women ever name children? Yes, sometimes. A wise-one, even though she be a woman, possesses this right. I named my own children and all of my grandchildren. . . . I have had five children, three girls and two boys. I lost a boy and a girl when they were babies. Now all my girls are gone. But my boy, Good, is living, and I have never known him to be bad. He lives up to the name I gave him.[13]

In the Judeo-Christian scriptures, names were also taken to be symbolic of a person's character. Moreover, as the result of a life-transforming experience many biblical characters actually had their names changed. Abram became Abraham, Jacob became Israel, Simon became Peter, and Saul became Paul. Even until fairly recently in Western culture, names were often chosen to influence a person's character by association with a specific moral quality, such as Faith and Hope, or with a special person, such as Mary, Peter, and Paul.

Often in Native American cultures an infant is not considered to be a real human being until it has received a name, and sometimes this does not happen for some time after birth. Furthermore, a person will acquire a number of different names in the course of a lifetime, as the result of a variety of events and/or experiences. Some of these names are public and official, while others may be extremely personal and private. Some names may well parallel the Western cultural practice of giving people "nicknames" on the basis of some specific characteristic or event in their lives. Sam Gill puts it like this:

> Practices associated with naming demonstrate the close association between the identity of a person and his or her names; and also suggest the great complexity associated with personality and character. While names distinguish a person among a community, they also help shape and mold a person within the various communities and domains of culture in which he or she must have a place.[14]

Each ceremony in the early life of a Native American child functions as a ritual of renewal, since each acknowledges and celebrates a crucial turning point in the individual's life and serves as a means of entry into a whole new phase of existence. Thus at each of these pivotal points the person is regenerated or starts over in his or her life adventure, and in this sense is renewed. Nowhere is this more clearly illustrated than in the rite of passage through which an individual passes from childhood to adulthood, roughly at the time of puberty. At this juncture the child is said to have "come of age."

The Tewa ceremony of "Water Pouring" is the means by which a Pueblo child becomes a full participant in the life of the community, usually between six and ten years of age. This rite of passage is not considered to be completed until it is followed by a ritual called the "Finishing," which takes place when a child is ten years old or more. In this event there is a clear distinction between boys and girls, with the former receiving membership in the *kiva* societies, for which there is no female counterpart. At this point in their lives, young Tewa are regarded as having entered into adulthood.[15]

As was noted earlier, the Navajo and the Apache share a common heritage which is grounded in their migratory history. Thus it is no surprise that they share many cultural beliefs and practices, among them the puberty rite for young girls about to become women. The following account of the "Sunrise Dance" is offered by Keith Basso and is representative of both Navajo and Apache rites:

> A major ritual among the Western Apache, this ceremony symbolically invests young women with physical and psychological attributes needed to fulfill adult responsibilities. The girl is dressed to represent White Painted Woman (Changing Woman, White Shell Woman), a prominent figure in Apache mythology whom the girl "becomes" for a 4-day period. . . . The girl's "sponsor," a woman of exemplary character and reputation who belongs to a different matrilineal clan . . . ties a piece of abalone shell in the girl's hair—another symbol of her identification with White Painted Woman. . . . The girl assumes the kneeling posture in which White Painted Woman was made pregnant in mythological times by the Sun. . . . While she lies facedown, the girl's shoulders, back, and legs are massaged by her sponsor, an action that assures the girl of physical strength as an adult. She is then instructed to run in each of the four directions, an act that is intended to provide her with quickness and endurance. Later, shortly before the ceremony ends, the girl and her sponsor are blessed with holy pollen by the girl's parents, and by all other participants who care to repeat the blessings.[16]

The "coming of age" process for young boys very often involved a "vision quest," which required them to spend several days alone in the wilderness, fasting and enduring hardship, even self-torture, until they encountered their particular "guardian spirit." This ritual was practiced by many groups in the Northeast woodland region, such as the Huron, and by almost every group on the Great Plains.

The vision quest ritual, as a puberty rite or ceremony of passage into adulthood, needs to be distinguished from dreams, on the one hand, and from other sorts of visions on the other hand. Dreams are often used as a source of insight or direction throughout a person's life, while visions are commonly encountered at times of crisis, such as disease, death, war, and childbirth. The visionary quest for one's guardian spirit constitutes a specific type of experience within the broader category of altered states of consciousness.[17]

The initiation rite whereby boys become men was frequently more low-key among some Plains groups. "One might say that if there is any initiation for the Cheyenne boy, it takes place on his first warpath. . . . Such a boy receives a new name, chosen from among those belonging to his family's most outstanding predecessors. He is now, indeed, a full-fledged adult."[18]

Black Elk, on the other hand, experienced his transition to manhood through participating in his first buffalo kill several years after receiving his vision at the age of nine. That vision came during a twelve-day coma and remained clearly in Black Elk's mind throughout his life. One might say that it was the first step of his passage into adulthood, a process which was completed with his first buffalo kill and his participation in a raid when he was thirteen. At the close of his life, Black Elk reflected on his initial vision:

> I am sure now that I was too young to understand it all, and that I only felt it. It was the pictures I remembered and the words that went with them; for nothing I have ever seen with my eyes was so clear and bright as what my vision showed me; and no words that I have ever heard with my ears were like the words I heard. I did not have to remember these things; they have remembered themselves all these years. It was as I grew older that the meanings came clearer and clearer out of the pictures and the words; and even now I know that more was shown to me than I can tell.[19]

Marriage, Family, and Clan

We have seen how the worldviews of a number of Native American peoples are expressed in the specific ceremonies and rituals of renewal associated with such shared events as planting, harvesting, and hunting, as well as with more individual events like birth, naming, and coming of age. Now we shall look at those rituals and customs by means of which diverse individuals and groups are brought together to form larger units within the broader society, as seen in the dynamics of marriage, family, and clan membership.

The general pattern of marriage among Native Americans is by and large the same across North America, but the specific rituals and customs involved differ greatly. We shall briefly consider four different patterns of marriage, family, and clanship: those of the Haida of the Northwest coast, the Cheyenne of the Plains, the Huron of the Eastern woodlands, and the Tewa Pueblo. These four present a diverse variety of patterns since they represent a wide geographical range.

These patterns of marriage, family, and clan are at least indirectly, if not directly, tied to the overall worldview of a particular group of people. Generally, for instance, the way a people understands the universe as reflecting gender, age, family, and social groupings will influence the way they structure their own classification systems for these realities. Moreover a people's perception of how the cosmos in general conducts itself also influences the classifications.

For example, some groups divide up and govern their families and clans according to a dualistic set of patterns because they experience the world around them as structured in this way. In addition, particular patterns of marriage and kinship are frequently drawn from observation of the way other species arrange and comport themselves. All these factors reflect the interaction between mores and practices and views of how the world, or reality, is put together.

Among the Haida, marriages are generally arranged by the couple's parents, often while the prospective spouses are children or even infants, with emphasis being placed on the father's lineage. At the ceremony, gifts of property and fishing rights are exchanged by both families. If one spouse dies the other is expected to marry a member of the deceased's lineage. Kinship relationships among the Haida follow the pattern outlined in chapter 4, according to which the father's sister and the mother's brother are called mother and father, respectively, and regarded as fulfilling the same functions as parents, with cousins being designated and related to in the same way as siblings.

Haida families live in small villages and in private houses which generally reflect the wealth of the individual owner. There does not seem to be any set pattern as to whether the family and/or property belongs to the lineage of either the husband or the wife; each nuclear family functions as a separate unit after marriage. Children are given a good deal of attention and training by their parents, but are also disciplined and instructed by their uncles and aunts. There is no special coming-of-age ceremony for boys, but for girls experiencing their first menstruation there are many specific rituals and taboos to be observed. Each family has two homes, a winter house in the woods away from the water for protection from the storms of the sea and a summer "camp" which is used during the summer and fall fishing season.

Each lineage among the Haida has a chief who renders judgment within it concerning family and property matters, while each village, composed of a number of families, is governed by a chief. Chieftainships are handed down within a lineage according to a matrilineal pattern, even though they are held by the oldest male in a given family or village. As with most Northwest coastal groups, there is a fairly rigid class or ranking system among the Haida. In addition to the "nobles," who possess a great deal of wealth and display it regularly in their homes and at special ceremonies, such as the Potlatch, there are individuals who do not have much wealth, and in former times there were also war captives who served as slaves of the nobles.

Haida society is divided into two main divisions or moieties, the Raven and the Eagle, by means of which the structure and evolution of community and lineage life are regulated. Each of these moieties contains around twenty lineages, although there seems to have been a wide fluctuation in size over the years. "Haida lineages trace their origin to several supernatural women of the Raven and Eagle moieties, and their autochthonous beginnings go back to a series of mythical 'story towns' . . . on the Queen Charlotte Islands."[20] Members of both moieties live together in the same villages, but each moiety has its own ritual symbols or "crests," as do the different lineages. These crests are carved on totem poles, painted on houses, and tattooed on bodies, as well as being incorporated into the designs on household items, clothes, weapons, and canoes.

On the Great Plains, Cheyenne marriages are not arranged by the parents, although courtship of a girl must be approved by both sets of parents as well as the potential bride's brother. Once approval has been granted, a long, elaborate ritual begins, involving the exchange of gifts, especially horses, and the furnishing of the young couple's new tepee. The independence of Plains young men, in contrast to the extreme interdependence of members of a Pueblo society, is clearly demonstrated in the courtship and marriage customs of the Cheyenne, for each individual is free to choose a mate and establish a separate dwelling.

However, the majority of new Cheyenne families place their homes near those of the bride's mother and her sisters. Thus the focus of any given group is matrilocal, even though the head of most families and residential groups is the oldest male. The sexual ethic of the Cheyenne people is one of severe restraint, even after marriage. Parents stand constant guard over their daughters in order to avoid any possibility of disgrace through promiscuity, while young men are raised to exhibit qualities of reservedness and dignity. G. B. Grinnell elaborates:

> The women of the Cheyennes are famous among all western tribes for their chastity. In old times it was most unusual for a girl to be seduced, and she who had yielded was disgraced forever. The matter at once became known, and she was taunted with it wherever she went. It was never forgotten. No young man would marry her.[21]

The kinship relationships of interwoven families among the Cheyenne actually become more important than either the nuclear family, together with grandparents, or the larger society. These relationships do not result in a residential grouping, nor are they bound together by lineages or clans, as among the Haida. Indeed, clans do not even exist among the Cheyenne. The basic subgroup is the band, the group of more or less closely related kinfolk who customarily camp together during the hunting season. Only when all the bands come together for one of the important yearly ceremonies or to go to war do the Cheyenne become a truly united people.[22]

Although the courtship and marriage customs of the Huron in the Northeast resemble those of the Cheyenne and other loosely knit Plains groups in many respects, there are important differences as well. While avoiding public displays of affection, between both married and unmarried partners, the Huron consider premarital sex to be normal for young people who have reached puberty. Both boys and girls are sexually active and jealousy is severely frowned upon. The Huron recognize different stages within romantic relationships and a couple is not considered married until children are born. After this, Huron couples remain monogamous and their relationship is formalized by the consent of both sets of parents. The right of divorce, especially for women, is taken seriously, and the kinship connections of the extended family mean that the support of a woman's mother and sisters is always available.[23]

The Huron nation is composed of four distinct tribes, but these seem to have undergone a good deal of fluctuation in recent centuries and do not function as a primary factor within the social life of the people. The eight distinct clans, which together include every Huron individual, operate as the basic unit within cultural life. These clans are named after animals, such as the bear, the turtle, and the beaver, and are thought of as kinship groups, although no strict accounts are kept as to the biological or genealogical connections of the members, and there are no territorial ramifications. The household traditionally consisted of several nuclear families living together in a common long house, with the older women exercising authority over their daughters and their daughters' husbands.

The Huron are both matrilineal and matrilocal, which means that inheritance and authority are traced through the women's lineage and that new husbands go to live with their wives' families. The clan structure serves to arbitrate in family blood feuds and to facilitate the performance of the basic rituals and ceremonies. All public offices are held by men, but the main responsibility of the chiefs is to moderate discussions and announce decisions reached by a consensus of all those affected by a course of action. Some chiefs have civil or peacekeeping duties, while others deal with wars and witch hunts. While chiefhood is determined by heredity, it is the older women of a clan who are responsible for selecting the best candidate, and as with the Iroquois, these women can depose their chiefs as well.[24]

The Rio Grande Tewa Pueblo people operate according to a moiety pattern rather than to one of clans; the entire Pueblo community is divided into two subgroups in relation to the two main seasons, summer and winter. This particular moiety pattern lacks any prohibition against people of different moieties marrying each other. Tewa marriage customs have also been strongly influenced by the teachings of the Roman Catholic Church, which has been a powerful force in the Rio Grande area for over four hundred years.

The common pattern of individual courtship and family consent is followed in the premarital period, with the mutual exchange of gifts and parental advice. There are two separate marriage ceremonies, one traditional and the other Catholic, and at this time the bride must join the moiety of her husband if she is not already a member. There are no special regulations regarding the location of the couple's home. Special circumstances allow for various forms of "adoption" from one moiety to another, and thus it is clear that lineage as such is not the ruling factor in Tewa society. It is only after marriage that men become eligible for political office, and it is this elaborate sociopolitical system that serves as the backbone of Tewa culture.

> A person's progression through the system may be symbolized by a vine which branches out and reaches into almost every household in the village. In the absence of a rule of descent, it is this vinelike network of ties which gives the individual a sense of community.[25]

The sociopolitical and religious structure of the Tewa is far too complex to attempt to summarize here. Suffice it to say that in addition to the moiety pattern there exists a three-level hierarchy of authority and function, each level of which is itself divided into two parts. Moreover, each of these levels has a spiritual counterpart in the supernatural world. Some of these levels pertain to the political governance of the pueblo, while others have to do with religious functions and official external relations. Essentially, every member of the Tewa community takes part in one or more leadership roles during his or her lifetime.[26]

There is a clear correlation between the social patterns and the worldview of each culture, especially with regard to the relationship between the natural environment and subsistence patterns. Groups located in coastal and/or wooded regions where the food supply is generally ample and travel is relatively minimal tend to have fairly loose-textured social customs and organizational systems, as there is little need for tight control. Those peoples who live in areas where life is more precarious, such as deserts, and those who must continuously roam across a vast area chasing animals represent extreme cases. The more difficult the life the tighter the social fabric, while the more mobile the lifestyle the less emphasis on clan and lineage.

At the same time, there is a strong correlation between the terrain and animal life that surround a given people and that people's views on the nature of spiritual reality. The peoples in the Southwest and on the Plains, who exist in relation to large areas of space and travel across them, incorporate notions such as journeys and quests more thoroughly into their views of the structure of reality. Moreover, the animals indigenous to a given area factor heavily into the religious views of its human inhabitants.

Perhaps the best way to summarize the relationship between Native Americans' worldviews and specific beliefs and practices on the socioreligious level is in terms of the notion of symbiosis. Worldviews help to define and shape cultures, while at the same time cultures influence the ways people experience the world around them. It is neither possible nor necessary to say which aspect of different groups' ways of being in the world comes first. These two dimensions of Native American reality are inextricably intertwined and must be studied together.

SUN DANCE, POTLATCH, SWEATLODGE, AND PEYOTE

No treatment of the ceremonies of Native American people would be complete without some discussion of the key rituals around which various cultures arrange their community life. In the previous sections we have discussed the cyclical rituals of planting, harvest, and the hunt, the rites of passage from birth and naming through puberty and marriage, and social structures. Consideration can now be given to the way in which some of the central rituals of different groups reflect their respective views of reality. We shall look at one ritual indigenous to people in each of four distinct regions: the Sun Dance of the Plains, the Potlatch of the Northwest, the Sweatlodge of the Huron in the Northeast, and the Peyote Ceremony of the Native American Church in the Southwest.

The Sun Dance is practiced throughout the Great Plains, although within each group it serves slightly different functions and takes a somewhat different form. While it may at one time have been associated with the great buffalo hunts, it is more commonly used nowadays as a means of expressing a personal vow or renewing various socioreligious commitments. Because of its self-torture aspects, the Sun Dance was outlawed by the U.S. government nearly a hundred years ago. For Plains Indians the ritual provides a way to demonstrate the depth of their sense of honor and courage, not unlike contact sports and mountain climbing in Western culture. In addition, the Sun Dance focuses the Native American belief in the power of both the sun and the sacred circle.

There is perhaps no better way to get a feel for the meaning of the Sun Dance in the lives of those who participated in it than to read Black Elk's account of one such ceremony during his childhood:

> Sitting Bull, who was the greatest medicine man of the nation at that time, had charge of this dance to purify the people and to give them power and endurance. It was held in the Moon of Fatness because that is the time when the sun is highest and the growing power of the world is strongest. . . . First a holy man was sent out all alone to find the *waga chun*, the holy tree that should stand in the middle of the dancing circle. . . . Then when they had gathered about the holy tree, some women who were bearing children would dance around it, because the Spirit of the Sun loves all fruitfulness. After this a band of young maidens came singing, with sharp axes in their hands. . . . The maidens chopped the tree down and trimmed off its branches. . . . Now when the holy tree had been brought home but was not yet set up in the center of the dancing place . . . there was a big feast and plenty for everybody to eat, and a big dance just as though we had won a victory. . . . The next day the tree was planted in the center by the holy men who sang sacred songs and made sacred vows to the Spirit. . . . The next day the dancing began, and those who were going to take part were ready, for they had been fasting and purifying themselves in the sweatlodges, and praying. First their bodies were painted by the holy men. Then each would lie down beneath the tree as though he were dead, and the holy men would cut a place in his back or chest, so that a strip of rawhide, fastened to the top of the tree, could be pushed through the flesh and tied. Then the man would get up and dance to the drums, leaning on the rawhide strip as long as he could stand the pain or until the flesh tore loose.[27]

The Potlatch, found among nearly all the peoples of the Northwest coastal region, is a public social event in which the sponsor presents a considerable amount of property and food to the invited guests. Later on, the guests usually reciprocate by hosting a feast of their own. This continuous giving of large gifts not only contributes to economic redistribution but also serves to establish and confirm social status. There are several different kinds and sizes of Potlatch ceremonies from everyday occurrences to those to which guests from other tribes are invited. These are called "doing a great thing" and involve huge amounts of food and material gifts, as well as a great deal of ceremony and drama.[28]

Like the Sun Dance, the Potlatch struck Euro-American officials as unacceptable, so it was outlawed by the Canadian government for a number of years around the end of the nineteenth century. Also like the Sun Dance, the Potlatch in modified form has been restored to life in recent years. In addition to its economic and social function, it has religious significance for those who practice it. Sam Gill points out that the gifts symbolize the life-giving forces that sustain the tribe and goes on to explain that

> The animal skins or their equivalent, when ritually circulated among the societies whose work is to make present the mythic order of reality, are thereby participating in the process that is so important to Kwakiutl religion and life; that is, the mediation of the primordial world of human ancestors (animal peoples) and the ordinary world of hunter and hunted. It is through the ritual circulation of goods in which this quality of life is inherent that Kwakiutl reality is integrated and unified. In this way the reciprocity that binds all interrelationships in the Kwakiutl world is complete.[29]

The sweatlodge ritual, nearly always reserved for men, is common to almost all Native American groups, except for the Inuit and the peoples of the Great Basin and High Plateau. In nearly every Native American culture it serves a variety of purposes, from curing physical illness, through forming a bond of friendship among men, to achieving spiritual purification and religious renewal for an entire community. Among the Crow, the sweatlodge is used in the ceremony for initiating young males and adoptees into full community membership, while in other cultures it is employed as part of the preparation for yearly festivals.

The Hupa of northwestern California use this ritual to mark the beginning of the salmon season. For them the sweatlodge itself symbolizes the structure of the cosmos, even as it does, along with the hogan, for the Navajo. Perhaps this similarity derives from the fact that both the Hupa and the Navajo are Athapascan speaking, though it is unclear just how the Hupa found their way into the mountains of California. Be that as it may, the fresh lighting of the fire within the sweatlodge, which begins the Hupa ceremonial cycle, symbolizes the renewal of life throughout the world.[30]

Among the Huron the sweatlodge has three main functions: to promote health, both physical and mental, to facilitate the work of a shaman, and to foster friendship. With respect to the goal of enhancing health it is important to bear in mind that the Huron, like most Native American peoples,

> ... draw no clear distinction between physical and mental states and did not attempt to distinguish between what happened to a person as a result of his own actions and what we would regard as accidents. The concept of health included an individual's happiness and personal fulfillment as well as his good or bad fortune.[31]

Thus sweating profusely in a sweatlodge ritual would help to cleanse both the bodies and the spirits of the participants, while at the same time uniting them in a common bond.

In addition, sometimes Huron shamans make use of the sweatlodge ritual as a means of determining the nature of a patient's ailment, whether physical or spiritual. In fact, the Huron seem especially concerned about illness and its cure, perhaps because they, like so many other Native American peoples, were decimated by diseases brought to North America by European explorers, traders, and settlers. The Huron have a number of different societies which seek to relieve illness through various dances involving symbolic masks, fire trials, and songs, as well as through sweating rituals.[32]

The Huron have also used the sweatlodge to promote friendship and bonding among their male members. The following passage describes a sweatlodge procedure among the Huron, a procedure which is typical of a great many Native American cultures:

When a man wished to sweat, he invited his friends to join him. The sweating was done inside a small, circular hut that was heated by placing hot stones in the center. . . . The men huddled closely inside the hut, their knees raised against their stomachs. Then someone outside covered the hut with skins and pieces of bark so that no heat could escape. To encourage sweating, one of the men inside the hut sang, while the rest shouted continuously as they did in their dances. . . . When the sweating was over, they closed their pores by jumping into a nearby river or washing in cold water.[33]

The Peyote Ceremony, which has become the central ritual of the Native American Church, was first introduced in Oklahoma in 1918. It soon spread throughout the Great Plains and the Southwest and has become especially well established among the Navajo. Although the use of peyote as an enhancer of spirituality through hallucinogenic experience has a long history, stretching back to the Aztecs, it seems to have been brought to North America by the Comanche, who lived along the southern stretches of the Rio Grande in west Texas. It spread informally to other Plains peoples, and finally to the Navajo in Arizona and New Mexico. It eventually merged with traditional Christian beliefs and became the central ritual of the newly formed Native American Church. The peyote plant itself is a cactus-like plant that produces small, nonaddictive mushroom-like buttons which are chewed in the ritual.

The Native American Church, which focuses on the use of peyote, began to have an influence among the Navajo in the early years of the twentieth century and became a dominant force in the 1930s. It was opposed by native traditionalists, Christian missionaries, and government officials alike. However, it continued to grow and finally won legal acceptance in the early 1970s.

Peyotists believe in an all-powerful, transcendent God, who, they say, is the same supreme being worshipped by all people everywhere. Peyote is a symbol of the Church, a means of communication with God, a power in its own right, and a cure of unique potency for spiritual and physical disease.[34]

Peyote ceremonies are held whenever a specific need arises and at traditional holiday celebrations, such as Thanksgiving, Christmas, Easter, and the Fourth of July. Specific needs include weddings and deaths, as well as blessings for any new endeavor and the curing of physical or psychological illness. The ceremony itself is complex and elaborate and is led by a "roadman" who supplies the necessary items and administers the rituals. It is generally held in a hogan and lasts from sunset to dawn. The ceremony includes songs, prayers, smoking, water rituals, and the chewing of peyote. The meeting is followed by a small breakfast and a feast at noon. Although some elements of traditional Navajo rituals are included, as well as some standard Christian rituals, the Peyote Ceremony is essentially distinct in its content and format.

Rituals and ceremonial rites embody and reflect the worldviews of their participants. The axis around which these worldviews revolve is the basic belief that all of reality, including the physical universe, supernatural beings, plant and animal life, and human beings, is a single, integrated, and unified whole. In Native American worldviews the origin, structure, and dynamic of this vast, intricate reality all bear witness to this primal unity.

Native American peoples' agricultural, hunting and fishing, and even plant-gathering seasons follow a cyclical pattern that reflects a purposeful, inner harmony among all that exists, and their various food-source ceremonies seek to honor and encourage this life force. The human life cycle from birth through childhood, marriage, and full community membership is marked by an acknowledgment of this overall cosmic pattern through rituals that express gratitude for it. In addition, the particular nonseasonal yet immensely important ceremonies of various peoples, such as the Sun Dance, the Potlatch, the sweatlodge, and the peyote rituals, all seek to embody specific aspects of this unified, harmonious cosmic order in order to achieve fuller participation in it, as well as to renew and replenish it.

NOTES

1. Åke Hultkrantz, *The Religions of the American Indians* (Berkeley: University of California Press, 1979), p. 104.

2. Alfonso Ortiz, *The Tewa World: Space, Time, Being, and Becoming in a Pueblo Society* (Chicago: University of Chicago Press, 1969), p. 100.

3. Ibid., p. 103.

4. Barbara Graymont, *The Iroquois* (New York: Chelsea House, 1988), p. 195.

5. Sam Gill, *Native American Religions: An Introduction* (Belmont, Calif.: Wadsworth, 1982), p. 126.

6. Hultkrantz, *Religions of the American Indians*, p. 105.

7. Howard Harrod, *Renewing the World* (Tucson: University of Arizona Press, 1987), p. 116.

8. E. Adamson Hoebel, *The Cheyennes* (New York: Harcourt Brace, 1988), pp. 115–16.

9. As quoted in James McNeley, *Holy Wind in Navajo Philosophy* (Tucson: University of Arizona Press, 1981), pp. 8–9.

10. Ibid., p. 39.

11. Ortiz, *The Tewa World*, p. 32.

12. Ibid., pp. 32–37.

13. Frank Linderman, *Pretty-Shield: Medicine Woman of the Crows* (Lincoln: University of Nebraska Press, 1972), pp. 19 and 145.

14. Gill, *Native American Religions*, p. 90.

15. Ortiz, *The Tewa World*, pp. 37–43.

16. See fig. 5, in Morris E. Opler, "The Apachean Culture Pattern and Its Origins," *Handbook of North American Indians*, ed. Alfonso Ortiz, vol. 10 (Washington, D.C.: Smithsonian Institution, 1983), p. 374.

17. Hultkrantz, *Religions of the American Indians*, pp. 74–79.

18. Hoebel, *The Cheyennes*, p. 100.

19. Black Elk, *Black Elk Speaks: Being the Life Story of a Holy Man of the Oglala Sioux*, as told through John G. Neihardt (Lincoln: University of Nebraska Press, 1979), p. 49.

20. Margaret B. Blackman, "Haida: Traditional Culture," in *Handbook of North American Indians*, ed. Wayne Suttles, vol. 7 (Washington, D.C.: Smithsonian Institution, 1990), pp. 240–54.

21. G. R. Grinnell, *The Cheyenne Indians*, vol. 1 (New Haven, Conn.: Yale University Press, 1923), p. 156.

22. Hoebel, *The Cheyennes*, pp. 36–37.

23. Bruce Trigger, *The Huron: Farmers of the North* (Fort Worth, Tex.: Holt, Rinehart, and Winston, 1990), pp. 78–79.

24. Ibid., pp. 65–68 and 80–82.

25. Ortiz, *The Tewa World*, p. 50.

26. Ibid., pp. 13–18.

27. Black Elk, *Black Elk Speaks*, pp. 97–98.

28. Helen Codere, "Kwakiutl Traditional Culture," in *Handbook of North American Indians*, ed. Suttles, vol. 7, pp. 368–72.

29. Gill, *Native American Religions*, p. 128.

30. Hultkrantz, *Religions of the American Indians*, p. 106.

31. Trigger, *The Huron*, p. 132.

32. Ibid., p. 116.

33. Ibid., pp. 117–18.

34. David F. Aberle, "Peyote Religion among the Navajo," *Handbook of North American Indians*, ed. Ortiz, vol. 10, p. 559.

Chapter Six

The Vital Balance

I n his book *The Vital Balance*, psychiatrist Karl Menninger offered the image of keeping one's balance as a helpful way of understanding mental health as well as mental illness. He suggested that when we see a person behaving oddly or disfunctionally we should remind ourselves that such an imbalance is caused by some invisible emotional baggage the person is carrying, just as we understand why someone carrying physical baggage may walk awkwardly. This notion of balance as the key to mental and emotional health lies at the heart of the Native American way of thinking about human life and values in general, and thus forms the axis for many peoples' approach to the task of living and dying well.

The Path of Life

One aspect of many Native American worldviews involves their concept of the human condition at the beginning of life. Generally the central image is that of a person starting out on the "path of life" and striving to follow this path without falling off or straying from it throughout one's alotted time on earth. The central idea is keeping one's balance on the path by honoring the traditional teachings and practices of one's people. It is believed that such a life is full of harmony and health, and enables a person to be useful to his or her family and community.

According to this way of thinking, every person starts out already on the proper path and simply strives to remain on it. This stands in marked contrast to the way nearly all the major "world religions" depict the human condition at the beginning of life. According to the dominant worldviews of both the West and the East, humans either come into a world that is illusory and/or evil or they arrive on the scene already out of harmony with the goals and values of divine reality. In either case, something is deemed to be drastically wrong at the very beginning of life and needs to be set right before humans can enter into the fullness and bliss for which they are intended.

Native American worldviews, however, do not begin by assuming that people start out with strikes already against them. The assumption is that everyone begins life already on the proper path and must do his or her best to remain on it as the years go by. It is understood that at various points in life all people will stray from this path, but such departures are thought of as temporary rather than as normative for human existence. Imbalances can be rectified by engaging in prescribed rituals and ceremonies, returning to the path of traditional beliefs and duties. Overall the Native American way of thinking sees life as a challenge to maintain one's balance on the right path, not as the task of overcoming an obstacle that one encounters at the very outset. Thus life is understood as essentially good rather than as evil. This is in remarkable contrast to many other worldviews.

The various stages and phases of an individual's life cycle have already been discussed. Our central concern now is with the main teachings and guidelines of some cultural groups which are aimed at helping a person maintain balance on the path of life. Subsequently we shall consider ways of returning to the path or regaining one's balance after having lost it, as well as some of the basic goals toward which the path of life leads. Here the immediate focus is on the general moral or ethical dimension of Native American worldviews.

The overarching theme is the notion of maintaining one's balance. Navajo writers explain this notion in the following way:

> Morals set the limits and boundaries of personal behavior and ethics teach social behavior or the way individuals order their behavior with one another. A large part of sacred tradition is devoted to maintaining a balance among the elements and forces of nature. By understanding ecological relationships and taking care to maintain them and learn from them, human beings maintain their own lives.[1]

One of the moral dilemmas confronting Native American peoples pertains to their sense of kinship with all of nature, and especially animals, on the one hand, and the necessity of procuring the sustenance for survival by killing and eating the animals among whom they live, on the other. This dilemma was faced quite bluntly by the Plains Indians, as Howard Harrod makes clear:

> The people sensed, and they reflected in their traditions the moral and religious problems involved in life feeding upon life. Unlike moderns, who are largely desensitized to the meanings surrounding their food supply, Plains Indians were extremely sensitive to the meaning of killing beings who were, in a deep sense, kinspersons. It is little wonder, then that this moral and religious dilemma is ritually addressed in the great tribal ceremonies, especially those which thematize the process of world renewal.[2]

Native American peoples have generally exercised great thoroughness and inventiveness in the use they have made of meat, hides, and bones, while at the same time paying homage to the animals they have killed, through prayers and rituals of thanksgiving. It is true that it was not always possible to control the number of buffalo, for example, that would die in a stampede over a prairie cliff and thus sometimes more animals were killed than could be used. With animals that do not run in herds, this possibility of overkill did not arise. Whenever possible Native American hunters have sought to show proper respect for the life of the animals they use and to make the most efficient use of them.

Turning to broader questions of personal moral behavior and character, by and large Native American cultures prize quiet dignity and honest loyalty in personality and behavior. A person is expected to embody responsibility and truthfulness in every aspect of life. The following description of Cheyenne parents' training of their children underscores the Plains Indians' ideal standards of character:

> On the basis of this well-established relationship, Cheyenne children are continuously exhorted by their elders: "Be brave, be honest, be virtuous, be industrious, be generous, do not quarrel! If you do not do these things people will talk about you in the camp; they will not

respect you; you will be shamed. If you listen to this advice you will grow up to be a good man or woman, and you will amount to something." The values of the Cheyennes [are] made explicit in a steady stream of sermonizing that expostulates what is deeply woven into everyday life. The values are reinforced by many explicit mechanisms of public and family approval.[3]

An interesting approach to the issue of moral responsibility and ethical behavior is found among the Navajo. The origin stories of the Navajo stress the limited involvement of divine beii gs in the affairs of humans. The former created the framework and proce ses which constitute the world in which we live, but they do not inter ene, either positively or negatively, in the lives of humans. Rather, the: beings set the boundaries and conditions within which people must work out their own solutions to the situations in which they find themselves.

So, the givens are sexual desire, gender, and other difference , birth, joy, beauty and increase on the one hand, and jealousy, worr grief, death, and ugliness on the other. These givens combine to form a whole, a package which although quite necessary, also produces great difficulties. To have any chance at solving these problems, one must begin by accepting these givens.[4]

The socialization process by which a Navajo child becomes a responsible member of the community is seen as a continuous effort to balance the needs and desires of the self and those of the larger society. On the one hand, it is said that each person must actively seek his or her own self-interest in every endeavor, must strive for individual self-realization and fulfillment. Such enlightened self-interest is thought to be best for the community in the long run. On the other hand, there is a strong imperative in Navajo culture against competition, against trying to put oneself at an advantage in relation to another person. These two seemingly opposed emphases create the paradox that structures Navajo behavior.

John Farella argues that these two angles of approach to moral behavior among the Navajo have been synthesized in practice on the basis of the very nature of their main form of livelihood, sheep herding:

[T]he question of "proper behavior" is such that the significant parameters are defined very broadly. Within these bounds it is left up to the
individual. Such a system is workable only if there is a minimum of
required social interaction. . . . It would have a better chance of
working in an environment where one's nearest neighbor was spatially
very distant.[5]

A different though related way to picture the basic path of life is in
terms of a labyrinth or maze. This image seems to have had general appeal
in many periods and places but is particularly well focused in the diagram
of the "Pima Maze." Actually, the diagram of the maze and the story behind
it have more affinity with those who used to be called the Papago, but who
have always called themselves "Tohono O'odham" (Desert People), than it
does with the so-called Pima, who call themselves "Akimel O'odham"
(River People). The former are located in the northern region of the
Sonora Desert in southern Arizona, while the latter reside further to the
north, along the rivers of central Arizona. The names "Pima" and "Papago"
were given to these people by their Spanish conquerors.

One account of the maze diagram centers around the legendary
Papago or O'odham figure, "Iitoi," who struggled to find his way to the
center of the world through all the twists and turns of his life. Another
account suggests that the man in the maze is "everyperson," traveling
through life as though through a maze, growing wiser and stronger as
death draws ever nearer. The way the maze is drawn makes it clear that
there is but one way to reach the center, the goal of life, and that once one
is there it is possible to turn and look back on the path in a final act of
acceptance and understanding before taking the final step. Here again the
image of the path of life is the overall basis for interpreting the moral
dimension of human existence, stressing the need to stay within the limits
prescribed by traditional teachings in order to reach the desired goal.

HARMONY AND HEALTH

The two basic concepts that underlie nearly every major Native American worldview are harmony and balance. It is the responsibility of the
entire community to see to it that a proper harmony is maintained among

the various aspects of the complex processes by which the world is woven together. Hence we have seen the strategic importance of ceremonies and rituals. The order and dynamic of reality are continuously renewed through harmonious participation in these patterns and processes.

The success of an individual results from the quality of his or her desire and ability to maintain a proper balance on the path of life. The various factors and challenges of an individual's life must be integrated in such a way as to enable the individual to avoid straying from the way that leads to harmony, health, and happiness. The main resources available in this endeavor, in addition to parental guidance and example, are traditional beliefs and teachings. When a person fails to achieve or maintain this desired balance, straying or falling from the prescribed path, he or she is said to have become "sick."

In general, Native Americans do not distinguish between different kinds of illness: the various dimensions of the human person are viewed as forming a single, unified whole. Although there are many types of imbalance and each must be treated in a specific manner, the major illnesses are usually treated by the intervention of a shaman or "medicine man," while minor ones are handled by means of herbal medicines.

The terms *shaman* and *medicine man* are frequently used interchangeably to describe individuals within a given culture who are called upon to "cure" or restore a sick person to health. The former term derives from the name used in Siberia for such a person, and has become the standard designation for healers among anthropologists, while the latter term derives from the expression used by the French Jesuit missionaries for anyone who intervened in a situation where things had gone wrong and stood in need of rectification. Their term *medicine* came to mean healing power, whether pertaining strictly to physical health or more broadly to "spiritual" health as well. Thus this term has come to serve as a general word for exceptional power in any form, as in the expression "big medicine." The Navajo actually refer to their healers as "singers" rather than as medicine men.[6]

Aside from the cases in which a person's ill health can be traced directly to a specific transgression, there are generally said to be two forms of sickness, namely, the intrusion of foreign objects or spirits into the body of the sick person and what is called "soul loss." In the former case the shaman seeks to restore the original and desired harmony of the person's life by removing whatever has entered and is creating the imbalance. Here the symptoms are generally either external injuries or internal pains. The shaman first determines the location of the foreign element and then seeks to extract it.

Determining exactly what and where the intruding element is may be accomplished either through some form of divination or through clairvoyance and may take some time. Once the disruptive element has been diagnosed and located, the shaman employs any number of different techniques to remove it, the most common of which are massaging, blowing, and sucking it away. Often an actual object, such as a seed or an insect, is displayed as the source of the sickness when it is not found to be a spiritual matter.

In cases of "soul loss," the sick person's inner spirit or soul is believed to have either wandered away or been taken away by some evil force. The task of the shaman in such cases is to send his or her (in some cases the shaman may be a female) own inner spirit in search of the missing soul in order to restore it to its rightful place. This reestablishes harmonious balance. In these situations the patient usually exhibits abnormal psychological symptoms, such as unconsciousness or delirium. Accordingly the shaman must seek an altered form of consciousness, by means of a trance or seance, in order to pursue and retrieve the lost spirit.[7]

Among many groups the role of shaman is inherited, while among others there is an established training procedure, much like a school, for filling the position. Frequently, however, a person receives a "calling," usually by means of a vision, that leads to this vocation. Such was the case with Black Elk who received his vision when he was only nine years old.

At the age of nineteen Black Elk performed his first cure, and thus was termed a "*wakan* man" or holy man. *Wakan* is the Lakota term for "spirit"; thus the Great Spirit is called "Wakan Tanka." A holy man is "one with spiritual power." Black Elk received his vision after hearing a series of voices calling him away to his spiritual "Grandfathers" as he began to feel increasingly ill, feverish, and swollen. At the beginning of his spiritual journey,

> I went outside the tepee, and yonder where the men with flaming spears were going, a little cloud was coming very fast. It came and

stooped and took me and turned back to where it came from, flying fast. And when I looked down I could see my mother and my father yonder, and I felt sorry to be leaving them.[8]

At the conclusion of his vision Black Elk was left alone on the plains and began walking toward his village. He entered his own tepee in time to see his parents kneeling over his body and to hear someone saying, "The boy is coming to; you had better give him some water." "Then I was sitting up; and I was sad because my mother and my father didn't seem to know I had been so far away."[9] Later he was told that he had been sick for twelve days, near death, and that he had been retrieved or cured by Whirlwind Chaser, a shaman who told Black Elk's father,"Your boy is sitting in a sacred manner. I don't know what it is, but there is something special for him to do, for just as I came in I could see a power like a light all through his body."[10]

Black Elk also gives a detailed account of his first healing of a sick little boy. Earlier he had found himself especially attracted to a rare herb and had made a special journey in order to collect some of it. When a man asked Black Elk to try to heal his sick son, Black Elk was afraid because he had never used his latent powers before. He began with the ritual of the sacred pipe, followed by a rumbling like thunder on his drum. Then he moved around the sick boy in a circle, moving clockwise, and seated himself on the west side of the tepee. Next, he called upon the Great Spirit, Wakan Tanka, for help, and rehearsed the different phases of his original vision in his mind. After drinking a little water and stamping on the ground four times, Black Elk put his mouth on the boy's stomach and "drew through him the cleansing wind of the north." Then he chewed some of the herb he had found, mixed it with water, and blew some of the liquid on the boy and in the four Cardinal Directions. Finally he told the boy to drink a little water and to walk with help around the inside of the tepee, "beginning at the south, the source of life." In a few days the boy was completely healed.[11]

Over against the powers of the shaman stand those of "witchcraft," the negative forces that can be employed by individuals and departed spirits to cause pain and illness. Although shamans have many different potions and rituals with which to combat such forces, one of the more common is the "masks" of good spirits that are used to frighten evil spirits away.

Among the Iroquois these masks, or more properly "false faces," are worn by a group of men who function as a healing society whenever there is an illness in the community or during certain annual ceremonies. "The faces represent spirit beings that have the power to heal. The Iroquois view illness as a disorder of the natural world caused by evil supernatural beings. The faces symbolize spirits that bring order and restore health."[12]

A entirely different type of medical activity has to do with plants and herbs. These are used for everyday ailments, such as headaches, upset stomachs, fevers, coughs, body aches, and even snake bite, paralysis, and internal bleeding. Knowledge of suitable herbs and potions is often widespread, but sometimes it seems advisable to invoke the special techniques known only to the shaman. Among the Cheyenne, for example, this decision is seen as moving into serious considerations:

> Here we move into theoretical medicine and supernaturalism. The basic Cheyenne assumption concerning serious illness is that it is caused by the intrusion of a tangible foreign object into the body of the person. . . . The cure is a ritual performance to locate and dislodge the element, followed by the doctor sucking on the spot. This results in removal of the object, which is then shown by the doctor to all those in the lodge.[13]

A quite different overall approach to the curing process is found among the Navajo people in the Four Corners area. The general Native American understanding of illness as the disruption of the natural order of things, on either the everyday or the cosmic level, prevails for the Navajo as well. Health is still viewed as the harmonious balance of all the forces participating in the ongoing processes of the world. When disruption occurs, "Harmony, balance and order are restored through the use of knowledge and the correct performance of orderly procedures in a controlled ritual environment. . . . Recovery occurs through sympathetic magic."[14]

The distinctive element in the Navajo approach involves the techniques employed. Unlike the Pueblo peoples of the Southwest, the Navajo do not have an organized system of religious ceremonies, a regularized ceremonial calendar, or any hierarchical spiritual leadership. Their rituals are always performed on special occasions by highly trained "singers" (*hataali*) and consist almost exclusively of chants, songs, and sandpaintings. Healing ceremonies take place in the hogan of the one who is ill and are under the strict direction of the singer. When the sand-painting appropriate to the specific problem is complete, the patient sits or lies upon it during the chanting ritual. The painting comprises symbolic representations of supernatural beings or holy people whose spiritual powers are thereby transmitted to the sick person. When the ceremony is over, the painting is swept away. Navajo sandpaintings are not considered as works of art in the Western sense. Once their healing purposes have been fulfilled they must be erased, since they embody powerful spiritual forces and should be kept from any possible inappropriate use.

The Navajo worldview places great emphasis on the power of speech and singing. The Navajo origin story tells how the world was created through speech by Talking Woman. Thus both storytelling and singing play crucial roles in Navajo rituals in general and in healing rituals in particular.

In this discussion, frequent use has been made of the concept of the supernatural, in reference both to divine beings and to spiritual reality. This mode of speech is common among anthropologists and historians of religion alike. However, it is somewhat misleading with respect to the worldviews of most Native Americans, since it presupposes a basic dichotomy between the natural world and a world transcendent to it, a distinction that is not characteristic of Native American modes of thought.

Like the ancient Hebrews, Native Americans generally see themselves existing in one, unified reality in which many different forces are active, some for good and others for evil. Even divine beings and holy people operate *within* this reality rather than interrupting it from the outside. The principles and processes that govern the world, then, are better understood as aspects of a common reality than as coming from two distinct worlds.

Native American worldviews are, for the most part, naturalistic. That is to say, they do not make the basic distinction between what are generally referred to in both Western and Eastern worldviews as "appearance" and "reality." In both of these approaches an initial dichotomy between this world and some other, "higher" world is postulated, and the goal of life is claimed to be the transcendence of this world into the other "more real" world. Native American thought does not begin with this dualistic assumption, and its inherent values are grounded in and directed toward this present world. Though some peoples do speak of a "spiritual world" beyond the present one, the former is generally viewed as an extension of the latter rather than as a separate reality.

LOYALTY AND COURAGE

Within the worldviews of all cultures certain values are focused and insisted on as a means of ensuring survival and minimal social cohesion, as well as individual meaning and prosperity. Nearly always included among these are loyalty and courage. The individuals who make up a given social group must maintain some degree of loyalty to the group, or community life is simply impossible. Likewise, especially in cultures that exist on the edge of survival, the courage to face the dangers of hunting and self-defense, as well as natural calamities, is highly valued. Native American peoples are no exception in this regard, as a brief survey of some representative ethical codes will demonstrate.

Within the culture of the Plains Indians, where broad latitude has been given for individual development and achievement, far greater emphasis has been placed on loyalty to one's immediate family than to any larger group. This is at least partly due to the Plains Indians' nomadic, hunting lifestyle. The same can be said for the culture of the Navajo, but for somewhat different reasons. Their lifestyle revolved around herding sheep and growing corn. The former activity resulted in Navajo families living at rather long distances from one another, and thus here as well the primary loyalty was directed inward toward the family unit. It is only in contemporary times that the Navajo, like many other peoples, have begun to function as a larger, united community.

Among the Crow, also, ties among family members are extremely strong, with connections and responsibilities determined according to matrilineal patterns. One cannot read Pretty-Shield's account of her childhood and not come away with a strong sense of the tightly woven family ties. While there were frequent opportunities for various Crow groups to gather together, in Pretty-Shield's account of life on the plains there is little reference to any strong sense of responsibility toward or sense of belonging to a wider social group. One of the few exceptions to this pattern was seen when numerous Crow groups came together to fight alongside General George Custer against the Sioux at the battle of Little Bighorn. The Sioux and the Crow were already traditional enemies, and the U.S. soldiers were seen as allies against the Sioux as well as against the Cheyenne.

As mentioned earlier, within the Crow family structure one's uncles, aunts, and cousins bear the same designations and the same responsibilities as one's mother, father, and siblings. Thus there is a tightly knit pattern of mutual loyalty within the broader kinship group. Not only does the mother's brother carry out disciplinary duties for her children and assume economic responsibility for her family should her husband die, but in the past a Crow brave frequently married an entire set of sisters. Pretty-Shield describes her own situation:

> A man could not take a woman from his own clan, no matter how much he might wish to have her. He had to marry a woman belonging to another clan, and then all their children belonged to their mother's clan. This law kept our blood strong. . . . My oldest sister, Standing-medicine-rock, was his first woman; then he took me, and finally, when my youngest sister, Two-scalps, became sixteen years old, she was also taken by my man, Goes-ahead, so that there were three lodges, all sisters, and all belonging to Goes-ahead.[15]

The Navajo also exhibit a stronger sense of loyalty to the family and clan than to the larger tribe or nation. Only in recent years have the Navajo found it necessary to stand together as a people in order to protect their rights against the inroads of white culture.

By way of contrast, the Pueblo people of the Southwest, as well as to some extent the peoples of the Northwest coastal region, follow a tighter pattern at the broad, cultural level. Correspondingly, they place a much greater emphasis on loyalty to the larger group than do the peoples previously discussed. Among the Pueblo peoples, who are far more sedentary and agriculturally based, equal if not primary loyalty is directed toward the maintenance of the overarching affiliation with the society at large. These people reveal a strong sense of territoriality and cultural self-protection, as was evident in the Pueblo Rebellion against the Spanish in 1680.

The Rio Grande and Hopi Pueblo cultures are situated within a rather small geographical area, and thus both can and must develop a loyalty that stretches beyond family and clan in order to achieve common goals and meet common needs. The Hopi, too, strongly resisted the Spanish incursions, and even banded together against one of their own villages that had converted to Catholicism, burning it to the ground in 1700.

While the Rio Grande Pueblos eventually absorbed the Catholic religion as parallel to their own, the Hopi have continued to resist outside influence and have remained relatively isolated until very recently. They continue to reveal an intense sense of loyalty to the Hopi nation as a whole, and to the preservation of its cultural heritage, even though as individuals the Hopi generally participate in the surrounding Eruo-American culture as well.[16]

While the courage generated by loyalty that motivated the Pueblo peoples to resist outside influences has been significant in their history, it has for the most part been expressed as an inner quality rather than an outwardly visible quality. The Pueblos' military rebellions against the Spanish were the exception rather than the norm. For their primary concern has been to ensure their own survival and integrity through inward cohesiveness based on loyalty to the larger group. Largely as a result of this emphasis, they have been able to a considerable degree to maintain themselves on their own land even up to the present.

The sort of loyalty and courage valued most highly among the Plains Indians pertains more to the individual and the family than to the larger social group. While this emphasis stood them in good stead in their battles with each other and the troops of the U.S. Army, it eventually led to their dissolution into ever smaller bands perpetually on the run or holed up in the mountains. Even the Navajo were scattered and hunted down piecemeal by the soldiers under Kit Carson's command, and then forced into the "Long Walk" of 1864. A more nomadic way of life evokes and requires a set of values which make it more difficult to resist massive and systematic invasion.

Among the Plains Indians the "warrior" role has always been the focus of the values of loyalty and courage. While all Native Americans honored those who exhibited such qualities, the Plains Indians developed this to the highest level. The Cheyenne, for example, had five special warrior clubs or associations that all young men joined. These competed against one another for honors. Each individual male was ranked and valued in terms of his accomplishments in combat with enemies.

> Living as they do in an atmosphere of chronic warfare, the Cheyennes, like other Plains tribes, emphasize military virtue. There are at least a hundred different situations in the ritual life of the people that invite ceremonial coup counting by an outstanding warrior. Public glory is the ever present reward of the man who fights bravely and well. Public ridicule and scornful songs sung by the women drive on the young men. . . . The fighting patterns of the Cheyennes are embellished with virtuosities that go far beyond the needs of victory. Display in bravery tends to become an end in itself. Prestige drives override the more limited military requirements for defeat of the enemy. The scoring is in the counting of coup—touching or striking an enemy with hand or weapons. . . . Actual killing and scalping get their credit, too, but they do not rate as highly as the show-off deeds.[17]

Since the conclusion of the "Indian Wars" in 1890, Cheyenne men have had to find other ways to express loyalty and courage. Because of removal to reservations, this became increasingly difficult and led to serious psychosocial confusion in many Plains cultures. This trend has recently been significantly reversed.

Other ways of embodying courage among Plains societies were ceremonial activities, such as the "vision quest" and the Sun Dance ritual, which have already been discussed. Within the value system of the Plains Indians, horse raiding was held in especially high regard, equal in worth to actually engaging in battle with the enemy. It was the availability of the horse, after all, that rendered life on the Plains far more viable in the first place, and thus it became imperative that each group should acquire and maintain as many horses as possible. Stealing them from one another thus became common.

One final comment needs to be made about "warfare" among Native Americans in general. Battles were conducted as minor avenues to economic and domestic enhancement rather than as all-out conflict as in Western culture. Most battles were the result of efforts to steal horses or kidnap women for wives, rather than attempts to "conquer" the enemy.

Indeed, such encounters were almost sporting contests rather than battles, since they were extremely limited in scope and were a regular, expected feature of life. Occasionally there were large-scale confrontations over territorial hunting rights, but even these often ended in some sort of mutual agreement. This limited and cultural understanding of "warfare" contributed strongly to Native Americans' inability to comprehend the scope and intent of westward expansion by white invaders. Large-scale conquest and territorial dominance were never part of Native American worldviews.

WISDOM AND BEAUTY

Within many Native American worldviews, life is approached as if it is a path or road along which a person walks, seeking to achieve and maintain a basic balance in the face of dangers and difficulties. To stay on the path, or to find one's way through the maze of human existence, in both personal and social life, is the proximate goal. Whenever a person strays or falls from the path, or is thrown off balance by external forces, ceremonies and healing rituals are available to enable the person to return to the path and continue the journey of life.

The ultimate goal of this journey is a life full of what is generally translated into English from Navajo as "beauty," "wisdom," or "health." As a person grows and matures in the process of achieving balanced progress along the path of life, his or her personality is increasingly characterized by a high degree of harmony and spiritual richness, together with an accumulation of wise understanding. Since it takes many years to acquire the experience necessary for such maturity, these qualities are generally regarded as the fruits or rewards obtained only by those who are nearing their final years. For such people have not only experienced a great deal, but they have also invested the effort required to reflect on their experience and learn from it. Long, broad experience, together with continual reflection, yields a life of harmony and wisdom. At the close of life a Native American hopes to be able to exhibit these highly valued qualities.

The concept central to this way of thinking for the Navajo people is *hozhò*, which is variously translated as "beauty," "happiness," "blessing," "wholeness," or even "health." This last rendition may seem paradoxical to the Western mind, since Westerners generally think of the end of life in terms of death rather than health. Westerners may have difficulty understanding how someone who is at the end of life can be said to have achieved final well-being or health.

There is a parallel here to the classical Greek notion of excellence (*areté*) which also may be translated as "beauty," in the sense of wholeness, or as "virtue" in the richest sense of the word. Both Plato and Aristotle believed that these qualities can only be attained after a lifetime of experience and reflection. Similarly, in the Native American viewpoint the concepts of old age and death are not antithetical to those of health and blessing. Indeed, they are complementary.

Gary Witherspoon has sought to interpret the intricacies of the Navajo concept of *hozhò* so as to highlight its emphasis on both fullness and termination. Since this notion is often associated with the verb *sa'ah*, which means to grow or mature, Witherspoon concludes that the term *sa'ah* contains "the Navajo concern for and emphasis upon life, their attitude toward birth and death, and particularly toward death of old age as the goal of life."[18] Thus when the ideas of *hozhò* and *sa'ah* are combined, death is seen as the fulfillment of life as well as its end. Even in English we have these two meanings for the word "end": as the goal, as in the expression "The end justifies the means," and as the termination of a process.

On the basis of his analysis of the many uses of the term *hozhò*, John Farella concludes that its most fundamental meaning pertains to the idea of completeness, in the sense of being whole both in oneself and as part of a larger whole. The root meaning is, then, a kind of integration or interrelatedness, but as Farella says, the source of this completeness "is the lack of completeness of the individual. As Westerners we often view the complete person as the man apart, the one who can go it alone. In the Navajo context the emphasis is on being a part of the past, the future, and of the world around us."[19] The essence of human existence is, in the Navajo worldview, interconnected with every aspect of the total reality constituting the world.

In Navajo spiritual life, nearly all the various chants and songs, such as those used in the Blessingway, Night Chant, and Flintway ceremonies, employ the term *hozhò* in one form or another. Like the Greek word *makarios* in Jesus' Sermon on the Mount, which can be translated as "happy" or "blessed," the word *hoꝣhò* can be rendered as either "in beauty" or "happily" in these chants, though perhaps "in health" or "in wholeness" might be more appropriate. It is the observance of a life of *hoꝣhò* that results in the all-encompassing notion of wisdom. The word is ued throughout this prayer from the Night Chant, which plays a vital part in a healing ceremony:

> Happily I recover
> Happily my interior becomes cool
> Happily I go forth
> My interior feeling cool, may I walk
> No longer sore, may I walk
> As it used to be long ago, may I walk
> Happily, with abundant dark clouds, may I walk
> Happily, with abundant showers, may I walk
> Happily, with abundant plants, may I walk
> Happily, on a trail of pollen, may I walk
> Happily, may I walk.[20]

The notion of the circle is crucial to the Native American understanding of spatial reality. The idea of the circle also incorporates the concept of completeness or beauty as harmony and balance. The Plains Indians emphasize the ritual significance of the circle as symbolizing the inclusiveness and completeness of all reality, and they frequently speak of the circle as the "sacred hoop." It is clear from Black Elk's words that this idea also carries connotations of health and wholeness, completeness and beauty, as well as balance:

> You have noticed that everything an Indian does is in a circle, and that is because the Power of the World always works in circles, and everything tries to be round. In the old days when we were a strong and happy people, all power came to us from the sacred hoop of the nation, and so long as the hoop was unbroken, the people flourished. . . . Even the seasons form a great circle in their changing, and always come back again to where they were. The life of a man is a circle from childhood to childhood. . . . Our tepees were round like the nests of birds, and

these were always set in a circle, the nation's hoop, a nest of nests, where the Great Spirit meant for us to hatch our children.[21]

In nearly all Native American worldviews a high premium is placed on knowledge of three basic kinds. First, knowledge of the community's traditions and belief systems is extolled as essential to a proper and prosperous life. This type of knowledge is generally conveyed through the telling of stories of origin and of legendary characters and events. It is also communicated through direct instruction and behavioral example, especially by family members. This is a familiar pattern in all cultures.

Second, general knowledge of the environment is necessary to survival for both individuals and societies. The crucial and diverse nature of such knowledge is revealed by the range of terrain and climate encountered by Native American peoples. The food sources available to a group are largely dependent on such factors and every member of the group must know the characteristics and patterns of the available animals, fish, nuts, berries, and fruit. The knowledge of how to make tools and clothing is also fundamental, as well as the knowledge of how to raise children and perform everyday practical tasks.

A third type of knowledge concerns the secrets and mysteries of spiritual traditions. This is not available to everyone; it is entrusted only to those who are committed to its mastery and proper use within the community. Sacred knowledge can be acquired through specialized training, vision quests, and traditional rites of passage. Sacred knowledge includes both information and techniques, on the one hand, and experiential encounters with divine beings and powers, on the other. Shamans are generally the primary guardians and dispensers of this form of knowledge, and they are regarded as truly possessing "wisdom."

Knowledge alone does not constitute wisdom, which requires a combination of experience and knowledge. This pattern is universal in human experience. Without the experience and traditions of the elders, no individual or culture can survive at all, let alone grow and develop.

Native Americans are not generally expected to ask "why?" in relation to what is being taught, at least in the early stages. A young Taos Pueblo woman explains that to have asked "why?" when she was being taught

... would have meant that I was learning nothing—that I was stupid. And in Western society if you don't ask why they think you are stupid. So having been raised to not ask why but to listen, become aware, I take for granted that people have some knowledge of themselves and myself—that is religion.[22]

The crucial element in all real wisdom would seem to be making sound judgments rather than acquiring either simple factual knowledge or specialized techniques. Judgment involves a mature ability to draw reasonable conclusions from a thoughtful consideration of the issues and factors in any situation. This understanding of wisdom is underscored by Luther Standing Bear, a Lakota Sioux:

> Conversation was never begun at once, nor in a hurried manner. No one was quick with a question, no matter how important, and no one was pressed for an answer. A pause giving time for thought was the truly courteous way of beginning and conducting a conversation. Silence was meaningful with the Lakota, and his granting a space of silence to the speechmaker and his own moment of silence before talking was done in the practice of true politeness and regard for the rule that, "thought comes before speech." ... I am going to venture that the man who sat on the ground in his tipi meditating on life and its meaning, accepting the kinship of all creatures, and acknowledging unity with the universe of things was infusing into his being the true essence of civilization.[23]

NOTES

1. P. Beck, A. L. Walters, and N. Francisco, *The Sacred* (Tsaile, Ariz.: Navajo Community College, 1992), p. 25.

2. Howard Harrod, *Renewing the World* (Tucson: University of Arizona Press, 1987), p. 165.

3. E. Adamson Hoebel, *The Cheyennes* (New York: Harcourt Brace, 1988), p. 98.

4. John Farella, *The Main Stalk: A Synthesis of Navajo Philosophy* (Tucson: University of Arizona Press, 1984), p. 147.

5. Ibid., pp. 192–93.

6. Åke Hultkrantz, *The Religions of the American Indians* (Berkeley: University of California Press, 1979), pp. 84–85.

7. Ibid., pp. 88–89.

8. Black Elk, *Black Elk Speaks: Being the Life Story of a Holy Man of the Oglala Sioux*, as told through John G. Neihardt (Lincoln: University of Nebraska Press, 1979), p. 22.

9. Ibid., p. 47.

10. Ibid., p. 49.

11. Ibid., pp. 198–203.

12. Barbara Graymont, *The Iroquois* (New York: Chelsea House, 1988), p. 149.

13. Hoebel, *The Cheyennes*, p. 94.

14. Nancy Parezo, *Navajo Sandpainting: From Religious Act to Commercial Art* (Albuquerque: University of New Mexico Press, 1991), p. 12.

15. Frank Linderman, *Pretty-Shield, Medicine Woman of the Crows* (Lincoln: University of Nebraska Press, 1972), pp. 130–31.

16. J. O. Brew, "Hopi Prehistory and History to 1850," in *Handbook of North American Indians*, ed. Alfonso Ortiz, vol. 9 (Washington, D.C.: Smithsonian Institution, 1979), pp. 519–22.

17. Hoebel, *The Cheyennes*, pp. 75–77.

18. Gary Witherspoon, "Central Concepts in the Navajo Worldview," *Linguistics* (1974): p. 49.

19. Farella, *The Main Stalk*, p. 181.

20. Quoted by Paula Gunn Allen, "The Sacred Hoop," in *The Remembered Earth: An Anthology of Contemporary Native American Literature*, ed. Geary Hobson (Albuquerque: University of New Mexico Press, 1980), p. 226.

21. Black Elk, *Black Elk Speaks*, pp. 194–96.

22. Beck, Walters, and Francisco, *The Sacred*, p. 49.

23. *Native American Wisdom* (Philadelphia: Running Press, 1993), pp. 58 and 88.

Chapter Seven

Tradition and/or Progress

For many years there was a large sign on the Navajo Reservation in Chinle, Arizona, that read: "Tradition is the Enemy of Progress." Although it is unclear whether this sign was erected by the U.S. government's Bureau of Indian Affairs or by the Navajo people themselves, this statement focuses the central issue facing Native American cultures in the years to come. The difficulty of keeping traditions alive in the face of the overwhelming influence of an encircling and largely domineering culture is staggering.

The invasion of North America by European explorers, settlers, and missionaries almost led to the total extinction of Native American people along with their customs and beliefs. Over the past twenty-five years there has been a resurgence of Native American cultures and a serious effort to find a middle road between total assimilation into Euro-American society on the one hand and the maintenance of the traditional ways of life on the other. Perhaps this "middle path" will become a reality for Native American peoples, as well as for their worldviews.

CONTACT AND CONQUEST

Following the arrival of Christopher Columbus in the West Indies in 1492, the European invasion and conquest of the Americas was soon in full swing. The Spanish *conquistadores* made their way from southern Mexico into the Sonora Desert and what is today the southwestern

United States in 1540–42 under the leadership of Coronado. Spanish outposts and missions were established throughout the region and even spread into California. The native peoples were conquered and forced into slave labor to meet the economic expectations of their conquerors. For the next two hundred years this pattern, which also included forced "conversion" to Catholicism, continued, interrupted briefly by the Pueblo Rebellion in 1680, led by a Tewa named Popé. By 1692 the Spanish had reconquered the Rio Grande region of New Mexico, which remained under Spanish, and later Mexican, control until annexed by the United States in the mid-1800s. The same pattern of conquest and forced labor was followed by the Spanish in the American southeast, but with a more limited and short-lived effect.

The French established trading routes and outposts throughout the Great Lakes area. They were not essentially interested in conquering and settling the New World, but were content to explore and trade with Native Americans and established friendly relations with them. French trappers found their way down the great river systems, all the way to what is now New Orleans. The French were major suppliers of guns and liquor to the Native Americans, as well as major transmitters of European diseases to which Native Americans had no immunity.

All along the Atlantic coast, the Dutch and the English founded colonies and sought to take over the surrounding areas. From Plymouth, Massachusetts, to Jamestown, Virginia, the English established themselves and began to spread westward. The entire eastern woodland area was soon populated by English colonists. There were, of course, many conflicts with Native American peoples along the way. The Dutch, on the other hand, sought to deal with Native American groups as sovereign nations, making treaties with them and purchasing land from them, mostly in the New England area and eastern Canada. Eventually the Dutch were driven out by the English.

The Pacific coastal region was explored by the Spanish and English, as well as by the Russians, in the second half of the eighteenth century, from northern Alaska to Southern California. The Spanish continued their *conquistador* pattern until they were expelled as Mexico gained its independence. Mexican dominance was ended by the United States' acquisition of the western territories, which also removed the English outposts from the Pacific coast. The Russian colonies, perhaps the most devastating of all to Native American cultures, were all abandoned by 1841. The Native American population was decimated by a combination of savage treatment and unfamiliar diseases.

Those who dwelt on the Great Plains, on the High Plateau, and in the Southwest came under constant pressure from the westward expansion of U.S. settlers and soldiers in the nineteenth century. They were systematically harassed, hunted down, forced to move from one fort to another, and finally placed on reservations far from or quite unlike their original homelands. The U.S. government repeatedly broke every treaty it had signed and continuously sought to destroy the native peoples. The final battle, after the eventual capture of Apache chief Geronimo in 1886, was at Wounded Knee, where hundreds of Native Americans, including women and children, were massacred on the Rosebud Reservation in South Dakota in 1890.

In 1834, U.S. President Andrew Jackson, himself a famous Indian fighter with the nickname "Sharp Knife," established a "permanent boundary" between whites and Native American peoples at the Mississippi River. All the land west of this boundary was officially designated "Indian Land." The boundary was shifted westward to the 95th meridian within a matter of months, and with the discovery of gold in California in 1848, hoards of prospectors and settlers flooded into the western states over the Sante Fe and Oregon Trails. Eventually what is now the State of Oklahoma was designated "Indian Territory" and nearly all Native American peoples were required to relocate there. As Dee Brown explains,

> To justify these breaches of the "permanent Indian frontier," the policy makers in Washington invented Manifest Destiny, a term which lifted land hunger to a lofty plane. The Europeans and their descendants were ordained by destiny to rule all of America. They were the dominant race and therefore responsible for the Indians—along with their lands, their forests, and their mineral wealth. Only the New Englanders, who had destroyed or driven out all their Indians, spoke against Manifest Destiny.[1]

A crucial source of difficulty in the conflict between the European and Native American cultures, aside from the arrogance and racism of the former, was a difference in worldviews regarding the proper relationship with the environment. Western culture focuses on the conquest and control of nature, on shaping it to fit the needs and desires of people, while the majority of Native American cultures encourage the adaptation of human life to the laws and patterns of nature. The rationale for this latter approach is that nature itself represents the larger whole and is taken to be the work of divine beings and processes. Thus, Native Americans were content to devise a lifestyle involving a reciprocal relation with nature and saw no need to "conquer" or significantly alter their environment. Moreover, the concept of land ownership generally had no place in Native American worldviews. The earth was seen as the life source of all creatures and thus could "belong" to no one.

Out of the centuries of conflict and war that the white intruders brought to indigenous cultures, certain episodes have come to symbolize the essence of the experience and the extent of the devastation. A brief review of a few of these episodes illustrates the scope and character of the contrast between the worldviews involved.

These events reflect the value systems and ideologies of various Native American peoples as against those of the domineering and dominating European culture. The question of guilt, while not the central concern of this review, cannot, of course, be ignored. The imperialism and the genocide systematically carried out by European invaders and the U.S. government stands as a lasting indictment of some of the values that lie at the heart of Western civilization and continue to get in the way of its best intentions. The record speaks for itself.

Throughout the three hundred years of "Indian Wars" many confrontations were experienced by Native Americans across the continent. Most of these ended in some sort of treaty between various governments and Indian peoples, treaties which were repeatedly broken by the former, leading to retaliation by the Native Americans and even more conflicts and treaties. Five major encounters were the Pueblo Rebellion, the Cherokee "Trail of Tears," the "Long Walk" of the Navajo, the "Flight of the Nez Perce," and the "Massacre at Wounded Knee."

By 1680 the Spanish had established themselves as rulers in the Rio Grande region of northern New Mexico. They sought to force the Native Americans to give up their own religious practices and beliefs in favor of

Catholicism. In the summer of 1680 a shaman named Popé, of the Tewa pueblo of San Juan, secretly organized a massive rebellion against the Spanish at the town of Santa Fe. After four days of fierce fighting the Spanish abandoned Santa Fe. Unfortunately the victory was short-lived for the Spanish reconquered the area twelve years later.

The Cherokee Nation, spread up and down the eastern mountains of Virginia, the Carolinas, and Georgia, lived for many years under an uneasy truce with the whites in the area, with only one major conflict in the early 1760s. However, in 1830 President Andrew Jackson signed the Indian Removal Act which required the Cherokee, among many other peoples, to relocate west of the Mississippi River. In 1838–39 the Cherokee were forced at gunpoint to march some eight hundred miles to a new reservation in what is now Oklahoma. During the journey, which has come to be known as the "Trail of Tears," at least 4,000 Cherokee died or were killed. A few managed to escape and continued to live in the Carolina mountains where they were later granted a small reservation.

The tensions between the Navajo people and the Mexican slave-raiders on the one hand, and the U.S. Army on the other, mounted during the mid-1800s. In 1862 the army assigned Colonel Kit Carson the task of rounding up all Navajos, driving them into Canyon de Chelly, and marching them to Fort Sumner, some three hundred miles to the east in the Pecos River Valley at Bosque Redondo. This march came to be known as the "Long Walk," a walk on which a great many Navajos died.

After several years of near starvation and rampant disease, the Navajo people were allowed to return to their native land, under a new treaty, to a reservation near the Chuska mountains. Here they began to rebuild their culture. Today the Navajo Nation is one of the largest and most prosperous of all Native American groups. This turn of events testifies to the spiritual resilience and courage inherent in the Navajo worldview, qualities that continue to serve the people well today, even as they did when the Europeans sought to annihilate them.

The Nez Perce, who dwelt on the high plains of what is now eastern Washington State and western Idaho, also experienced continual difficulties as a result of intrusions into their hunting grounds. After having their reservation territory relocated several times, in 1863 they were granted land in northwest Oregon that was supposed to be theirs forever.

But the United States opened the area to white settlers again. In 1877 a fateful conflict with U.S. soldiers took place as a peace treaty was being signed. Chief Joseph led his people on a long, arduous journey to escape from the army. The chase led eastward through the Bitterroot Mountains and into eastern Montana. Chief Joseph believed that if the Nez Perce could get to Canada they would be safe. After a fierce battle near the border, Chief Joseph surrendered, his people having dwindled from nearly seven hundred to about four hundred, including only eighty braves. It was here that he delivered his now famous speech, ending with the words, "I will fight no more forever."

The Cheyenne and Sioux were also subdued in 1877 but the final blow came in 1890 at Wounded Knee in South Dakota where hundreds of people had gathered to take part in a Ghost Dance ritual. The prophet Wovoka had attracted a large following with his message of Native American revival and the banishment of Euro-American culture, and many people believed themselves to be invincible when they wore the special Ghost Dance shirts. The U.S. Army sought to break up the outlawed ceremony and opened fire on the Native Americans, killing at least 150 men, women, and children, all of whom were buried in a common grave. This massacre marked the end of Native American resistance and seemingly the end of Native American culture as well.

RESERVATIONS AND CONVERSIONS

The betrayals and atrocities perpetrated by white invaders and their culture, whether in wars and conquests, or in imprisonment on reservations, as described below, are powerfully detailed in Dee Brown's *Bury My Heart at Wounded Knee*. He concluded his introduction with the following words:

> This is not a cheerful book, but history has a way of intruding upon the present, and perhaps those who read it will have a clearer understanding of what the American Indian is, by knowing what he was. . . .
> And if the readers of this book should ever chance to see the poverty, the hopelessness, and the squalor of a modern Indian reservation, they may find it possible to truly understand the reasons why.[2]

Vine Deloria Jr., a Native American author, has summed up the depth of the whites' culpability in the near destruction of Native American people and their culture in terms of the very Christian imagery which provided much of the impetus for it. Even as Christ is said to have died for the sins of the world, so Deloria suggests that the death of General George Custer should be understood as symbolizing the punishments white people should pay for their sins against the Native American. Thus Deloria entitled his book *Custer Died for Your Sins*.[3]

The removal of Native Americans from their homes and their relocation on lands designated by the U.S. Government began in the middle of the nineteenth century with the concept of a "permanent Indian Territory" and the Removal Act of 1830. Fifty-two treaties were signed between 1853 and 1856 alone, and a total of 370 had been ratified by 1877 when Chief Joseph finally surrendered. The greatest number of reservations were established in the twenty years between 1867 and 1887, with the aim of segregating Native American peoples from white society. Eventually, instead of one large area for all, different peoples were given small parcels of land in different parts of the continent. The territories of the Pacific Northwest, in Washington and Oregon, served as the initial locales for this experiment.

Eventually this separatist policy gave way to the notion that Native Americans should be assimilated into the mainstream of American culture by being forced to abandon their traditional culture, including their languages and religious beliefs, in favor of the ideas and customs of white society as taught to them in missionary and government schools. In 1887 Congress passed the General Allotment Act which broke up the reservations and gave the head of each family 160 acres of land on which to farm. Between this time and 1924, when Native Americans were finally granted citizenship, government and church schools sought to "civilize" Native American children by educating them in the ways of Euro-American culture. By 1928 the allotment policy was judged to be a total failure.

Under the leadership of Franklin Roosevelt and his Commissioner of Indian Affairs, John Collier, Congress passed the Indian Reorganization Act in 1934, which completely reversed the policies of assimilation and allotment and

. . . gave legal sanction to tribal landholdings; returned unsold allotted lands to tribes, made provisions for the purchase of new lands; encouraged tribal constitutions, systems of justice, and business corporations; expanded educational opportunities through new facilities and loans, with an emphasis on reservation day schools instead of off-reservation boarding schools; advocated the hiring of Indians by the Bureau of Indian Affairs and Indian involvement in management and policy making at national and tribal levels . . . and granted Indians religious freedom.[4]

Between the world wars, U.S. policies toward Native Americans vacillated greatly. More treaties were broken and greater efforts were made to relocate Native Americans to urban areas, contributing to even greater confusion. However, in 1946 the Indian Claims Commission was set up to allow Native American peoples to reclaim their stolen lands and to receive monetary compensation for broken treaties. In the 1970s and 1980s this commission returned 48,000 acres to the Taos Pueblo in New Mexico, 21,000 acres to the Yakima in the State of Washington, and roughly the same amount of land to Native American peoples in Maine.

In recent decades there has been a marked increase in Native American self-determination and a reversal of the assimilation process. Today nearly half of the total Native American population lives off the reservations, working in urban areas. Nevertheless, a great many people return to the reservations regularly for social, cultural, and religious activities. So, although there is an ongoing process of assimilation into mainstream American culture, Native Americans are also finding ways to regenerate and maintain their traditional cultures.

One complex aspect of the reservation system concerns the role and character of religion within it. From the very beginning of the white, Christian invasion and conquest of Native America, religion has been at the center of nearly every turn of events. Throughout the centuries the dominant belief has been that Native Americans are pagans who stand in need of both civilization and salvation, and indeed a great many of them have converted to Christianity.

The ways in which people have adapted to or adopted the Christian faith are diverse, running the full gamut from total rejection of Native American beliefs and practices to nearly complete resistance to all attempts at Christianization. Many Protestant missionary efforts, especially those of the Presbyterians, Methodists, and Mormons, have been quite successful, when conducted in connection with medical and educational endeavors. Those who have converted to some brand of Protestant Christianity generally abandon their traditional religions and can be said to represent one end of the spectrum.

At the other end of the religious spectrum stand those who have always strongly resisted every effort to convert them. The Hopi probably represent the most striking example of resistance. From the very beginning of their encounter with the Spanish *conquistadores* and missionaries, all but one of the Hopi pueblos refused to have anything to do with the ideas and practices of the newcomers. Since that time Hopi leaders have been extremely hesitant to have much to do with either Protestants or Catholics, although the Mormons have had some success.

In the middle of the spectrum, between these two extreme responses to conversion efforts, stand those who have worked out some sort of relationship between their traditional religion and Christianity. One such relationship is that developed by the Yaqui of the Sonora Desert in northern Mexico and southern Arizona. The Yaqui gradually synthesized their own religion with Catholicism, producing a fascinating blend of the two. The celebration of the Easter season on the Yaqui reservations clearly embodies this cultural and religious synthesis.

A different relationship between traditional spirituality and Christianity has been developed by the Pueblos of the Rio Grande region. The Pueblo peoples accepted Catholicism while continuing to hold on to their own indigenous beliefs and practices. As the Tewa socioreligious calendar demonstrates, these peoples simply run their religious ceremonies and rituals according to two parallel cyclical patterns without denying either one.

There are various syntheses of Native American religion and Protestant Christianity. The Native American Church straightforwardly incorporates elements of both Native American belief and Christian teaching into its peyote ceremonies. In addition, the apocalyptic Ghost Dance faith that arose at the close of the nineteenth century exhibited a direct Christian influence in its promise of a coming upheaval and the installation of a new order on earth. Even traditional Apache religion began to show signs of Christian influence in the teachings of Silas John Edwards on western Apache reservations after 1921.

The foregoing discussion reveals a very strong contrast between the worldview of Western civilization on the one hand and the worldviews of Native Americans on the other. It has been suggested that the Native American way of relating to the surrounding environment in general and to other forms of life in particular is one of adaptation, of learning to fit in, rather than trying to alter and control these realities for one's own ends. Thus, Native Americans rarely if ever set out to conquer other peoples or tried to force them to change their spiritual beliefs and practices. In short, conquest and proselytization are not part of Native American worldviews. The Western worldview is very different.

ASSIMILATION AND RESISTANCE

Since 1950 the basic pattern for Native Americans has been one of assimilation into mainstream white culture. However, this process has not been rapid or smooth in spite of government poverty programs in the 1970s and the new self-determination policies introduced in the 1980s. A great many Native Americans find themselves caught in a "no man's land" between life on the reservation, which does not come close to their traditional way of life, and life in large cities where they sometimes find few opportunities for work or vocational training.

> The newfound cultural isolation of the cities has led many to opt for the poverty of the reservation. Those that do stay in the urban centers fall into at least three recognizable patterns: first, skilled laborers, often living on the edges of cities in Indian enclaves; second, those remaining oriented to their home reservations or rural communities, journeying back and forth depending on seasonal jobs; and third, an Indian middle class interspersed in white neighborhoods.[5]

Native Americans have the shortest lifespan of any ethnic group in the United States; the highest infant mortality rate; the highest suicide rate; the lowest per capita income; the highest unemployment rate; the highest school dropout rate; the poorest housing; and the most inadequate health care.[6] The causes of this abysmal situation are many and complex. Native Americans by and large live on unproductive land, start out without any monetary capital, lack adequate education, and still carry the stigma of being "savages," lazy, immoral, and dirty. All these factors go together, along with the psychology of being conquered cultures and dislocated people in the midst of an alien and dominating society, to produce a self-perpetuating cycle of defeatism and depression. Both assimilation and self-determination are still a long way off.

Perhaps the most devastating aspect of this whole situation has been the degree to which Native Americans have been separated from their particular homelands and from the earth in general. Within essentially every Native American worldview the earth, with its seasonal patterns and cycles, its fruitfulness, and its abundance of animal life, plays a crucial role. Throughout their centuries-long existence, Native American peoples have structured nearly every aspect of their cultural beliefs and practices around the earth as the mother of all life and meaning. Having their entire way of viewing the world and reality almost completely destroyed in a few generations, while not being enabled to find a place within the new, dominant culture, has left a great many feeling abandoned and hopeless.

Fortunately, there has been an increasing tendency in recent decades to restore to Native Americans the occupancy of their original lands, together with their traditional fishing and hunting rights. Many groups have won legal battles for the restoration of these rights in the highest state and federal courts, but this progress has been overshadowed by the fact that the federal government has cut back aid to Native Americans by nearly 50 percent over the last twenty years, as well as by the continual destruction of their lands by logging and strip-mining. Many groups, such as the Navajo, now face a dilemma: whether or not to tear up their sacred land in order to profit from the valuable resources that lie underground, such as coal and oil, so they can meet their subsistence needs. Although the U.S. government has recently passed a law protecting Native American sacred sites, it is not being enforced with much consistency.

It was not until around 1970 that organized Native American self-awareness and political activism became a force to be reckoned with at the national level. Finding inspiration in the civil rights movement of Martin Luther King and the anti-Vietnam protests, some leaders began to organize their people around issues and events that would call attention to the oppression and exploitation which had become the accepted lot of most Native Americans.

This more forceful resistance was triggered by a new organization, AIM (the American Indian Movement), under the leadership of Dennis Banks and Russell Means. This group began to occupy federally held property, such as Alcatraz Island, Fort Lawton in Seattle, and Mount Rushmore. In 1972 AIM took over the the Sioux Pine Ridge Reservation at the site of the 1890 Wounded Knee massacre. After seventy-one days of altercations, negotiations, and shootings, two Native Americans were left dead and a federal marshal wounded. Although the leaders in such encounters have frequently been arrested and imprisoned, they continue to speak out on behalf of Native American rights.

The dilemma that confronts today's Native Americans is a result of the dichotomized understanding of them that has characterized Western society from the initial point of contact. On the one hand, Native American peoples have been denigrated and vilified as pagan savages who must either be destroyed or "civilized" according to white definitions. On the other hand, they have been romanticized and sentimentalized as peaceful "noble savages" whose way of life symbolized all that is good and beautiful. Unfortunately, neither of these alternatives suggests or even leaves room for an activist posture whereby Native Americans can play a real role in determining their own lives and rebuilding their culture. In both scenarios the Euro-American culture prefers to marginalize the Native American, as a vile enemy or as a beautiful icon.

RENAISSANCE AND THE FUTURE

The activists' efforts to call attention to the rights and values of Native American peoples served as a catalyst for the rebirth of Native American culture among many groups. The heart of this renaissance consists in a renewed belief in the fundamental values of Native American worldviews and in the self-worth of people. In many ways and places Native Americans have become more self-confident, with increased pride in their traditional beliefs and practices, as well as in their own worth as persons. There are three main manifestations of this.

The first is in the political realm. The activists already referred to became the fulcrum for a fresh understanding of the possibilities of participation in the political processes that determine the realities of Native American life. Not only have Native Americans continued to make their presence felt and appreciated at both the local and national level, but they have taken renewed interest in the governance of their own groups. No longer are they simply at the beck and call of the Bureau of Indian Affairs and the federal government. This aspect of the Native American renaissance holds great potential for greater control of their own destiny.

A second manifestation of this renaissance is in the economic realm. Increasingly, Native American groups are seeking to make the most of their skills and crafts, as well as the resources of their traditional lands and reservations. Today there are far fewer "middlemen" between Native American artisans and buyers, and many groups are successfully operating resorts and casinos on their reservations. The result is that a great deal of money is now available to members for education and health facilities. To be sure, there are some problems attendant on such enterprises, but the fact remains that Native Americans are taking the initiative in finding ways to reaffirm and reshape their own cultural destiny.

The third way in which the Native American renaissance manifests itself is in a renewed cultural life. In addition to a growing awareness of and commitment to what is called the "Pan-Indian" movement, which seeks to unite all Native American peoples for political and cultural purposes, many tribes and nations are finding ways to enhance their own participation in their traditional culture. Perhaps the most important and dramatic development in this regard is the increasing interest in Native-American-sponsored schools throughout the country, schools that teach traditional culture and languages along with other subjects and modern technologies.

Just in the past two decades, for instance, over two dozen tribal community colleges have sprung up around the country, following the lead of the Navajo Community College (now the Diné Community College) in the Four Corners area. This development has been paralleled by the enormous growth in the number of courses and departments in Native American studies in the curricula of both state and private colleges and universities. A growing number of Native Americans have graduated or are graduating from college and are teaching and publishing scholarly work on nearly every aspect of Native American culture. Writers like N. Scott Momaday and Leslie Silko, and artists like R. Gorman and R. Carlos Nakai, along with scholars such as Vine Deloria Jr. and the recently deceased Alfonso Ortiz, have become well-known and influential in their fields. The new Smithsonian National Museum of the American Indian and the magazine *Native Peoples* also attest to the strength and quality of the cultural rebirth.

By far the most important aspect of this cultural renewal is the teaching of Native American languages to young people. The pivot of any culture is its language, since it is by this means that the stories and customs of a people, as well as traditional beliefs and rituals, are transmitted from one generation to another. Due to the strenuous efforts of white missionaries and government officials to stamp out Native American languages over the past four hundred years, it is not surprising that many tongues have disappeared completely and many others now have only a few speakers. Today, however, there is a strong revival of interest in native languages and the practice of them.

One other element that contributes a great deal to the renaissance of Native American cultures today is the ever-growing interest in intergroup "powwows" or festivals, among both Native Americans and whites. In addition to the economic aspects of these events, where a wide variety of foods and craft products are sold, attention is generally centered on dance exhibitions and contests. Nearly every part of the country has numerous festivals of this nature, and even though a degree of touristic interest and voyeurism is always involved, these gatherings are a great source of pride and bonding for the participants, as well as an informative and moving experience for most of the non-Native American audience.

The need for this cultural rebirth to succeed is clearly expressed in the words of Luther Standing Bear, a Lakota man of wisdom:

> When the Indian has forgotten the music of his forefathers, when the sound of the tomtom is no more, when noisy jazz has drowned the melody of the flute, he will be a dead Indian. When the memory of his heros are no longer told in story, and he forsakes the beautiful white buckskin for factory shoody, he will be dead. When from him has been taken all that is his, all that he has visioned in nature, all that has come to him from infinite sources, he then, truly, will be a dead Indian. His

spirit will be gone, and though he walk crowded streets, he will in truth be—dead.[7]

The essential yet difficult task facing the Native Americans who are seeking to effect this cultural renaissance is to find a way of incorporating the values of the modern, dominant culture that may prove useful to them, while preserving the main values of traditional culture. Fostering one of these sets of values at the expense of the other will only lead to the total eradication of the Native American way of life, through either complete assimilation or ultimate extinction. Some sort of synthesis of the two worldviews is an absolute necessity. Here is how Vine Deloria has expressed the dilemma facing his people:

> The important aspect of Indian tribal religions . . . has been their insistence on developing and maintaining a constant relationship with the spiritual forces that govern the lives of humans. As ceremonies have lost their content, with the changing of lifestyles, they have been forgotten or abandoned. The recent efforts of Indian activists to reclaim tribal land have highlighted the dilemma of today's religious Indian. A traditional Indian finds himself still experiencing the generalized presence of spiritual forces; at the same time he finds himself bound by the modern technology of communications and transportation, which speed his world far beyond its original boundaries.[8]

There are at least two major aspects of Native American worldviews that should help to facilitate the required synthesis. The first is the central idea of balance and harmony, which serves as the axis of the Native American understanding of both the natural environment and human existence. This notion has traditionally enabled Native Americans to adjust to the various developments and difficulties with which they have been confronted through the centuries. Since their first contact with white, European society this pivotal idea has been put to its most severe test and the results have not always been good. Nevertheless, in the midst of the current rebirth of Native American culture the concept of balance and harmony may well be reasserting itself. Native peoples may at last be in the process of regaining their center.

A second aspect of Native American worldviews, especially characteristic of the Navajo and Iroquois understanding of life and reality, is flexibility. The Iroquois Confederation was originally created to bring an end to the constant, ferocious warfare among the peoples of the upper Northeast region. This confederation, based on the Tree of Peace, required a great deal of flexibility and adjustment on the part of the tribes which initially entered into it. As one of their current chiefs, Oren Lyons, has said, "Even though we should by now be obsolete, we are still here and we shall continue to be here in the years to come."[9]

The Navajo are an Athapascan-speaking people who most likely migrated from western Canada about five hundred years ago. Clearly it is an advantage for migrating peoples to emphasize flexibility and adaptation as they make their way among different and sometimes hostile cultural groups. Upon arriving in the Southwest, the Navajo adopted several important aspects of the surrounding Pueblo societies, such as sheep herding and weaving. Through the years they have managed to combine tradition and progress in a remarkable way. David Brugge summarizes this crucial characteristic:

> It is very probable that Blessingway . . . was the core of a nativistic reassertion of the Athabaskan way of life with mechanisms for the integration of foreign elements that were compatible with it . . . to allow for the symbolic Navajo-ization of foreign traits that gives Navajo culture its incorporativeness, so that entire technologies can be integrated into the culture without causing basic changes, and the culture can be adapted relatively easily to changing conditions. The flexibility of Navajo material culture seems to be in part due to the fact that permissive and restrictive injunctions relating to material culture are considered to be largely a private matter for the individual to observe according to his own beliefs. . . .[10]

Brugge goes on to offer what he calls the "ceremonial break," the practice of interrupting the pattern of a ritual, blanket, or piece of pottery, of incorporating an imperfection into the design, as an example of the Navajo understanding of openness toward the incomplete and/or the unexpected. Such "incompleteness" carries with it the possibility, indeed the necessity, of being flexible with regard to whatever the future brings. This is a characteristic that will stand all Native American peoples in good stead in the years to come.

Once again we see the fundamental contrast between the worldviews of Native Americans and the worldview that dominates Western society. Native Americans by and large prize adaptation and flexibility in relation to their environment, whether physical or social, while Westerners seek to conquer and/or control the environment. As the world continues to "shrink," politically and economically, the ideology of adaptation will prove far more useful in the quest for the survival and well-being of all peoples in the future.

NOTES

1. Dee Brown, *Bury My Heart at Wounded Knee* (New York: Henry Holt, 1970), p. 8.

2. Ibid., p. xiv.

3. Vine Deloria Jr., *Custer Died For Your Sins: An Indian Manifesto* (New York: Avon, 1969).

4. Carl Waldman, *Atlas of the North American Indian* (New York: Facts on File, 1985), p. 194.

5. Ibid., p. 200.

6. Ibid., p. 201.

7. Luther Standing Bear, *Land of the Spotted Eagle* (Boston: Running Press, 1933), p. 255.

8. Vine Deloria Jr., "Religion and the Modern American Indian," in *Current History* (December 1974), p. 253.

9. Oren Lyons, PBS interview, "The Faith Keepers," with Bill Moyers, 1990.

10. David Brugge, *Navajo Pottery and Ethnohistory* (Window Rock, Ariz.: Navajoland Publications, 1963), p. 22.

Conclusion

A Primal Vision

A brief summary of the major themes emerging from this introduction to Native American worldviews seems appropriate at this point. When taken together these themes constitute the "primal vision" at the heart of the Native American way of understanding and interacting with the world. A summary of these themes runs the risk of oversimplification, but it also provides a sense of closure.

Three broad themes serve to integrate the various emphases characterizing many Native American approaches to life and the surrounding world, both material and social. One theme pertains to the natural environment, and might be called "ecological awareness." A second theme has to do with Native Americans' understanding of the social, relational network in which they live, or the "web of community." A third theme involves their approach to self-understanding or personal values, that is, their way of achieving a sense of "individual integrity."

ECOLOGICAL AWARENESS

Native American ecological awareness pivots on the distinction between *adapting* to the environment and *altering* the environment to suit one's own needs. There may not be an absolutely clear separation between these two positions, but there is still a significant difference of degree between them. For the most part Native American worldviews opt for the adaptive mode in relating to the natural environment; they seek to fit in with nature rather than alter it.

Although it frequently goes unnoticed, at the time of their initial contact with Europeans, Native North Americans were all "Stone Age" people. This simply means that they did not have metal tools, or the wheel. Nevertheless, Native American culture was sophisticated in social and religious terms. Moreover, their technology was well developed in making the maximum use of the natural environment.

The use of spears, bows and arrows, bone needles and knives, as well as the extensive use of herbs and roots for medicinal purposes, are all well-known aspects of the Native American way of life. In addition, Native Americans' knowledge of animal migration and breeding patterns, as well as the locations, varieties, and uses of plants, berries, and nuts, was extraordinary. The Plains Indians' thorough and intricate use of the bison as a source of food, clothing, and shelter materials, along with the desert dwellers' extensive use of the cactus, epitomize Native Americans' ability to utilize the available natural resources.

Technology has always provided humans with the means of turning nature to their best advantage in the struggle for survival and Native Americans were no exception. However, for the most part they put their technology to work as a means of harmonizing their way of life with nature rather than attempting to control and alter nature simply to meet their own purposes. In short, they saw themselves as part of the natural order rather than as existing apart from or above it.

Had the Native Americans been able to develop their technology more fully, they too might have begun to alter their natural environment more extensively, even as Euro-Americans have done. There is, in fact, some evidence to indicate that on occasion they did waste their resources, as with bison kills in which not all the animals could be used and in the burning of vast areas to clear land for farming. However, for the most part Native Americans were content to live with their natural surroundings as they found them, altering their surroundings only sufficiently to enable them to live above the survival threshold.

One interesting example of this general attitude is the fact that the hunters and gatherers of the Southwest knew how to plant and grow corn at least five hundred years before any of them bothered to do so. Corn was transported from Mesoamerica long before it became a staple in North America. According to recent research, by and large hunting and gathering societies spend far less time acquiring their food than agricultural societies do, and perhaps that is why Native American peoples of the Southwest resisted the growing of corn for so long.

Most Native Americans saw themselves as part of the fabric of nature and not as its most important element. It was common practice not to kill any more animals than could be used at any one time and among many peoples a ritual was used to express gratitude to the animal being killed for providing sustenance. The relationship to nature was reciprocal rather than unilateral.

The Native American attitude toward the environment included the belief that the natural order is only one facet of the cosmic spiritual reality which encompasses and pervades both the heavens and the earth. Although Euro-Americans have generally regarded such beliefs as mere "animism," in the environmental crisis with which we are now confronted, we have already begun to pay the price for stripping nature of its sacredness. Native American worldviews, however, generally see reality as a vast, complex spiritual dynamic in which each life form, including supernatural beings, plays a significant but limited role.

A related aspect of Native American ecological awareness is the concern with spatial and temporal orientation. All peoples living close to the earth must pay a great deal of attention to the Cardinal Directions, the seasons, and weather patterns. Hunters and gatherers, as well as subsistence farmers, must be aware of these factors as they vary by time and place. The sky, the positions and movements of the heavenly bodies in it, the landmarks on the horizon, and the weather patterns were all crucial to Native American life.

Native Americans were unusually sensitive to the world of nature that surrounded them, and found it natural to be at one with it. They were in touch with the rhythms of nature and experienced them in their own daily lives in a way that for the most part Westerners no longer do. Since human beings are, after all, composed of natural elements, and are born, live, and die like all other organisms, this sort of ecological awareness seems as necessary as it is natural.

THE WEB OF COMMUNITY

A second theme in the primal vision of Native Americans is the quality of their participation in the social web or fabric of their community and family. Their culture was embedded in the kinship and political inter-connections woven by marriage and the need for leadership. The "extended family" was common and crucial in Native American life. Indeed, one's actual mother and father were in practice no more impor-tant than one's uncles, aunts, cousins, brothers, sisters, and grandparents.

The privileges and responsibilities of each family member were usu-ally rather specific and served to keep a group together. The Native American family functioned as a wide and vibrant web that kept every person connected to and participating in the ongoing life of the commu-nity. As has been noted, for example, the customs of surviving brothers marrying their dead brother's wives, and of aunts and uncles "adopting" orphaned children, enabled those involved to continue their lives with a minimum of stress and proved extremely valuable in societies where death was a constant possibility.

Political leadership, too, was a matter of close-knit relationships for most Native American peoples. Though the leaders were almost always men, in many if not most cases women played a significant role in choosing and/or advising them. Moreover, major decisions were gener-ally worked out through discussion and consensus among the elders. Thus the notion of ruling "chiefs" is inaccurate.

The thread that held these two aspects of community life, the familial and the political, together was the ceremonial pattern. Although certain rituals were sometimes the responsibility of shamans, by and large the ceremonies in which all the people participated were tied to the cyclical patterns of the hunting and/or farming seasons. This ceremonial thread bound the people to their common past, as well as to one another. Family life and political reality merged in the ongoing reenactment of the group's heritage and in the continual renewal of the world's structure.

At the heart of ceremonial life was the telling of the traditional sto-ries in which were embodied practical advice as well as the cosmic value system. In these stories, people encountered the heroes and villains, the places and events, and the morals to be drawn from them, by which they could regulate and motivate their everyday lives.

The traditional stories ranged from mythic tales of the first people and divinities in primordial time, through accounts of the exploits of culture heroes, to stories of the people's distant and recent history. Generally speaking, specific elders were understood to be the storytellers, and they told the stories from memory with little or no variation. These stories provided the cultural framework and value structure for the group, especially for the children.

It may be very difficult for some of us to grasp, let alone appreciate, the nature and significance of this oral approach to the preservation of a heritage and the instilling of the values of a culture. This is similar to the difficulty some older adults may encounter when confronted by the electronic revolution that younger people find easy to accept. Conversely, today's young people are often hard pressed to appreciate the significance adults attach to books, letters, and documents. In all of these cases, however, it would take but a single generational gap for any society to lose its entire accumulated knowledge and cultural heritage.

The ritual character of storytelling carried with it a great deal of power and authority, which in turn had a unifying effect on Native American people. A collection of accepted stories provided a center around which a group could unite and from which they could obtain guidelines for decision and action. A large part of this unity depended on the vitality of the language of the group. This is why the loss of so many Native American tongues today is so tragic, and why the revival of interest in those that remain alive has become so crucial. The values of a community are embedded in its stories, and its stories are woven within its language.

INDIVIDUAL INTEGRITY

A third broad theme in the Native American primal vision is focused on the notion of harmonious existence or personal integrity. It might be thought that Native Americans do not see themselves as individuals among others, but only as members of the larger group. While there is some truth to this, since for the most part community concerns and goals take precedence over those of the individual, in all cases the individual continues to have choices to make and personal goals to achieve.

Among the Plains Indians there is a strong emphasis on the achievements of individual male warriors, yet in the end these exploits and accomplishments are valued because they contribute to the overall well-being of the community. Among the Hopi, while a strong emphasis is placed on conformity, as in other Pueblo societies, there is also ample room for individual development and distinctiveness.

Generally speaking, among Native Americans life is thought to stretch out or unfold in the form of a path or trail defined by the values that create meaningful existence and lead to a long, happy, and useful life. The primary task in life is to proceed along this path maintaining one's balance and integrity by avoiding all opportunities or temptations to stray.

When an individual has wandered from the path, there are specific rituals to assist her or him in returning to it. The individual always remains a part of the broader community, since the healing rituals are administered and participated in by relatives and elders, and frequently by the entire community. Thus the community and the individual coexist in a symbiotic relationship.

Another aspect of personal or individual integrity is seen in the understanding of holistic health. Striving to maintain one's balance on the path of life is akin to achieving a fundamental harmony within oneself and in relation to all surrounding forces, both natural and social. Such harmony is conceived of by many groups as an essential condition of health or wholeness, so that when a person slips off the basic path of life he or she is viewed as sick, and the rituals invoked to restore the person to the path of harmony and balance are referred to as "medicines" or "healings."

A central feature of this way of thinking is the absence of any distinction between mental and physical health or sickness. Each person is viewed as an integral whole, including physical and spiritual dimensions, to be sure, but nonetheless a unitary being. The dualistic view of the person characteristic of Western thinking on selfhood, as made up of a body inhabited by a spirit, soul, and/or mind is foreign to the Native American mind.

This is not to deny the fact that in the Native American approach to these issues, just as in the Western way, situations may occur in which serious harm is done to a person through ignorance, prejudice, and/or negligence. Superstition and personal bias may enter into any approach to sickness and health, and guidelines are generally invoked in any culture to guard against such harmful possibilities. However, it seems increasingly clear that the holistic understanding of health characteristic of Native American worldviews needs to be taken seriously.

An additional feature of the Native American approach to personal integrity is the importance of flexibility or adaptability. In addition to adjusting one's life to the contours of both the community and the natural environment, a Native American must seek to adjust to the various twists and turns of daily life and circumstance. The balance one needs on life's path is not static but dynamic. It is more like that of a tightrope walker than that of a pedestrian. At every step there is a new challenge to be met.

A mature and balanced person learns to bend with circumstances and so to progress toward the health and wholeness embodied in the Navajo notion of *hozhò*, which encompasses Western concepts of health, beauty, balance, peace, and harmony. *Hozhò* entails the dynamic centeredness exhibited by a master potter creating a bowl on the wheel. While the clay remains centered on the wheel, the interaction between it and the potter continuously gives rise to fresh developments requiring further decisions and adjustments.

The quality of personal flexibility is often a mark of Native Americans, both as specific groups and as a whole. In response to the pressures of invasion and conquest by Europeans, they adapted their lives to meet fresh circumstances. The Pueblo peoples, the Navajo, the Cherokee, and the Nez Perce, to name but a few, are examples of people who not only endured great hardship but eventually came to terms with the reality imposed upon them. They have not only survived, but in some cases even prospered.

The threefold primal vision shared by many Native American worldviews presents a comprehensive and viable alternative to much that has come to characterize the Western way of being in the world. While Native American cultural values may be more tradition-oriented than those of the West, such values have much to offer a culture which overemphasizes individualism and material gain. The Native American way seeks to ensure that people stay in close relationship with the natural environment and pursue wisdom and harmony.

The core of the Native American primal vision is contained in the advice, "Face the sun, walk in wisdom." To face the sun is to orient life, both individually and collectively, toward nature and the Spirit of the cosmos in an intelligent and reverent manner. To walk in wisdom is to understand and live according to those principles that contribute to health and balance in individual life as well as in the life of the community. This is the genius of Native American worldviews.

Appendix

Representative Readings

The essays comprising this appendix have been included to provide some first-hand readings to complement th chapters. Some of these essays are direct accounts from Nativ cans while others were written by persons who were in con Native American peoples at a very early stage.

Although these readings are in no way exhaustive, they do effort to provide a representative sampling of diverse Native *I* groups from different geographical and cultural locales. The in to give the reader a sense of the texture and tone of Native A ways of thinking about the world and their own place in it. Th ities and differences between and among these worldviews c tional light on Native American understandings of their experi

The first essay presents the Iroquois story of their moder hero, Handsome Lake, who brought the Iroquois people their n tional religious and moral code. Entitled "The Dekanawida Le gives an account of the person generally referred to as Hiawatl translated by Seth Newhouse and published in 1916 in A Parker's *Constitution of the Five Nations.*

The second essay is a collection of reports by a number of Oglala/Lakota Indians, often called the "Sioux," which provide in their view of the way reality is put together. The collection is entitle Metaphysics" and is taken from J. R. Walker's *The Sun Dance and C emonies of the Oglala Division of the Teton Dakota,* first published in the pological Papers of the American Museum of Natural History in 19

The third essay tells the story of "Creation and the Origin of Corn" from the Zuni Pueblo peoples as related by Frank Hamilton Cushing, who lived among the Zuni for several years in the early 1800s. It is taken from his book, *Zuni Breadstuff*, first published in 1884 and reprinted in 1920.

The fourth essay relates the Navajo account of their emergence from previous underground worlds into the present world. It is entitled "The Fourth World: The Glittering World," and is taken from *Navajo History*, edited by Ethelou Yazzie and published in 1971.

The fifth essay gives the Hopi story of their emergence from the previous underground worlds into this one and is called "How the People Came Out of the Underworld." It is taken from *Truth of a Hopi* by Edmund Nequatewa, published by Northland Press, Flagstaff, Arizona, in 1967, and reprinted here with the permission of Northland Press.

The sixth essay provides an account of the history of the Potlatch Ceremony among the Kwakiutl people of the Northwest coastal region. This ceremony was outlawed by the Canadian government and has only recently been "officially" reinstated. The account is given by Gloria Cranmer Webster, who comes from a long line of Kwakiutl chiefs, and is entitled "The Contemporary Potlatch." It was first published in *Chiefly Feasts*, edited by Aldona Jonaitis and published by the American Museum of Natural History in 1991. The essay appears here by courtesy of the American Museum of Natural History.

The final essay in this collection details several origin stories of the Cherokee peoples of the Southeast. These and many other stories were collected toward the end of the nineteenth century by James Mooney, one of the earliest ethnologists working with Native American peoples. These accounts were edited by J. W. Powell and the selections here are taken from Powell's collected reports to the Smithsonian Institution's Bureau of American Ethnology in 1897–98.

THE DEKANAWIDA LEGEND

Dekanawida's Birth and Journey

North of the beautiful lake (Ontario) in the land of the Crooked Tongues, was a long winding bay and at a certain spot was the Huron town, Ka-ha-nah-yenh. Near by was the great hill, Ti-ro-nat-ha-ra-da-donh. In the village lived a good woman who had a virgin daughter. Now strangely this virgin conceived and her mother knew that she was about to bear a child. The daughter about this time went into a long sleep and dreamed that her child should be a son whom she should name Dekanawida. The messenger in the dream told her that he should become a great man and that he should go among the Flint people to live and that he should also go to the Many Hill Nation and there raise up the Great Tree of Peace. It was true as had been said the virgin gave birth to a boy and the grandmother greatly disliked him and she rebuked her daughter.

"You refuse to tell me the father of the child," she said, "and now how do you know that great calamity will not befall us, and our nation? You must drown the child."

So then the mother took the child to the bay and chopped a hole in the ice where she customarily drew water and thrust him in, but when night came the child was found at his mother's bosom. So then the mother took the child again and threw him in the bay but at night the child returned. Then the third time the grandmother herself took the child and drowned him but in the morning the child nestled as before on its mother's own bosom.

So the grandmother marveled that the child, her grandson, could not be drowned. Then she said to her daughter:

"Mother, now nurse your child for he may become an important man. He can not be drowned, we know, and you have borne him without having marriage with any man. Now I have never heard of such an occurrence nor has the world known of it before."

Beginning with that time the mother took great care of her child and

Translated by Seth Newhouse and published in Arthur C. Parker, *The Constitution of the Five Nations* (Albany: University of the State of New York, 1916).

nursed him. She named him Dekanawida in accord with the instruction of her dream.

The child rapidly grew and was remarkably strong and healthy. His appearance was noticed for its good aspect and his face was most handsome.

When Dekanawida had grown to manhood he was greatly abused by the Huron people because of his handsome face and his good mind. He was always honest and always told what he believed was right. Nevertheless he was a peculiar man and his people did not understand him.

Many things conspired to drive him away for the Crooked Tongues had no love for such a man. Their hearts were bitter against a man who loved not war better than all things.

After a journey by canoe across the lake he came into the hunting territory of the Flint Nation. He journeyed on to the lower fall of the river of the Flint Nation and made a camp a short way from the fall on the flat land above it. He sat beneath a tall tree and smoked his pipe in quiet meditation.

A man of the Flints passed by and seeing the fire and the stranger approached him cautiously to discover what weapon he bore, if any. Carefully the man of the Flint reconnoitered but saw no weapon, but only the stranger quietly smoking. Returning to the town a short distance away the presence of the odd stranger was reported. Then the chiefs and their men went out and assembled about the man who smoked. One of the head men was delegated to question the stranger and so he asked "From whence came you?"

"I am from Ka-ka-na-yenh," the stranger replied.

"I am of the Wyandots, whom you call the Crooked Tongues because our speech is slightly different," answered the stranger, "My mother is a virgin woman."

"Then," said the speaker, "By what name are you known?"

"I am Dekanawidah, so named because my virgin mother dreamed that it should be so and no one else shall ever be named by this name."

"What brought you here to us," asked the speaker.

So then Dekanawidah answered, "The Great Creator from whom we all are descended sent me to establish the Great Peace among you. No longer shall you kill one another and nations shall cease warring upon each other. Such things are entirely evil and he, your Maker, forbids it. Peace and comfort are better than war and misery for a nation's welfare."

Then answered the speaker of the Flints, "All that you say is surely true and we are not able to contradict it. We must have proof, however, before we submit ourselves to you whereby we may know that you indeed possess rightful power to establish the Great Peace."

So answered Dekanawida, "I am able to demonstrate my power for I am the messenger of the Creator and he truly has given me my choice of the manner of my death."

"Choose then," said the speaker, "a manner of destruction for we are ready to destroy you." Dekanawida replied, " By the side of the falls at the edge of a precipice stands a tall tree. I will climb the tree and seat myself in the topmost branches. Then shall you cut down the tree and I shall fall into the depths below. Will not that destroy me?"

Then said the speaker, "Let us proceed at once."

Dekanawida ascended the tree and it was chopped down. A multitude of people saw him fall into the chasm and plunge into the water. So they were satisfied that he was surely drowned. Night came but Dekanawida did not appear and thus were the people sure of his death, and then were they satisfied.

The next morning the warriors saw strange smoke arising from the smoke hole of an empty cabin. They approached cautiously and peering in the side of the wall where the bark was loosened they saw Dekanawidah. He was alive and was not a ghost and he was cooking his morning meal.

So the watchers reported their discovery and then were the chiefs and people truly convinced that indeed Dekanawidah might establish the Great Peace.

The Troubled Nations

The Ongwe-oweh had fought long and bravely. So long had they fought that they became lustful for war and many times Endeka-Gakwa, the Sun, came out of the east to find them fighting. It was thus because the Ongwe-oweh were so successful that they said the Sun loved war and gave them power.

All the Ongwe-oweh fought other nations sometimes together and sometimes singly and, ah-gi! ofttimes they fought among themselves. The nation of the Flint had little sympathy for the Nation of the Great Hill, and sometimes they raided one another's settlements. Thus did brothers and Ongwe-oweh fight. The nation of the Sunken Pole fought the Nation of the Flint and hated them, and the Nation of the Sunken Pole was Ongwe.

Because of bitter jealousy and love of bloodshed sometimes towns would send their young men against the young men of another town to practise them in fighting.

Even in his own town a warrior's own neighbor might be his enemy and it was not safe to roam about at night when Soi-ka-Gakwa, our Grandmother, the Moon, was hidden.

Everywhere there was peril and everywhere mourning. So men were ragged with sacrifice and the women scarred with the flints, so everywhere there was misery. Feuds with outer nations, feuds with brother nations, feuds of sister towns and feuds of families and of clans made every warrior a stealthy man who liked to kill.

Then in those days there was no great law. Our founder had not yet come to create peace and give united strength to the Real Men, the Ongwe-oweh.

In those same days the Onondagas had no peace. A man's life was valued as nothing. For any slight offence a man or woman was killed by his enemy and in this manner feuds started between families and clans. At night none dared leave their doorways lest they be struck down by an enemy's war club. Such was the condition when there was no Great Law.

South of the Onondaga town lived an evil-minded man. His lodge was in a swale and his nest was made of bulrushes. His body was distorted by seven crooks and his long tangled locks were adorned by writhing living serpents. Moreover, this monster was a devourer of raw meat, even of human flesh. He was also a master of wizardry and by his magic he destroyed men but he could not be destroyed. Adodarhoh was the name of the evil man.

Notwithstanding the evil character of Adadarhoh the people of Onondaga, the Nation of Many Hills, obeyed his commands and though it cost many lives they satisfied his insane whims, so much did they fear him for his sorcery.

The time came, however, when the Onondaga people could endure him no longer. A council was called to devise a way to pacify him and to entreat him to cease his evil ways. Hayonwatha called the council for he had many times sought to clear the mind of Adodarhoh and straighten his crooked body. So then the council was held in the house of Hayontawatha. It was decided that half the people should go by boat across the creek where it widens and that others should skirt the shore. Adodarhoh was not in his nest in the swale but in a new spot across the wide place in the creek.

The boats started and the people walked. From the bushes that over-hung the shore a loud voice sounded. "Stand quickly and look behind you for a storm will overwhelm you."

In dismay the people arose in their canoes and turned about. As they did so the canoes overturned and the men were plunged into the water and many were drowned. A few escaped and then all survivors returned to the village. So had Adodarhoh frustrated the attempt to meet with him.

Again the people prepared to conciliate Adodarho. Three times they agreed to attempt the undertaking. So on the second occasion they go by canoe and by land, those who go by canoe follow the shore and those who go by land walk on the pebbles close to the water's edge.

Again the cunning Adodarho sees them and calling down Hagoks he shook him, and the people in a wild rush scramble for the feathers, for the plumes of Hagoks are most beautiful and men are proud when their heads are adorned with them. There is a tumult and blows are struck. Evil feelings arise and in anger the people return to the village still con-tending. The mission of conciliation is forgotten.

The next day Ayonhwatha called the people to their promise and for the third time to attempt a council with Adodarho. Moreover, they promised to obey every instruction and listen neither to a voice outside nor an omen nor any commotion.

Another council was held in the lodge of a certain great dreamer. He said, "I have dreamed that another shall prevail. He shall come from the north and pass to the east. Hayonwhatha shall meet him there in the Mohawk country and the two together shall prevail. Hayonwhatha must not remain with us but must go from us to the Flint land people."

So when the journey across the lake was attempted there was a divi-sion and the dreamer's council prevailed.

Then the dreamer held two councils and those who believed in him conspired to employ Ohsinoh, a famous shaman.

Hayonwhatha had seven daughters whom he loved and in whom he took great pride. While they lived the conspirators knew he would not depart. With the daughters dead they knew the crushing sorrow would sever every tie that bound him to Onondaga. Then would he be free to leave and in thinking of the welfare of the people forget his own sorrow.

Hayonwhatha could not call the people together for they refused further to listen to his voice. The dreamer's council had prevailed.

At night Osinoh climbed a tree overlooking his lodge and sat on a large limb. Filling his mouth with clay he imitated the sound of a screech owl. Calling the name of the youngest daughter he sang:

> "Unless you marry Osinoh
> You will surely die, -whoo-hoo!"

Then he came down and went to his own home.

In three days the maiden strangely died. Hayonwhatha was disconsolate and sat sitting with his head bowed in his hands. He mourned, but none came to comfort him.

In like manner five other daughters passed away and the grief of Hayonwhatha was extreme.

Clansmen of the daughters then went to the lodge of Hayonwhatha to watch, for they knew nothing of Osinoh's sorcery. They gathered close against the large trees and in the shadows of bushes. The clansmen suspected some evil treachery and were there to discover it.

There was no moon in the sky when Osinoh came. Cautiously he came from habit but he was not afraid. He drove his staff in the ground, he breathed loud like a magic totem animal snorting and then he climbed the tree. He spat the clay about the tree to imitate the screech owl and as he did he said: " Si-twit, si-twit, si-twit." Then he sang:

> "Unless you marry Osinoh
> You will surely die, -whoo-hoo!"

The morning came and Osinoh descended. As he touched the ground a clansman shot an arrow and transfixed him. Prostrate fell Osinoh and the clansman rushed at him with a club.

Osinoh looked up. "You are unable to club me," he said. "Your arm has no power at all. It weakens. Today I shall recover from this wound. It is of no purpose to injure me."

It was true indeed; the clansman could not lift the club to kill Osinoh. Then Osinoh arose and went home and in three days the daughter died. So perished all by the evil magic arts of Osinoh.

The grief of Hayonwhatha was terrible. He threw himself about as if tortured and yielding to the pain. No one came near him so awful was his sorrow. Nothing would console him and his mind was shadowed with the thoughts of his heavy sorrow.

"I shall cast myself away, I shall bury myself in the forest, I shall become a woodland wanderer," he said. Thus he expressed his desire to depart. Then it was known that he would go to another nation.

Hayonwhatha "split the heavens," Watanwhakacia, when he departed and his skies were rent asunder.

Toward the south he went and at night he camped on the mountain. This was the first day of his journey. On the second day he descended and camped at the base of the hill. On the third day he journeyed onward and when evening came he camped in a hickory grove. This he named O-nea-no-ka-res-geh, and it was on the morning he came to a place where round jointed rushes grew. He paused as he saw them and made three strings of them and when he had built a fire he said: "This would I do if I found anyone burdened with grief even as I am. I would console them for they would be covered with night and wrapped in darkness. This would I lift with words of condolence and these strands of beads would become words with which I would address them."

So at this place he stayed that night and he called the spot O-hon-do-gon-wa, meaning Rush-land.

When daylight came he wandered on again and altering the course of his journey turned to the east. At night he came to a group of small lakes and upon one he saw a flock of ducks. So many were there and so closely together did they swim that they seemed like a raft.

"If I am to be truly royanch (noble)," he said aloud to himself, "I shall here discover my power." So then he spoke aloud and said: "Oh you who are 'floats' lift up the water and permit me to pass over the bottom of the lake dryshod."

In a compact body the ducks flew upward suddenly and swiftly, lifting the water with them. Thus did he walk down the shore and upon the bottom of the lake. There he noticed lying in layers the empty shells of the water snail, some shells white, and others purple. Stooping down he filled a pouch of deer skin with them, and then passed on to the other shore. Then did the ducks descend and replace the water.

It was here that Hayonwhatha desired for the first time to eat. He then killed three ducks and roasted them. This was the evening of the fifth day.

In the morning he ate the cold meat of the roasted ducks and resumed his journey. This was the sixth day and on that day he hunted for small game and slept.

On the morning of the seventh day he ate again and turned his way to the south. Late in the evening he came to a clearing and found a bark field hut. There he found a shelter and there he erected two poles, placed another across the tops and suspended three shell strings. Looking at them he said: "Men boast what they would do in extremity but they do not do what they say. If I should see anyone in deep grief I would remove these shell strings from the pole and console them. The strings would become words and lift away the darkness with which they are covered. Moreover what I say I would surely do." This he repeated.

A little girl discovered smoke arising from the field lodge and she crept up and listened. She advanced and peered in a chink in the bark. Then she ran homeward and told her father of the strange man.

"The stranger must be Hayonwhatha," said the father, "I have heard that he has departed from Onondaga. Return, my daughter, and invite him to our house."

The girl-child obeyed and Hayonwhatha went to her house. "We are about to hold a council," the father said, "Sit in that place on one side of the fire and I will acquaint you with our decisions."

The council was convened and there was a great discussion. Before darkness every evening the council dissolved and at no time was Hayonwhatha called upon for advice nor was anything officially reported to him.

On the tenth day of his journey during the debate in the council Hayonwhatha quietly left and resumed his wandering. Nothing had been asked of him and he felt himself not needed by the people. Late in the evening he came to the edge of another settlement and as was his custom he kindled a fire and erected a horizontal pole on two upright poles. On this he placed three strings of the wampum shells. Then he sat down and repeated his saying: "Men boast what they would do in extremity but they do not do what they promise. If I should see any one in deep grief I would remove these shells from this pole and console him. The shells would become words and lift away the darkness with which they are covered. Moreover, I truly would do as I say." This he repeated.

The chief man of the village saw the smoke at the edge of the forest and sent a messenger to discover who the stranger might be. Now when the messenger reached the spot he saw a man seated before a fire and a horizontal pole from which three strings of small shells were suspended. He also heard the words spoken as the stranger looked at the strings. So then when he had seen all he returned and reported what he had seen and heard.

Then said the chief man, "The person whom you describe must truly be Hayonwhatha whom we have heard left his home at Onondaga. He it is who shall meet the great man foretold by the dreamer. We have heard that this man should work with the man who talks of the establishment of peace."

So then the chiefs sent a messenger who should say, "Our principal chief sent me to greet you. Now then I wish you would come into our village with me."

Hayonwhatha heard the messenger and gathered up his goods and went into the village and when he had entered the chief's house the chief said, "Seat yourself on the opposite side of the fire so that you may have an understanding of all that we do here in this place."

Then Hayonhwatha sat there for seven days and the chiefs and people talked without arriving at any decision. No word was asked Hayonhwatha and he was not consulted. No report was made officially to him. So he did not hear what they talked about.

On the eighteenth night a runner came from the south. He was from the nation residing on the seashore. He told the chiefs of the eminent man who had now come to the town on the Mohawk river at the lower falls. Then the messenger said: "We have heard of the dream of Onodaga which told of the great man who came from the north. Now another great man who shall now go forward in haste to meet him shall change his course and go eastward to meet in the Flinty land village (Kanyaka-hake), the great man. There shall the two council together and establish the Great Peace." So said the messenger from the salt water seashore, who came to tell Hayonwhatha to journey cast.

So the chiefs of the town where Hayonhwatha was staying chose five men as an escort for Hayonhwatha. They must go with him until he reached the house where Dekanawida was present. So then on the next day the chief himself went with the party and watched carefully the health of Hayonhwatha. The journey lasted five days and on the fifth day the party stopped on the outskirts of the town where Dekanawida was staying and then they built a fire. This was the custom, to make a smoke so that the town might know that visitors were approaching and send word that they might enter without danger to their lives. The smoke was the signal of friends approaching.[1] The Mohawks (People of the Flinty Country) knew the meaning of the signal so they sent messengers and invited the party into the village.

When Hayonhwatha had entered the house where the people had gathered the chief asked him whom he would like to see most. Then Ayonhwatha answered, "I came to see a very great man who lately came from the north." The chief said, "I have with you two men who shall escort you to the house where Dekanawida is present." Then the people went out and the two men escorted Hayonhwatha to Dekanawida. This was on the twenty-third day. Then Dekanawida arose when Hayon-hwatha had entered and he said: "My younger brother I perceive that you have suffered from some deep grief. You are a chief among your people and yet you are wandering about."

Hayonhwatha answered, "That person skilled in sorcery, Osinoh, has destroyed my family of seven daughters. It was truly a great calamity and I am now very miserable. My sorrow and my grief have been bitter. I can only rove about since now I have taken myself away from my people. I am only a wanderer. I split the heavens when I went away from my house and my nation."

Dekanawida replied, "Dwell here with me. I will represent your sorrow to the people here dwelling."

So Hayonhwatha had found some one who considered his distress and he did stay. Then Dekanawida told of his suffering and the people listened.

The five escorts were then dismissed and Hayonhwatha gave thanks to them and told them to return to their own region again. Then the escorts said, "Now today it has happened as was foretold in a dream. The two are now together. Let them now arrange the Great Peace." Then they returned home.

When Dekanawida laid the trouble before the council he promised to let Hayonhwatha know their decision. The chiefs deliberated over the sad events and then decided to do as Dekanawida should say. He then should remedy the trouble. Then Dekanawida went in perplexity to his lodge and as he came to it he heard Hayonhwatha say, "It is useless, for the people only boast what they will do, saying 'I would do this way,' but they do nothing at all. If what has befallen me should happen to them I would take down the three shell strings from the upright pole and I would address them and I would console them because they would be covered by heavy darkness." Dekanawida stood outside the door and heard all these words. So then Dekanawida went forward into the house and he went up to the pole, then he said: "My younger brother, it has now become very plain to my eyes that your sorrow must be removed. Your griefs and your rage have been great. I shall not undertake to remove your sorrow so that your mind may be rested. Have you no more shell strings on your pole?"

Hayonhwatha replied, "I have no more strings but I have many shells in a tanned deer's skin." So he opened his bundle and a great quantity of shells fell out. So then Dekanawida said, "My younger brother, I shall string eight more strands because there must be eight parts to my address to you." So then Hayonhwatha permitted the stringing of the shells and Dekanawida made the strings so that in all there were thirteen strings and bound them in four bunches. These must be used to console the one who has lost by death a near relative. "My younger brother, the thirteen strings are now ready on this horizontal pole. I shall use them. I shall address you. This is all that is necessary in your case."

So then he took one bunch off the pole and held it in his hand while he talked. While he talked one after another he took them down and gave one to Hayonhwatha after each part of his address.

The words that he spoke when he addressed Hayonhwatha were eight of the thirteen condolences.

When the eight ceremonial addresses had been made by Dekanawida the mind of Hayonhwatha was made clear. He was then satisfied and once more saw things rightly.

Dekanawida then said, "My younger brother, these thirteen strings of shell are now completed. In the future they shall be used in this way: They shall be held in the hand to remind the speaker of each part of his address, and as each part is finished a string shall be given to the bereaved chief (Royaneh) on the other side of the fire. Then shall the Royaneh hand them back one by one as he addresses a reply; it then can be said, 'I have now become even with you.'"

Dekanawida then said, "My junior brother, your mind being cleared and you being competent to judge, we now shall make our laws and when all are made we shall call the organization we have formed the Great Peace. It shall be the power to abolish war and robbery between brothers and bring peace and quietness.

"As emblems of our Royoneh titles we shall wear deer antlers and place them on the heads of Royaneh men."

Hayonhwatha then said, "What you have said is good, I do agree."

Dekanawida said, "My younger brother, since you have agreed I now propose that we compose our Peace song. We shall use it on our journey to pacify Adodarhoh. When he hears it his mind shall be made straight. His mind shall then be like that of other men. This will be true if the singer remembers and makes no error in his singing from the beginning to the end, as he walks before Adodarhoh."

Hayonhwatha said, "I do agree, I truly believe the truth of what you say."

Then Dekanawida said, "My younger brother, we shall now propose to the Mohawk council the plan we have made. We shall tell our plan for a confederation and the building of a house of peace. It will be necessary for us to know its opinion and have its consent to proceed."

The plan was talked about in the council and Dekanawida spoke of establishing a union of all the nations. He told them that all the chiefs must be virtuous men and be very patient. These should wear deer horns as emblems of their position, because as he told them their strength came from the meat of the deer. Then Hayonhwatha confirmed all that Dekanawida had said.

Then the speaker of the Mohawk council said, "You two, Dekanawida and Hayonhwatha, shall send messengers to the Oneida (People of the Stone) and they shall ask Odatshedeh if he will consider the plan."

When Odatshedeh had been asked he replied, "I will consider this plan and answer you tomorrow."

When the tomorrow of the next year had come, there came the answer of the Oneida council, "We will join the confederation."

So then the Mohawks (Kanyenga) sent two messengers to Onondaga asking that the nation consider the proposals of Dekanawida. It was a midsummer day when the message went forth and the Onondaga council answered, "Return tomorrow at high sun." So the two great men returned home and waited until the next midsummer. Then the midday came and the Onondaga council sent messengers who said, "We have decided that it would be a good plan to build the fire and set about it with you." Dekanawida and Hayonhwatha heard this answer.

So then at the same time Dekanawida and Hayonhwatha sent messengers to the Cayuga nation and the answer was sent back. The Cayugas said they would send word of their decision tomorrow, upon the midsummer day. The next year at midsummer the Cayugas sent their answer and they said, "We do agree with Dekanawida and Hayonhwatha."

Now the People of the Great Hill were divided and were not agreed because there had been trouble between their war chiefs, but messengers were sent to them but the Senecas could not agree to listen and requested the messengers to return the next year. So when the messengers returned the councils did listen and considered the proposals. After a year had passed they sent messengers to say that they had agreed to enter into the confederacy.

Then Dekanawida said, "I now will report to the Mohawk council the result of my work of five years." Hayonhwatha then said, "I do agree to the report."

The Establishment of the Great Peace

Dekanawida requested some of the Mohawk chiefs to call a council, so messengers were sent out among the people and the council was convened.

Dekanawida said, "I, with my co-worker, have a desire to now report what we have done on five successive midsummer days, of five successive years. We have obtained the consent of five nations. These are the Mohawks, the Oneidas, the Onondagas, the Cayugas and the Senecas. Our desire is to form a compact for a union of our nations. Our next step is to seek out Adodarhoh. It is he who has always set at naught all plans for the establishment of the Great Peace. We must seek his fire and look for his smoke."

The chief speaker of the council then said, "We do agree and confirm all you have said and we wish to appoint two spies who shall volunteer to seek out the smoke of Adodarhoh."

Two men then eagerly volunteered and Dekanawida asked them if they were able to transform themselves into birds or animals, for such must be the ability of the messengers who approached Adodarhoh. The two men replied, "We are able to transform ourselves into herons and cranes."

"Then you will not do for you will pause at the first creek or swamp and look for frogs and fish."

Two men then said, "We have magic that will transform us into humming birds. They fly very swiftly."

"Then you will not do because you are always hungry and are looking for flowers."

Two other men then said, "We can become the Dare, the white crane."

"Then you will not do because you are very wild and easily frightened. You would be afraid when the clouds move. You would become hungry and fly to the ground looking about for ground nuts."

Then two men who were crows by magic volunteered but they were told that crows talked too loudly, boasted and were full of mischief.

So then in the end two men who were powerful by the magic of the deer and the bear stepped before the council and were chosen. The speaker for the council then reported to Dekanawida that the spies were ready to go. Then they went.

Now Dekanawida addressed the council and he said, "I am Dekanawida and with me is my younger brother. We two now lay before you the laws by which to frame the Ka-ya-neh-renh-ko-wa. The emblems of the chief rulers shall be the antlers of deer. The titles shall be vested in certain women and the names shall be held in their maternal families forever." All the laws were then recited and Hayonhwatha confirmed them.

Dekanawida then sang the song to be used when conferring titles. So in this way all the work and the plans were reported to the Mohawk council and Hayonhwatha confirmed it all. Therefore the council adopted the plan.

When the spies returned the speaker of the council said, " Ska-non-donh, our ears are erected." Then the spies spoke and they said, "At great danger to ourselves we have seen Adodarhoh. We have returned and tell you that the body of Adodarhoh has seven crooked parts, his hair is infested with snakes and he is a cannibal."

The council heard the message and decided to go to Onondaga at midsummer.

Then Dekanawida taught the people the Hymn of Peace and the other songs. He stood before the door of the longhouse and walked before it singing the new songs. Many came and learned them so that many were strong by the magic of them when it was time to carry the Great Peace to Onondaga.

When the time had come, Dekanawida summoned the chiefs and people together and chose one man to sing the songs before Adodarhoh. Soon then this singer led the company through the forest and he preceded all, singing the Peace songs as he walked. Many old villages and camping places were passed as they went and the names were lifted to give the clan name holders. Now the party passed through these places:

> Old Clearing
> Overgrown with bushes
> A temporary place
> Protruding rocks
> Between two places
> Parties opposite at the council fire
> In the Valley
> Drooping Wing
> On the Hillside
> Man Standing
> I have daubed it
> Lake Bridge
> Between two side hills
> Lake Outlet
> At the forks

Long Hill
Broken Branches Lying
The Spring
White
Corn Stalks on both sides
Two Hillsides
The Old Beast

All these places were in the Mohawk country.

Now they entered the Oneida country and the great chief Odat-shedeh with his chiefs met them. Then all of them marched onward to Onondaga, the singer of the Peace Hymn going on ahead.

The frontier of the Onondaga country was reached and the expedition halted to kindle a fire, as was customary. Then the chiefs of the Onondagas with their head men welcomed them and a great throng marched to the fireside of Adodarhoh, the singer of the Peace Hymn leading the multitude.

The lodge of Adodarhoh was reached and a new singer was appointed to sing the Peace Hymn. So he walked before the door of the house singing to cure the mind of Adodarhoh. He knew that if he made a single error or hesitated his power would be weakened and the crooked body of Adodarhoh remain misshapen. Then he hesitated and made an error. So another singer was appointed and he too made an error by hesitating.

Then Dekanawida himself sang and walked before the door of Adodarhoh's house. When he finished his song he walked toward Adodarhoh and held out his hand to rub it on his body and to know its inherent strength and life. Then Adodarhoh was made straight and his mind became healthy.

When Adodarhoh was made strong in rightful powers and his body had been healed, Dekanawida addressed the three nations. He said, "We have now overcome a great obstacle. It has long stood in the way of peace. The mind of Adodarhoh is now made right and his crooked parts are made straight. Now indeed may we establish the Great Peace.

"Before we do firmly establish our union each nation must appoint a certain number of its wisest and purest men who shall be rulers, Rodiyaner. They shall be the advisers of the people and make the new rules that may be needful. These men shall be selected and confirmed by their female relations in whose lines the titles shall be hereditary. When these are named they shall be crowned, emblematically, with deer antlers."

So then the women of the Mohawks brought forward nine chiefs who should become Rodiyaner and one man, Ayenwaehs, as war chief.

So then the women of the Oneidas brought forward nine chiefs who should become Rodiyaner, and one man, Kahonwadironh, who should be war chief.

So then the Onondaga women brought forward fourteen chiefs who should become Rodiyaner, and one man, Ayendes, who should be war chief.

Each chief then delivered to Dekanawida a string of lake shell wampum a span in length as a pledge of truth.

Dekanawida then said: "Now, today in the presence of this great multitude I disrobe you and you are not now covered by your old names. I now give you names much greater." Then calling each chief to him he said: "I now place antlers on your head as an emblem of your power. Your old garments are torn off and better robes are given you. Now you are Royaner, each of you. You will receive many scratches and the thickness of your skins shall be seven spans. You must be patient and henceforth work in unity. Never consider your own interests but work to benefit the people and for the generations not yet born. You have pledged yourselves to govern yourselves by the laws of the Great Peace. All your authority shall come from it.

"I do now order that Skanawateh shall in one-half of his being be a Royaneh of the Great Peace, and in his other half a war chief, for the Rodiyaner must have an ear to hear and a hand to feel the coming of wars."

Then did Dekanawida repeat all the rules which he with Ayonhwatha had devised for the establishment of the Great Peace.

Then in the councils of all the Five Nations he repeated them and the Confederacy was established.

NOTE

1. In those days it was necessary to build a fire on the outskirts of a village about to be entered. If necessary to kill an animal for food, its pelt must be hung on a tree in plain sight because it is the property of the nation in whose territory it is killed. This information was given to me by Albert Cusick and Seth Newhouse.

OGLALA METAPHYSICS: SWORD, FINGER, ONE-STAR, AND TYON, THROUGH J. R. WALKER

Wakan

by Sword

Wakan means very many things. The Lakota understands what it means from the things that are considered *wakan*; yet sometimes its meaning must be explained to him. It is something that is hard to understand. Thus *wasica wakan* means a white man medicineman; but a Lakota medicineman is called *pejuta wacasa*. *Witcasa wakan* is the term for a Lakota priest of the old religion. The white people call our *wicasa wakan*, medicineman, which is a mistake. Again, they say a *wicasa wakan* is making medicine when he is performing ceremonies. This is also a mistake. The Lakota call a thing a medicine only when it is used to cure the sick or the wounded, the proper term being *pejuta*. When a priest uses any object in performing a ceremony that object becomes endowed with a spirit, not exactly a spirit, but something like one, the priests call it *tonwan* or *ton*. Now anything that thus acquires *ton* is *wakan*, because it is the power of the spirit or quality that has been put into it. A *wicasa wakan* has the power of the *wakan* beings.

The roots of certain plants are *wakan* because they are poisonous. Likewise some reptiles are *wakan* because if they bite they would kill. Again, some birds are *wakan* because they do very strange things and some animals are *wakan* because the *wakan* beings make them so. In other words anything may be *wakan* if a *wakan* spirit goes into it. Thus a crazy man is *wakan* because the bad spirit has gone into him.

From J. R. Walker, *The Sun and Other Ceremonies of the Oglala Division of the Teton Dakota*, Anthropological Papers of the American Museum of Natural History, vol. 16, pt. 2 (1917). Walker, a physician, lived among the Oglala (a division of the Teton Sioux) for many years; he befriended Sword, Finger, One-Star, Tyon, and other shamans and was initiated into their practices.

Again, if a person does something that cannot be understood, that is also *wakan*. Drinks that make one drunk are *wakan* because they make one crazy.

Every object in the world has a spirit and that spirit is *wakan*. Thus the spirit or the tree or things of that kind, while not like the spirit of man, are also *wakan*.

Wakan comes from the *wakan* beings. These *wakan* beings are greater than mankind in the same way that mankind is greater than animals. They are never born and never die. They can do many things that mankind cannot do. Mankind can pray to the *wakan* beings for help. There are many of these beings but all are of four kinds. The word *Wakan Tanka* means all of the *wakan* beings because they are all as if one. *Wakan Tanka Kin* signifies the chief or leading *Wakan* being, which is the Sun. However, the most powerful of the *Wakan* beings is *Nagi Tanka*, the Great Spirit who is also *Taku Skanskan*; *Taku Skanskan* signifies the Blue, in other words, the Sky.

Iya is a *Wakan Tanka*, but he is an evil *Wakan Tanka*. Mankind is permitted to pray to the *Wakan* beings. If their prayer is directed to all the good *Wakan* beings they should pray to *Wakan Tanka*; but if the prayer is offered only to one of these beings, then the one addressed should be named.

Wakan Tanka is pleased with music. He likes to hear the drums and the rattles. When any of the *Wakan* beings hear the drum and the rattles they always give attention. He is also fond of the smoke of sweetgrass and evil *Wakan* beings are afraid of the smoke of sage. All of the *Wakan*, both the good and evil, are pleased with the smoke of the pipe.

The *Wicasa Wakan* or priests, speak for all the *Wakan* beings. *Wakan Tanka* gives them the power that makes them *Wakan* and by which they can put *ton* into anything. Each priest has an object for himself into which *ton* has been put. This is called a *Wasicun*. A *Wasicun* is one of the *Wakan* beings. It is the least of them, but if its *ton* is from a powerful being it may be more powerful than many of the *Wakan* beings. This *Wasicun* is what the priests do their work with, but the white people call it the medicine bag, which is a mistake, for there are no medicines in it. A medicine bag is a bag that doctors have their medicines in. If a man has a *Wasicun* he may pray to it, for it is the same as the *Wakan* being whose *ton* (*wan*) is in it.

The earth and the rock and the mountains pertain to the chief *Wakan*. We do not see the real earth and the rock, but only their *tonwanpi*.

When a Lakota prays to *Wakan Tanka* he prays to the earth and to the rock and all the other good *Wakan* beings. If a man wishes to do evil things he may pray to the evil *Wakan*.

Wakan Tanka

by Sword

When *Wakan Tanka* wishes one of mankind to do something he makes his wishes known either in a vision or through a shaman. . . . The shaman addresses *Wakan Tanka* as *Tobtob Kin*. This is part of the secret language of the shamans. . . . *Tobtob Kin* are four times four gods while *Tob Kin* is only the four winds. The four winds is a god and is the *akicita* or messenger of all the other gods. The four times four are: *Wikan* and *Hanwikan*; *Taku Skanskan* and *Tatekan* and *Tob Kin* and *Yumnikan*; *Makakan* and *Wohpe*; *Inyankan* and *Wakinyan*; *Tatankakan*; *Hunonpakan*; *Wanagi*; *Waniya*; *Nagila*; and *Wasicunpi*. These are the names of the good Gods as they are known to the people.

Wakan Tanka is like sixteen different persons; but each person is *kan*. Therefore, they are all only the same as one. . . . All the God persons have *ton*. *Ton* is the power to do supernatural things. . . . Half of the good Gods are *ton ton* (have physical properties) and half are *ton ton sni* (have no physical properties). Half of those who are *ton ton* are *ton ton yan* (visible), and half of those who are *ton ton sni* are *ton ton yan sni* (invisible). All the other Gods are visible or invisible as they choose to be. . . . All the evil Gods are visible or invisible as they choose to be. . . . The invisible Gods never appear in a vision except to a shaman. . . . Except for the Sun dance, the ceremonies for the visible and the invisible Gods differ. The Sun dance is a ceremony the same as if *Wikan* were both visible and invisible. This is because *Wi* is the chief of the Gods. . . .

Skan

by Finger

I heard you exclaim when a meteorite fell and heard you address the people immediately afterwards. Then I saw you burning sweet-grass. Will you tell me why you did this?

You are a white man's medicineman and you want to know the mysteries of the Lakota. Why do you want to know these things?

The old Indians who know these things will soon be dead and gone and as the younger Indians do not know them they will be lost. I wish to write them so they will be preserved and your people can read them in years to come. Will you tell them to me?

My father was a shaman and he taught me the mysteries of the shamans and I will tell them to you. What is it you want to know?

When the meteor fell you cried in a loud voice, "*Wohpa. Wohpe-e-e-e.*" Why did you do this?

Because that is *wakan.*

What is *wohpa*?

It is what you saw. It is one of the stars falling.

What causes the stars to fall?

Taku Skanskan.

Why does *Taku Skanskan* cause the stars to fall?

Because he causes everything that falls to fall and he causes everything to move that moves.

When you move what is it that causes you to move?

Skan.

If an arrow is shot from a bow what causes it to move through the air?

Skan.

What causes a stone to fall to the ground when I drop it?

Skan.

If I lift a stone from the ground what causes the movement?

Skan. He gives you power to lift the stone and it is he that causes all movement of any kind.

Has the bow anything to do with the movement of an arrow shot from it?

Taku Skanskan gives the spirit to the bow and he causes it to send the arrow from it.

What causes smoke to go upward?

Taku Skanskan.

What causes water to flow in a river?

Skan.

What causes the clouds to move over the world?

Skan.

Are *Taku Skan* and *Skan* one and the same?

Yes. When the people speak to him, they say *Taku Skanskan*. When a shaman speaks of him, he says *Skan*. *Skan* belongs to the *wakan* speech used by the shamans.

Is *Skan*, *Wakan Tanka*?

Yes.

Is he *Wakan Tanka Kin*?

No. That is *Wi*, the Sun.

Are *Wi* and *Skan* one and the same?

No. *Wi* is *Wakan Tanka Kin* and *Skan* is *Nagi Tanka*, the Great Spirit.

Are they both *Wakan Tanka*?

Yes.

Are there any other *wakan* that are *Wakan Tanka*?

Yes. *Inyan*, the Rock and *Maka*, the Earth.

Are there any others?

Yes. *Wi Han*, the Moon; *Tate*, the Wind; *Wakinyan*, the Winged; and *Wohpe*, the Beautiful Woman.

Are there any others that are *Wakan Tanka*?

No.

Then there are eight *Wakan Tanka*, are there?

No, there is but one.

You have named eight and say there is but one. How can this be?

That is right. I have named eight. There are four, *Wi*, *Skan*, *Inyan*, and *Maka*. These are the *Wakan Tanka*.

You named four others, the Moon, the Wind, the Winged, and the Beautiful Woman and said they were *Wakan Tanka*, did you not?

Yes. But these four are the same as the *Wakan Tanka*. The Sun and the Moon are the same, the *Skan* and the Wind are the same, the Rock and the Winged are the same, and the Earth and the Beautiful Woman are the same. These eight are only one. The shamans know how this is, but the people do not know. It is *wakan* (a mystery).

Did the *Wakan Tanka* always exist?

Yes. The Rock is the oldest. He is grandfather of all things.

Which is the next oldest?

The Earth. She is grandmother of all things.

Which is next oldest?

Skan. He gives life and motion to all things.

Which is the next oldest after *Skan*?

The Sun. But he is above all things and above all *Wakan Tanka*.

Lakota have told me that the Sun and *Taku Skanskan* are one and the same. Is that true?

No. Many of the people believe that it is so, but the shamans know that it is not so. The Sun is in the sky only half the time and *Skan* is there all the time.

Lakota have told me the *Skan* is the sky. Is that so?

Yes. *Skan* is a Spirit and all that mankind can see of him is the blue of the sky. But he is everywhere.

Do you pray to *Wakan Tanka*?

Yes, very often.

To which of the eight you have named do you pray?

When I pray I smoke the pipe and burn (sweetgrass) and *Wohpe* carries my prayer to the *Wakan Tanka*. If the prayer is about things of great importance, it is carried to the Sun; if about my health or my strength it goes to *Skan*; if about my implements, to *Inyan*; if about food or clothing and such things, to the Earth.

Are such prayers ever carried to the Moon, or the Wind, or the Winged, or to *Wohpe*?

They may be carried to the Moon and to the Wind; but this is the same as if to the Sun or *Skan*. Lakota do not pray to the Winged. They defy him. They do not pray to *Wohpe*, for she carries all prayers. The Lakota may pray to any *Wakan*, but if to a *Wakan* that is below *Wakan Tanka*, such must be named in the prayer and it will be carried to the one named.

You say *wohpa* is a falling star. Is *Wohpe* in any way related to a falling star?

She first came like a falling star.

Where did she come from?

From the stars.

What are the stars?

Waniya.

What are *waniya*?

They are ghosts. *Skan* takes from the stars a ghost and gives it to each babe at the time of its birth and when the babe dies the ghost returns to the stars.

Is *Wohpe* a ghost?

She is *Wakan Tanka*. A ghost is *Wakan*, but it is not *Wakan Tanka*.

Has a Lakota ever seen *Wohpe*?

Yes. When she gave the pipe to the Lakota she was in their camp for many days.

How did she appear at that time?

Like a very beautiful young woman. For this reason the people speak of her as the Beautiful Woman. The people do not speak of her as *Wohpe*. Only the shamans call her that.

Lakota have told me that her *ton* is in the pipe and in the smoke of the sweetgrass. Is that true?

It was a shaman who told you that. When the people say *ton* they mean something that comes from a living thing, such as the birth of anything or the discharge from a wound or a sore or the growth from a seed. Only shamans speak of the *ton* of the *Wakan*. Such *ton* is *wakan* and the shamans only know about it. The people are afraid to talk of such *ton* because it is *wakan*. The people smoke the pipe and burn sweet grass because *Wohpe* will do no harm to anyone.

You say the Rock is the grandfather of all things and the Earth the grandmother of all things. Are the Rock and the Earth as a man and wife?

Some shamans think they are, and some think they are not.

Who were the father and mother of all things?

The *Wakan* have no father or mother. Anything that has a birth will have a death. The *Wakan* were not born and they will not die.

Is anything about a Lakota *wakan*?

Yes. The spirit, the ghost, and the *sicun*.

Do these die?

No. They are *wakan*.

What becomes of them when the body dies?

The spirit goes to the spirit world, the ghost goes to where *Skan* got it, and the *sicun* returns to the *Wakan* it belongs to.

What is the *sicun*?

It is the *ton* of a *Wakan*. *Skan* gives it at the time of the birth.

What are its functions?

It remains with the body during life, to guard it from danger and help it in a *wakan* manner.

How does the spirit get to the spirit world?

It goes on the spirit trail.

Where is the spirit trail?

It can be seen in the sky at night. It is a white trail across the sky.

Is it made of stars?

No. It is like the clouds, so that nothing but *Wakan* can travel on it. No man knows where it begins or where it ends. The Wind alone knows where it begins. It moves about. Sometimes it is in one direction and sometimes in another.

How does the ghost go to the place where *Skan* got it?

The ghost is like smoke and it goes upward until it arrives at the stars.

What becomes of the body when it dies?

It rots and becomes nothing.

Sicun

by Sword

The word *sicun* is from the sacred language of the shamans. It signifies the spirit of a man. This spirit is given to him at birth to guard him against the evil spirits and at death it conducts him to the land of the spirits, but does not go there itself. In the course of his life a man may choose other *sicun*. He may choose as many as he wishes but such *sicun* do not accompany him after death; if he has led an evil life no *sicun* will accompany him.

A shaman should direct a person in the choice of his *sicun*. When the Lakota chooses a *sicun* such is the *ton* of a *Wakan* or it may be the *ton* of anything. When one chooses a *sicun* he should give a feast and have a shaman to conduct the ceremony, for no one can have the knowledge necessary to conduct his own ceremony unless he has learned it in a vision. One's *sicun* may be in any object as in a weapon or even in things to gamble with or in a medicine. But the *sicun* that a man receives at birth is never found in anything but his body. This *sicun* is like one's shadow.

No one ever had the *ton* of the Sun for a *sicun*, for the Sun will not be a *sicun* for anyone. On the other hand, the *ton* of the Sky, while a very powerful *sicun*, may be secured through old and wise shamans. The *sicun* of the earth is the next most powerful and next in rank is the *sicun* of the rock. The *sicuns* of the bear and the buffalo are often chosen, but that of the bear more frequently. A shaman's *Wakan* bag is his *sicun* and all *sicun* are considered *wakan*. A doctor's medicine is his *sicun* and the implements used by a shaman in any ceremony are the *sicun* of that shaman. Implements that are in such *sicun* will not be appropriate in a ceremony. A person may lend his *sicun* to another. The term *wasicun* is applied to any object used as a *sicun* or it may represent anything which is *wakan*. If a ceremony by which one gets a *wasicun* is performed in the most acceptable manner that *wasicun* will be the same in essence as the *wakan* thing it represents. An evil man cannot secure a good *sicun*, but may secure an evil one. If the ceremony be performed, a *sicun* is secured. Then that *sicun* must do as it is directed to do by the one who chooses it; but the chooser must know the songs that belong to it.

Sicun

by One-Star

A *sicun* is like a spirit. It is the *ton-ton sni*, that is, it is immortal and cannot die. A Lakota may have many many *sicunpi*, but he always has one. It is *wakan*, that is, it is like *Wakan Tanka*. It may be the spirit of anything. A shaman puts the spirit in a *sicun*. The bear taught the shamans how to do this. A Lakota should know the songs and if he sings them his *sicun* will do as he wishes. One *sicun* may be more powerful than another. The *sicun* may be of the Great Spirit. If it is opposed by the *sicun* of herbs it is the most powerful. The *sicun* of a good spirit is more powerful than the *sicun* of a bad spirit. The power of sweetgrass is always the spirit of the spirit that is with the south wind. This is always pleasing to the good spirits. The bad spirits do not like the smoke of the sweetgrass. The smoke of sage will drive bad spirits away. A medicin-eman knows the songs of his medicines and they are his *sicun*. The *sicun* that has the power of the spirit should be colored. Red is the color of the sun; blue, the color of the moving spirit; green the color of the spirit of the earth; and yellow is the color of the spirit of the rock. These colors are also for other spirits. Blue is the color of the wind; red is the color of all spirits. The colors are the same for the friends of the great spirits. Black is the color of the bad spirits. A man who paints red is pleasing to the spirits. A *sicun* is a man's spirit. A man's real spirit is different from his *sicun* spirit. *Ni* is also like a spirit. It is a man's breath. It is the spirit of smoke. It is the spirit of steam. It is the spirit of the sweatlodge. It purifies the body. The bear taught these things to the shamans.

The Number Four

by Tyon

In former times the Lakota grouped all their activities by fours. This was because they recognized four directions: the west, the north, the east, and the south; four divisions of time: the day, the night, the moon, and the year; four parts in everything that grows from the ground: the roots, the stem, the leaves, and the fruit; four kinds of things that breathe: those that crawl, those that fly, those that walk on four legs, and those that walk on two legs; four things above the world: the sun, the moon, the sky, and the stars; four kinds of gods: the great, the associates of the great, the gods below them, and the spiritkind; four periods of human life: baby-hood, childhood, adulthood, and old age; and finally, mankind has four fingers on each hand, four toes on each foot and the thumbs and the great toes taken together form four. Since the Great Spirit caused every-thing to be in fours, mankind should do everything possible in fours.

The Circle

by Tyon

The Oglala believe the circle to be sacred because the Great Spirit caused everything in nature to be round except stone. Stone is the imple-ment of destruction. The sun and the sky, the earth and the moon, are round like a shield, though the sky is deep like a bowl. Everything that breathes is round like the body of a man. Everything that grows from the ground is round like the stem of a plant. Since the Great Spirit has caused everything to be round mankind should look upon the circle as sacred, for it is the symbol of all things in nature except stone. It is also the symbol of the circle that marks the edge of the world and therefore of the four winds that travel there. Consequently it is also the symbol of the year. The day, the night, and the moon go in a circle above the sky. Therefore the circle is a symbol of these divisions of time and hence the symbol of all time.

For these reasons the Oglala make their *tipis* circular, their camp-circle circular, and sit in a circle in all ceremonies. The circle is also the symbol of the *tipi* and of shelter. If one makes a circle for an ornament and it is not divided in any way, it should be understood as the symbol of the world and of time. If, however, the circle be filled with red, it is the symbol of the sun; if filled with blue, it is the symbol of the sky. If the circle is divided into four parts, it is the symbol of the four winds; if it is divided into more than four parts, it is the symbol of a vision of some kind. If a half circle is filled with red it represents the day; filled with black, the night; filled with yellow, a moon or month. On the other hand, if a half circle is filled with many colors, it symbolizes the rainbow.

One may paint or otherwise represent a circle on his *tipi* or his shield or his robe. The mouth of a pipe should always be moved in a circle before the pipe is formally smoked.

Invocation

by Sword

Before a shaman can perform a ceremony in which mysterious beings or things have a part, he should fill and light a pipe and say:

"Friend of *Wakinyan*, I pass the pipe to you first. Circling I pass to you who dwell with the father. Circling pass to beginning day. Circling pass to the beautiful one. Circling I complete the four quarters and the time. I pass the pipe to the father with the sky. I smoke with the Great Spirit. Let us have a blue day."

The pipe is used because the smoke from the pipe, smoked in communion, has the potency of the feminine god who mediates between godkind and mankind, and propitiates the godkind. When a shaman offers the pipe to a god, the god smokes it and is propitiated. In this invocation, when the shaman has filled and lighted the pipe, he should point the mouth toward the west and say, "Friend of *Wakinyan*, I pass the pipe to you first." Thus he offers the pipe to the west wind, for the west wind dwells in the lodge of *Wakinyan* and is his friend. The pipe should be offered to the west wind first, because the birthright of precedence of the oldest was taken from the firstborn, the north wind, and given to the second born, the west wind, and the gods are very jealous of the order of their precedence.

When he has made this offering the shaman should move the pipe toward the right hand, the mouthpiece pointing toward the horizon, until it points toward the north. Then he should say: "Circling, I pass to you who dwells with the grandfather." Thus he offers the pipe to the north wind, for because of an offense against the feminine god, the Great Spirit condemned the north wind to dwell forever with his grandfather, who is Wazi, the wizard. Then the shaman should move the pipe in the same manner, until the mouthpiece points toward the east and say: "Circling, pass to beginning day." This is an offering to the east wind, for his lodge is where the day begins and he may be addressed as the "beginning day." Then the shaman should move the pipe in the same manner until the mouthpiece points toward the south, and say: "Circling, pass to the beautiful one." This is an offering to the south wind, for the "beautiful one" is the feminine god who is the companion of the south wind and dwells in his lodge, which is under the sun at midday. It pleases the south wind to be addressed through his companion rather than directly.

The four winds are the *akicita* or messengers of the gods and in all ceremonies they have precedence over all other gods and for this reason should be the first addressed.

When the offering has been made to the south wind the shaman should move the pipe in the same manner until the mouthpiece again points toward the west, and say: "Circling, I complete the four quarters and the time." He should do this because the four winds are the four quarters of the circle and mankind knows not where they may be or whence they may come and the pipe should be offered directly toward them. The four quarters embrace all that are in the world and all that are in the sky. Therefore, by circling the pipe, the offering is made to all the gods. The circle is the symbol of time, for the day time, the night time, and the moon time are circles above the world, and the year time is a circle around the border of the world. Therefore the lighted pipe moved in a complete circle is an offering to all the times.

When the shaman has completed the four quarters and the time he should point the mouthpiece of the pipe toward the sky and say: "I pass the pipe to the father with the sky." This is an offering to the wind, for when the four winds left the lodge of their father, the wind, he went from it, and dwells in the sky. He controls the seasons and the weather, and he should be propitiated when good weather is desired.

Then the shaman should smoke the pipe and while doing so, should say: "I smoke with the Great Spirit. Let us have a blue day."

CREATION AND THE ORIGIN OF CORN

F irst, there was sublime darkness, which vanished not until came the "Ancient Father of the Sun," revealing universal waters. These were, save him, all that were.

The Sun-father thought to change the face of the waters and cause life to replace their desolation.

He rubbed the surface of his flesh, thus drawing forth *yep'-na*.[1]

The *yep'-na* he rolled into two balls. From his high and "ancient place among the spaces," (*Te'-thlä-shi-na-kwin*), he cast forth one of these balls and it fell upon the surface of the waters. There, as a drop of deer suet on hot broth, so this ball melted and spread far and wide like scum over the great waters, ever growing, until it sank into them.

Then the Sun-father cast forth the other ball, and it fell, spreading out and growing even larger than had the first, and dispelling so much of the waters that it rested upon the first. In time, the first became a great being—our Mother, the Earth; and the second became another great being—our Father, the Sky. Thus was divided the universal fluid into the "embracing waters of the World" below, and the "embracing waters of the Sky" above. Behold! this is why the Sky-father is blue as the ocean which is the home of the Earth-mother, blue even his flesh, as seem the far-away mountains—though they be the flesh of the Earth-mother.

Now while the Sky-father and the Earth-mother were together, the Earth-mother conceived in her ample wombs—which were the four great underworlds or caves—the first of men and creatures. Then the two entered into council that they might provide for the birth of their children.

"How shall it be?" said the one to the other. "How, when born forth, shall our children subsist, and who shall guide them?"

"Behold!" said the Sky-father. He spread his hand high and abroad with the hollow palm downward. Yellow grains like corn he stuck into all the lines and wrinkles of his palm and fingers. "Thus," said he, "shall I, as it were, hold my hand ever above thee and thy children, and the

---

From Frank Hamilton, Cushing's *Zuñi Breadstuff*, first published 1884; reprinted 1920 (New York: Museum of the American Indian, Heye Foundation).

yellow grains shall represent so many shining points which shall guide and light these, our children, when the Sun-father is not nigh."

Gaze on the sky at night-time! Is it not the palm of the Great Father, and are the stars not in many lines of his hand yet to be seen?

"Ah yes!" said the Earth-mother, "yet my tiny children may not wander over my lap and bosom without guidance, even in the light of the Sun-father; therefore, behold!"

She took a great terraced bowl into which she poured water; upon the water she spat, and whipping it rapidly with her fingers it was soon beaten into foam as froths the soap-weed, and the foam rose high up around the rim of the bowl. The Earth-mother blew the foam. Flake after flake broke off, and bursting, cast spray downward into the bowl.

"See," said she, "this bowl is, as it were, the world, the rim its farthest limits, and the foam-bounden terraces round about, my features, which they shall call mountains whereby they shall name countries and be guided from place to place, and whence white clouds shall rise, float away, and, bursting, shed spray, that my children may drink of the water of life, and from my substance add unto the flesh of their being. Thou has said thou wilt watch over them when the Sun-father is absent, but thou art the cold being; I am the warm. Therefore, at night, when thou watchest, my children shall nestle in my bosom and find there warmth, strength and length of life from one day light to another."

Is not the bowl the emblem of the Earth, our mother? for from it we draw both food and drink, as a babe draws nourishment from the breast of its mother, and round, as is the rim of a bowl, so is the horizon, ter-raced with mountains, whence rise the clouds. Is not woman the warm, man the cold being? For while woman sits shivering as she cooks by the fire in the house-room, man goes forth little heeding the storms of winter, to hunt the feed and gather pine-faggots.

Yet alas! men and the creatures remained bounden in the lowermost womb of the Earth-mother, for she and the Sky-father feared to deliver them as a mother fears for the fate of her first offspring.

Then the Ancient Sun pitied the children of Earth. That they might speedily see his light, he cast a glance upon a foam cap floating abroad on the great waters. Forthwith the foam cap became instilled with life, and bore twin children, brothers one to the other, older and younger, for one was born before the other. To these he gave the *k'ia'-al-lan*, or "water-shield," that on it they might fly over the waters as the clouds—from which it was spun and woven—float over the ocean; that they might blind with its mists the sight of the enemy as the clouds darken the earth with rain-drops. He gave them for their bow, the rainbow, that with it they might clear men's trails of enemies, as the rain-bow clears away the storm-shadows; and for their arrows gave he them the thunder-bolts, that they might rive open the mountains, as the lightning cleaves asunder the pine trees; and then he sent them abroad to deliver, guide and protect the children of earth and the Sky-father. With their bow they lifted from his embraces the Sky-father from the bosom of the Earth-mother, "for," said they, "if he remain near, his cold will cause men to be stunted and stooped with shivering and to grovel in the earth," as stunted trees in the mountains delve under the snow to hide from the cold of the Sky-father. With their thunder-bolts they broke open the mountain which gave entrance to the cave-wombs of the Earth-mother, and upon their water-shields they descended into the lowermost of the caves, where dwelt the children of earth—men and all creatures.

Alas! It was dark as had been the world before the coming of the Sun, and the brothers found men and the beings sadly bewailing their lot. When one moved it was but to jostle another, whose complaints wearied the ears of yet others; hence the brothers called a council of the priest-chiefs—even ere the coming forth of men such lived—and they made a ladder of tall canes which they placed against the roof of the cavern. Up this rushed the children of earth. Some, climbing out before of their own wills, found deliverance from the caves above and, wandering away, became the ancestors of nations unknown to us; but our fathers followed in the footsteps of the older and younger brothers. Does not the cane grow jointed to-day, showing thus the notches which men traversed to day-light?

In the second cave all was still dark, but like starlight through cloud rifts, through the cleft above showed the twilight. After a time the people murmured again, until the two delivered them into the third world where they found light like that of early dawn. Again they grew discontented, again were guided upward, this time into the open light of the Sun— which was the light of this world. But some remained behind, not escaping until afterward; and these were the fathers of the Western nations whom our ancients knew not.

Then indeed for a time the people complained bitterly, for it was then that they *first* saw the light of the Sun-father, which, in its brilliancy, smote them so that they fell grasping their eye-balls and moaning. But when they became used to the light they looked around in joy and wonderment; yet they saw that the earth seemed but small, for everywhere rolled about the great misty waters.

The two brothers spread open the limbs of the Earth-mother, and cleft the western mountains with their shafts of lightning and the waters flowed down and away from the bosom of the Earth-mother, cutting great cañons and valleys which remain to this day. Thus was widened the land, yet the earth remained damp. Then they guided the people eastward.

Already before men came forth from the lower worlds with the priest-chiefs, there were many gods and strange beings. The gods gave to the priests many treasures and instructions, but the people knew not yet the meaning of either. Thus were first taught our ancients incantations, rituals and sacred talks (prayer), each band of them according to its usefulness. These bands were the "Priesthood"—*Shi'-wa-na-kwe*; the "Hunter-band"—*Sa'-ni-a-k'ia-kwe*; the "Knife-band"—*A'tchi-a-k'ia-kwe* or Warrior, and the *Ne'-we-kwe*, or Band of Wise Medicine Men. The leaders of each band thus came to have wonderful knowledge and power—even as that of the gods! They summoned a great council of their children—for they were called the 'Fathers of the People'—and asked them to choose such things as they would have for special ownership or use. Some chose the macaw, the eagle, or the turkey; others chose the deer, bear, or coyote; others the seeds of earth, or *a'-tâ-a*, the spring vine, tobacco, and the plants of medicine, the yellow-wood and many other things. Thus it came about that they and their brothers and sisters and their children, even unto the present day, were named after the things they chose in the days when all was new, and thus was divided our nation into many clans, or gentes (*A'-no-ti-we*) of brothers and sisters who may not marry one another but from one to the other. To some of the elders of these bands and clans was given some thing which should be, above all other things, precious. For instance, the clans of the Bear and Crane were given the *Mu'-et-ton-ne*, or medicine seed of hail and snow. For does not the bear go into his den, and appears not the crane when come storms of hail and snow?

When more than one clan possessed one of these magic medicines they formed a secret society—like the first four—for its keeping and use. Thus the Bear and Crane peoples became the "Holders of the Wand"— who bring the snow of winter and are potent to cure the diseases which come with them. In time they let into their secret council others, whom they had cured, that the precious secrets of their band might not be wasted. Thus it was that one after another were formed the rest of our medicine bands, who were and are called the finishers of men's trails, because, despite disease and evil, they guard and lengthen our lives; but in the "days of the new" there were only four bands.[2]

To the Eagle, Deer and Coyote peoples was given the *Nal'-e-ton*, or "Deer Medicine Seed," which the Hunter-band still guards; and to the Macaw, Sun and Frog peoples the *Kia'-et-ton*, or the "Medicine Seed of Water," which the priesthood and the Sacred Dance, or *Kâ'-kâ*, still hold— without the administration of which the world would dry up and even the insects of the mountains and hollows of earth grow thirsty and perish. Yet, not less precious was the gift to the "Seed-people," or *Ta'-a-kwe*. This was the *Tchu'-et-ton*, or the "Medicine Seed of Corn"—for from this came the parents of flesh and beauty, the solace of hunger, the emblems of birth, mortal life, death and immortality. To the Badger people was given the knowledge of Fire, for in the roots of all trees, great and little—which the badger best knows how to find—dwells the essence of fire.[3]

To all of these peoples it was told that they should wander for many generations toward the land whence the Sun brings the day-light (East-ward) until at last they would reach the "middle of the world," where their children should dwell forever over the heart of our Earth-mother until their days should be numbered and the light of Zuñi grow dark.

Toward this unknown country the "twin brothers of light" guided them. In those times a day meant a year, and a night another, so that four days and nights meant eight years. Many days the people wandered east-ward, slaying game for their flesh-food, gathering seeds from grasses and weeds for their bread-food, and binding rushes about their loins for their clothing; they knew not until afterward, the flesh of the cotton and yucca-mothers.

The earth was still damp. Dig a hole in a hill-side, quickly it filled with water. Drop a seed on the highest table-land and it without waiting shot forth green sprouts. So moist, indeed, was the soil, that even foot-prints of men and all creatures might be traced whithersoever they tended. The beings and strange creatures increased with men, and spread over the world. Many monsters lived, by whose ferocity men perished.

Then said the twin brothers: "Men, our children, are poorer than the beasts, their enemies; for each creature has a special gift of strength or sagacity, while to men has been given only the power of guessing. Nor would we that our children be webfooted like the beings that live over the waters and damp places."

Therefore, they sent all men and harmless beings to a place of security; then laid their water shield on the ground. Upon it they placed four thunder-bolts, one pointed north, another west, another south, and the other eastward. When all was ready they let fly the thunder-bolts. Instantly the world was covered with lurid fire and shaken with rolling thunders, as is a forest to-day burned and blasted where the lightning has fallen. Thus as the clay of vessels is burned to rock, and the mud of the hearth crackled and reddened by fire, so the earth was mottled and crackled and hardened where now we see mountains and masses of rock. Many of the great monsters and prey-beings were changed in a twinkling to enduring rock or shriveled into twisted idols which the hunter and priest-warrior know best how to prize. Behold, their forms along every mountain side and ravine, and in the far western valleys and plains, still endure the tracks of the fathers of men and beings, the children of earth. Yet some of the beings of prey were spared, that the world might not become over-filled with life, and starvation follow, and that men might breathe of their spirits and be inspired with the hearts of warriors and hunters.

Often the people rested from their wanderings, building great houses of stone which may even now be seen, until the Conch of the Gods sounded, which lashed the ocean to fury and beat the earth to trembling.[4] Then the people started up, and gathering the few things they could, again commenced their wanderings; yet often those who slept or lingered were buried beneath their own walls, where yet their bones may sometimes be found.

Marvelous both of good and evil were the works of the ancients. Alas!

there came forth with others, those impregnated with the seed of sorcery. Their evil works caused discord among men, and, through fear and anger, men were divided from one another. Born before our ancients, had been other men, and these our fathers sometimes overtook and looked not peacefully upon them, but challenged them—though were they not their older brothers? It thus happened when our ancients came to their fourth resting place on their eastward journey, that which they named *Shi-po-lo-lon-K'ai-a*, or "The Place of Misty Waters," there already dwelt a clan of people called the *A'-ta-a*, or Seed People, and the seed clan of our ancients challenged them to know by what right they assumed the name and attributes of their own clan. "Behold," said these stranger-beings, "we have power with the gods above yours, yet can we not exert it without your aid. Try, therefore, your own power first, then we will show you ours." At last, after much wrangling, the Seed clan agreed to this, and set apart eight days for prayer and sacred labors. First they worked together cutting sticks, to which they bound the plumes of summer birds which fly in the clouds or sail over the waters. "Therefore," thought our fathers, "why should not their plumes waft our beseechings to the waters and clouds?" These plumes, with prayers and offerings, they planted in the valleys, and there, also, they placed their *Tchu'-e-ton-ne*. Lo! for eight days and nights it rained and there were thick mists; and the waters from the mountains poured down bringing new soil and spreading it over the valleys where the plumed sticks had been planted. "See!" said the fathers of the seed clan, "water and new earth bring we by our supplications."

"It is well," replied the strangers, "yet *life* ye did not bring. Behold!" and they too set apart eight days, during which they danced and sang a beautiful dance and prayer song, and at the end of that time they took the people of the seed clan to the valleys. Behold, indeed! Where the plumes had been planted and the *tchu'-e-ton* placed grew seven corn-plants, their tassels waving in the wind, their stalks laden with ripened grain. "These," said the strangers, "are the severed flesh of seven maidens, our own sisters and children. The eldest sister's is the yellow corn; the next, the blue; the next, the red; the next, the white; the next, the speckled; the next, the black, and the last and youngest is the sweet-corn, for see! even ripe, she is soft like the young of the others. The first is of the North-land, yellow like the light of winter; the second is of the West, blue like the great world of waters; the third is of the South, red like the Land of Everlasting Summer; the fourth is of the East, white like the land whence the sun brings the daylight; the fifth is of the upper regions, many-colored as are the clouds of morning and evening, and the sixth is of the lower regions, black as are the caves whence came we, your older, and ye, our younger brothers." "Brothers indeed be we, each one to the other," said the people to the strangers, "and may we not journey together seeking the middle of the world?" "Aye, we may," replied the strangers, "and of the flesh of our maidens ye may eat, no more seeking the seeds of the grasses and of your water we may drink, no more wondering whither we shall find it; thus shall each help the other to life and contentment. Ye shall pray and cut prayer-plumes, we shall sing, and dance shall our maidens that all may be delighted and that it may be for the best. But beware! no mortal must approach the persons of our maidens."

Thenceforward, many of the A'-ta-a and the seed clan journeyed together, until at last the Sun, Macaw, and some other clans-people found the middle of the world; while others yet wandered in search of it, not for many generations to join their brothers, over the heart of the Earth-mother, which is *Shi-wi-na-kwin*, or the "Land of the Zuñis."

Day after day, season after season, year after year, the people of the seed clan and the A'-ta-a, who were named together the Corn-clan, or people, prepared, and their maidens danced the dance of the *thla-he-kwe*,[5] or "Beautiful Corn Wands," until their children grew weary and yearned for other amusements.

Sometimes the people saw over Thunder-mountain thick mists floating and lowering. At such times, near the Cave of the Rainbow, a beautiful halo would spring forth, amidst which the many-colored garments of the rainbow himself could be seen, and soft, sweet music, stranger than that of the whistling winds in a mountain of pines, floated fitfully down the valley. At last the priests and elders gathered in council and determined to send their two chief warriors (Priests of the Bow) to the cavern of the rainbow, that it might be determined what strange people made the sights and sounds. "Mayhap it will prove some new dancers, who will throw the light of their favor on our weary hearts and come to cheer us and delight our children." Thus said they to the warriors when they were departing.

No sooner had the warriors reached the cave-entrance than the mists enshrouded them and the music ceased. They entered and were received by a splendid group of beings, bearing long brightly-painted flutes, amongst whom the leader was Pai'-a-tu-ma, the father of the *Ne'-we* band, and the God of Dew.

"Enter, my children," said he, "and sit. We have commanded our dancers to cease and our players to draw breath from their flutes, that we might listen to your messages; for 'not for nothing does one stranger visit the house of another.' "

"True," replied the warriors. "Our fathers have sent us that we might greet you, and the light of your favor ask for our children. Day after day the maidens of the corn-people dance one dance which, from oft repeating, has grown undelightful, and our fathers thought you might come to vary this dance with your own, for that you knew one we were taught by your music, which we sometimes heard."

"Aha!" replied Pai'-a-tu-ma, "it is well! We will follow; but not in the day-time—in the night-time we will follow. My children," said he, turning to the flute-players, "show to the strangers our custom."

The drum sounded till it shook the cavern; the music shrieked and pealed in softly surging unison, as the wind does in a wooded cañon after the storm is distant, and the mists played over the medicine bowl around which the musicians were gathered, until the rainbow fluttered his bright garments among the painted flutes. Maidens filed out brandishing wands whence issued tiny clouds white as the down of eagles, and as the sounds died away between the songs the two warriors in silent wonder and admiration departed for their home.

When they returned to their fathers in Zuñi, they told what they had seen and heard. Forthwith the fathers (priest-chiefs and elders) prepared the dance of the corn-maidens. A great bower was placed in the court of the pueblo, whither went the mothers and priests of the Seed-clan. The priests of the Macaw, Sun and Water clans were there. A terrace of sacred meal was marked on the ground, an altar set up over its base, and along its middle were placed the *E'-ta-e* or Medicine Seeds of corn and water. Along the outer edges were planted the sticks of prayer, plumed with the feathers of summer birds, and down in front of the altar and terrace were set basket-bowls covered with sacred mantles made of the flesh of the

Cotton-mother (Goddess of Cotton), whose down grows from the earth and floats in the skies (cotton and the clouds are one in the Zuñi mythology). By the side of each basket-bowl sat a mother of the clan, silent in prayer and meditation. To the right were the singers, to the left the corn maidens. Night was coming on. The dance began and a fire was built in front of the bower beyond where the maidens danced. More beautiful than all human maidens were those maidens of the corn, but as are human maidens, so were they, irresistibly beautiful.

As the night deepened, the sound of music and flutes was heard up the river, and then followed the players of the rainbow-cave with their sisters, led by the God of Dew. When the players entered and saw the maidens their music ceased and they were impassioned. And when their turn came for leading the dance, they played their softest strains over their medicine bowl—the terraced bowl of the world—whence arose the rainbow. The people were delighted, but the corn maidens were sad; for no sooner had the dancing ceased a little than the flute players sought their hands and persons. In vain the corn maidens pleaded they were immortal virgins and the mothers of men! The flute players continually renewed their suits 'till the next day, and into the night which followed, while the dance went on. At last the people grew weary. The guardian warrior-priests nodded, and no longer wakened them. Silently the corn maidens stole up between the basket-trays and the sleeping people. There, passing their hands over their persons they placed something under the mantles, vanishing instantly as do the spirits of the dying, leaving only their flesh behind. Still the people slept, and ere long even the flute-players and dancers ceased. When the sun came out the people awoke. Then every one cried to the others "Where are our maiden mothers, our daughters?" Yet not even the warriors knew; for only of the flesh of the maidens (corn) could be found a little in the trays under the mantles. Then the place was filled with moaning among the women and upbraidings among the men, each blaming every other loudly until the priests cried out to silence their wranglings, and called a council. Then said they:

"Alas, we have laden our hearts with guilt, and sad thoughts have we prepared to weigh down our minds. We must send to seek the maidens, that they desert us not. Who shall undertake the journey?"

"Send for the eagle," it was said. The two warrior-priests were commanded to go and seek him.

Be it known that while yet the earth was young her children, both men and the creatures, spoke as men alone now speak, any one with any other. This the aged among all nations agree in saying, and are not those who grow not foolish with great age the wisest of men? Their words we speak!

Therefore, when the two warriors climbed the mountain whereon the eagle dwelt, and found only his eaglets at home, the little birds were frightened and tried to hide themselves in the hole where the nest was built. But when the warriors came nearer they screamed: "Oh do not pull our feathers; wait 'till we are older and we will drop them for you."

"Hush," said the warriors, "we seek your father."

But just then the old eagle, with a frown on his eyebrow, rushed in and asked why the warriors were frightening his "pinfeathers."

"We came for you, our father. Listen. Our mothers, the beautiful corn maidens, have vanished, leaving no trace save of their flesh. We come to beseech that you shall seek them for us."

"Go before!" said the eagle, smoothing his feathers, which meant that he would follow. So the warriors returned.

Then the eagle launched forth into the sky, circling higher and higher up, until he was smaller than a thistle-down in a whirlwind. At last he flew lower, then into the bower of the dancers where the council awaited him.

"Ah, thou comest!" exclaimed the people.

"Yes," replied the eagle. "Neither a blue-bird nor a wood-rat can escape my eye," said he, snapping his beak, "unless they hide under rocks or bushes. Send for my younger brother; he flies nearer the ground than I do."

So the warriors went to seek the sparrow-hawk. They found him sitting on an ant hill, but when he saw them he would have flown away had they not called out that they had words for him and meant him no harm.

"What is it?" said he. "For if you have any snare-strings with you I'll be off."

"No, no! we wish you to go and hunt for our maidens—the corn maidens," said the warriors,—"your old brother, the eagle, cannot find them."

"Oh, that's it; well, go before—of course he can't find them! He climbs up to the clouds and thinks he can see under every tree and shadow as the Sun, who sees not with eyes, does."

The sparrow-hawk flew away to the north and the east and the west, looking behind every cliff and copsewood, but he found no trace of the maidens, and returned, declaring as he flew into the bower, "they can not be found. They are hiding more snugly than I ever knew a sparrow to hide," said he, ruffling his feathers and gripping the stick he settled on as though it were feathers and blood.

"Oh, alas! alas! our beautiful maidens!" cried the old women; "we shall never see them again!"

"Hold your feet with patience, there's old heavy nose out there; go and see if he can hunt for them. He knows well enough to find their flesh, however so little that may be," said an old priest, pointing to a crow who was scratching an ash-heap sidewise with his beak, trying to find something for a morning meal. So the warriors ran down and accosted him.

"O caw!" exclaimed the crow, probing a fresh place, "I am too hungry to go flying around for you stingy fellows. Here I've been ever since perching-time, trying to get a mouthful; but you pick your bones and bowls too clean, be sure for that!"

"Come in, then, grandfather, and we'll give you a smoke and something to eat," said the two warriors.

"Caw, haw!" said the old crow, ruffling up his collar and opening his mouth wide enough to swallow his own head. "Go before!" and he followed them into the dance-court.

"Come in, sit and smoke," said the chief priest, handing the crow a cigarette.

At once the old crow took the cigarette and drew such a big whiff into his throat that the smoke completely filled his feathers, and ever since then crows have been black all over, although before that time they had white shoulder-bands and very blue beaks, which made them look quite fine.

Then the crow suddenly espied an ear of corn under one of the mantles, for this was all the maidens had left; so he made for the corn and flew off with it, saying as he skipped over the houses, "I guess this is all you'll see of the maidens for many a day," and ever since then crows have been so fond of corn that they steal even that which is buried. But bye and bye the old crow came back, saying that he had a "sharp eye for the *flesh* of the maidens, but he could not find any trace of the maidens themselves."

Then the people were very sad with thought, when they suddenly heard Pai'-a-tu-ma joking[6] along the streets as though the whole pueblo were listening to him. "Call him," cried the priests to the warriors, and the warriors ran out to summon Pai'-a-tu-ma.

Pai'-a-tu-ma sat down on a heap of refuse, saying he was about to make a breakfast of it. The warriors greeted him.

"Why and wherefore do you two cowards come not after me?" inquired Pai'-a-tu-ma.

"We do come for you."

"No, you do not."

"Yes, we do."

"Well! I won't go with you," said he, forthwith following them to the dance-court.

"My little children," said he, to the gray-haired priests and mothers, "good evening;"—it was not yet mid-day—"you are all very happy, I see."

"Thou comest," said the chief priest.

"I do not," replied Pai'-a-tu-ma.

"Father," said the chief priest, "we are very sad and we have sought you that we might ask the light of your wisdom.

"Ah, quite as I had supposed; I am very glad to find you all so happy. Being thus you do not need my advice. What may I not do for you?"

"We would that you seek for the corn-maidens, our mothers, whom we have offended, and who have exchanged themselves for nothing in our gaze."

"Oh, *that's all*, is it? The corn maidens are not lost, and if they were I would not go to seek them, and if I went to seek for them I could not find them, and if I found them I would not bring them, but I would tell them you 'did not wish to see them' and leave them where they are not—in the Land of Everlasting Summer, which is not their home. Ha! you have no prayer-plumes here, I observe," said he, picking up one each of the yellow, blue and white kinds, and starting out with the remark—

"I come."

With rapid strides he set forth toward the south. When he came to the mouth of the "Cañon of the Woods," whence blows the wind of summer in spring-time, he planted the yellow-plumed stick. Then he knelt to watch the eagle down, and presently the down moved gently toward the north, as though some one were breathing on it. Then he went yet farther, and planted the blue stick. Again the eagle down moved. So he went on planting the sticks, until very far away he placed the last one. Now the eagle plume waved constantly toward the north.

"Aha!" said Pai'-a-tu-ma to himself, "It is the breath of the corn maidens, and thus shall it ever be, for when *they* breathe toward the northland, thither shall warmth, showers, fertility and health be wafted, and the summer birds shall chase the butterfly out of Summer-land and summer itself, with my own beads and treasures shall follow after." Then he journeyed on, no longer a dirty clown, but an aged, grand god, with a colored flute, flying softly and swiftly as the wind he sought for.

Soon he came to the home of the maidens, whom he greeted, bidding them, as he waved his flute over them, to follow him to the home of their children.

The maidens arose, and each taking a tray covered with embroidered cotton, followed him as he strode with folded arms, swiftly before them.

At last they reached the home of our fathers. Then Pai'-a-tu-ma gravely spoke to the council.

"Behold, I have returned with the lost maidens, yet may they not remain or come again, for you have not loved their beautiful custom—the source of your lives—and men would seek to change the blessings of their flesh itself into suffering humanity were they to remain amongst you.

"As a mother of her own blood and being gives life to her offspring, so have these given of their own flesh to you. Once more their flesh they give to you, as it were their children. From the beginning of the new Sun each year, ye shall treasure their gift, during the moon of the sacred fire, during the moon of the snow-broken boughs, during the moon of the great sand-driving winds, during the moon of the lesser sand-driving winds, ye shall treasure their flesh. Then, in the new soil which the winter winds and water have brought, ye shall bury their flesh as ye bury the flesh of the dead, and as the flesh of the dead decays so shall their flesh decay, and as from the flesh of the dead springs the other being (the soul), so from their flesh shall spring new being, like to the first, yet in eight-fold plenitude. Of this shall ye eat and be bereft of hunger. Behold these maidens, beautiful and perfect are they, and as this, their flesh, is derived from them, so shall it confer on those whom it feeds perfection of person and beauty, as of those whence it was derived." He lifted the tray from the head of the maiden nearest him. She smiled and was seen no more; yet when the people opened the tray it was filled with yellow seed-corn. And so Pai'-a-tu-ma lifted the trays, each in turn, from the heads of the other maidens, and, as he did so, each faded from view. In the second tray the people found blue corn; in the third, red; in the fourth, white; in the fifth, variegated; and in the sixth, black. These they saved, and in the spring-time they carefully planted the seeds in separate places. The breaths of the corn maidens blew rain-clouds from their homes in Summer-land, and when the rains had passed away green corn plants grew everywhere the grains had been planted. And when the plants had grown tall and blossomed, they were laden with ears of corn, yellow, blue, red, white, speckled and black. Thus to this day grows the corn, always eight-fold more than is planted, and of six colors, which our women preserve separately during the moons of the sacred fire, snow-broken boughs, great sand-driving winds and lesser sand-driving winds.

It was Pai'-a-tu-ma who found the corn maidens and brought them back. He took the trays from their heads and gave them to the people; hence, when in winter, during the moon of the sacred fire, the priests gather to bless the seed-corn for the coming year, the chief-priest of the *Ne'-we-kwe* hands the trays of corn-seed into the estufa.

Ever since these days, the beautiful corn maidens have dwelt in the Land of Everlasting Summer. This we know. For does not their sweet-smelling breath come from that flowery country, bringing life to their children, the corn-plants? It is the south wind which we feel in spring-time.

Thus was born *Tâ-a*, or the "Seed of Seeds."

NOTES

1. Or the "substance of living flesh." This is exemplified as well as may be by the little cylinders of cuticle and fatty-matter that may be rubbed from the person after bathing. [F.H.C.]

2. It may be seen that the Zuñis have here their own way of accounting for their primitive social organization into *Gentes* and *Phratries*—organizations well

nigh universal in the ancient world, as with the society of the early Greeks and Romans, and still prevalent amongst savage tribes of today. [F.H.C.]

3. In ancient times when desirous of making fire, and even today when kindling the sacred flame, the Zuñis produced and still produce, the first spark by drilling with a hard stick like an arrow-shaft into a dry piece of soft root. An arrow-shaft is now used by preference, as it is the emblem of lightning. [F.H.C.]

4. Doubtless this refers to the earthquake. Ruins may sometimes be found in the Southwest, buried like Pompeii beneath the ashes and lava of ancient eruptions, thus pointing either to a remote origin of the Pueblo or a recent cessation of volcanic action in New Mexico and Arizona. [F.H.C.]

5. Unexceptionably this is one of the most beautiful of the native ceremonials, and is one of the few sacred dances of the Zuñis in which women assume the leading part. It is still performed with untiring zeal, usually during each summer, although accompanied by exhausting fasts and abstinences from sleep. Curiously enough, it was observed and admirably, though too briefly described, by Coronado . . . nearly three hundred and fifty years ago.

It was with this ceremonial that the delighted nation welcomed the water which my party brought in 1882 from the "Ocean of Sunrise." As I was then compelled to join the watch of the priests and elders, I had ample leisure during two sleepless days and nights to gather the above and following story from the song which celebrates the origin of the custom, but which both in length and poetic beauty far surpasses the limits and style of the present paper. [F.H.C.]

6. The *Ne'-we-kwe*, of whom the God of Dew, or *Pai'-a-tu-ma*, was the first Great Father, are a band of medicine priests belonging, as explained heretofore, to one of the most ancient organizations of the Zuñis. Their medical skill is supposed to be very great—in many cases—and their traditional wisdom is counted even greater. Yet they are clowns whose grotesque and quick-witted remarks amuse most public assemblies of the Pueblo holiday. One of their customs is to speak the opposite of their meaning; hence too, their assumptions of the clown's part at public ceremonials, when really their office and powers are to be reversed. Their grotesque costuming and face-painting are quite in keeping with their assumed characters, and would, were it possible, justify the belief that our own circus clowns were their lineal descendants or copyists. Often so like are human things, though geographically widely severed. [F.H.C.]

THE FOURTH WORLD: THE GLITTERING WORLD

Locust's Tests

Wíineeshch'íjdii (Locust) was the first Being to come into the Fourth World. When he emerged, he was afraid because he saw water everywhere and also many monsters. One of the original inhabitants (monsters) of this world asked Locust from where he had come. Locust answered that he had come from the world beneath this Glittering World. Locust told him that other Beings were coming into this world to live. The monster said that no one could live here unless Locust could pass certain tests. Locust agreed. The first test was to sit in the same place for four days. Locust said he would do that. As the reader knows, a locust has a shell skin which he sheds at certain times; so Locust left his shell skin and made it look as if he were sitting in the same place. While his skin sat there, he burrowed back to the lower world and told the Beings what was happening in the upper world. Locust returned before the four days were up and passed the test.

Next the monster drew an arrow through his body, putting it in his mouth and drawing it out the other end. He challenged Locust to do the same. When Locust equalled the feat, the monster said that he and the rest of the Beings in the lower world could come and live in this world.

Sacred Mountains

In the Fourth World First Man and First Woman formed the four main sacred mountains from the soil that First Man had gathered from the mountains in the Third World. When the Beings had assembled the things with which to dress the mountains, they traveled by rainbow to the east to plant the sacred Mountain of the East, *Sis Naajiní*. They put down a blanket of white shell. On top of that they sprinkled some of the soil First Man had brought from the world below, and they placed more white shell. This was wrapped up and planted to the east. *Yoołgai Ashkii* (White Bead Boy, or Dawn Boy) was told to enter the Mountain of the East.

From *Navajo History*, ed. Ethelou Yazzie (Chinle, Ariz.: Rough Rock Press, 1971).

Tsoodził (the Mountain of the South) was planted the same way, except that it had a turquoise blanket, soil and pieces of turquoise. *Dootł'izhii At'ééd* (Turquoise Girl) was told to go and live in the Mountain of the South.

Dook'o'ooshíd (the Mountain of the West) was made on an abalone blanket and out of soil and pieces of abalone. *Diichiłí Ashkii* (Abalone Shell Boy) entered the Mountain of the West.

Dibé Nitsaa (the Mountain of the North) was made of an obsidian blanket, soil and pieces of obsidian. *Bááshzhinii At'ééd* (Obsidian Girl) entered the Mountain of the North.

First Man and First Woman fastened the various mountains to the earth. *Sis Naajiní* was fastened with a bolt of white lightning. They covered the mountain with a blanket of daylight and decorated it with black clouds and male rain. The *Shash* (Bear) was sent to guard the doorway of White Bead Boy.

Tsoodził was fastened to the earth with a stone knife. This Mountain of the South was covered with a blue cloud blanket. The mountain was decorated with dark mists and female rain. *Tl'iish Tsoh* (Big Snake) was sent to guard the doorway of Turquoise Girl.

Dook'o'ooshíd was fastened with a sunbeam. This mountain was covered with a yellow cloud. It was decorated with black clouds and male rain. *Niłch'í Diłhił* (Black Wind) was told to guard the doorway for Abalone Boy.

Dibé Nitsaa was fastened to the earth with a rainbow. The mountain was covered with a blanket of darkness, and it was decorated with obsidian. *Atsiniłtl'ish* (lightning) was sent to guard Obsidian Girl's doorway.

Fire and Sweat Bath

The Holy People decided they wanted to make fire and were uncertain about the fire-making procedure. After discussing the matter, they discovered that one of the people had carried flint from the Third World. With it they made the first fire, using the flint on four kinds of wood which were gathered from the four directions. The kinds of wood were fir, piñon, spruce and juniper. The fire made such a noise that it frightened the people. They put another piece of wood on the fire to quiet it, but that did not solve the problem. Finally, one of the people took a branch from another tree and brought it in to calm the fire. The fire quieted down immediately. At that time, the *Honeeshjish* (first poker) was discovered, and the people made a prayer and song for the poker.

The men decided that they wanted to build a sweat bath. The first sweat bath was larger than a hogan. All of the men crowded into the sweat bath, but it would not get warm. Then Lightning came and suggested that they send someone over to a distant place where there was a *Ch'idí* (blanket). A person was sent to bring back the blanket. Owl Man and Owl Woman also had blankets. All of the blankets were used to cover the doorway of the sweat bath, and they helped to get the bath warm. There, in the *Táchééh* (first sweat bath), First Man sang some ceremonial chants and songs. The chants and songs used became sweat bath chants, songs and prayers.

Hogans

In the sweat bath the men discussed how to build a home. After the bath, when the men returned to where the women were staying, they learned that the women had made a simple forked shelter out of sunflower stalks.

However, *Haashch'ééłti'í* (Talking God) showed the people how to make a home out of logs.

The people constructed a hogan of five logs, following Talking God's instructions. The first two logs came from east and west, the next two from south and north, and the fifth from the northeast. In blessing the hogan, they blessed only four sides. Today only four sides of a hogan are blessed. On the roof, where they placed the end of the east log, they put white shell; under the south log, turquoise; under the west log, abalone; under the north log, obsidian, and under the fifth log, jewels from all directions. Where the logs came together at the roof top, they tied feathers of different birds. The tips of the logs are thought to be the eyes of the hogan.

First Man and First Woman told the people that in the future when they built a hogan they must do the same thing and also put pollen underneath and on top. They requested that the hogan be blessed with white and yellow cornmeal, with pollen and with powder from prayer sticks.

After the logs were up and the smaller logs were being added, the people wondered which way the doorway should face. They decided that since all prayers and songs started in the east, they should have the doorway facing east. After deciding upon the doorway, they selected a place where the ashes from the hogan's fire were to be put. Neither charred wood nor bones were to be left inside. This was the first *Ałch'i' adeez'á* (Male hogan) ever built.

The Male hogan was used only for ceremonial gatherings and other religious matters. Food could be brought in when it was time to feed the men engaged in religious activities, but the remains had to be removed as soon as they finished eating. (Some say that the first Male hogan is still in existence, somewhere near the Place of Emergence, and that, at this place, there is still a petrified ladder.)

Sun, Moon, and Stars

The people had the same light as they had had in the worlds below, but they wanted a stronger light to awaken them in the morning; and they wanted a light at night. Also, the people wished to straighten out the night and day and the seasons so that there would be some order in their lives.

They laid stars on a blanket on the ground. *Haashch'ééshzhiní* (Black God) placed the *Sǫ'tsoh* (North Star). First Man placed the *Náhookǫs* (Big Dipper) while First Woman put the *Náhookǫs* (Little Dipper) into the sky. First Man also placed the *Dilyéhé* (Seven Stars) which Black God claimed represented parts of his body. When First Man and First Woman had named the main stars and placed them in the sky, they instructed the stars to guard the sky and man.

Before First Man was finished placing each star in a particular, pres-elected place in the sky, Coyote came along and asked what they were doing. Coyote picked up a star and put it in the south and said it was his *Sǫ'Doo Nídízídí* (Morning Star). Later, Coyote saw how slowly the naming and placing of the stars was progressing, so he took a corner of the blanket and flipped the remaining stars into the sky. First Man scolded Coyote, but Coyote felt he had done a good job.

After the stars had been placed in the sky, First Man and First

Woman still wanted to make something that would give strong daylight. They spread six unwounded buckskins on the ground. On them they placed a large, perfect, round turquoise. They marked the great turquoise with a mouth and nose and eyes. They made a streak of yellow below the mouth, across the face. They then placed another layer of six more unwounded buckskins. This became *Jóhónaa'éí* (the Sun).

The different Beings discussed where they would put the Sun. Some thought it should be placed on the highest mountain, but they finally decided to place it in the sky. The next question was how the Sun should move. Should it move up and down? Should it move in a circle without going down? It was decided that it would pass from east to west to give light all over the world.

Next they placed a perfect white shell on a buckskin. This large, perfect white shell was to become *Tl'éhonaa'éí* (the Moon).

After some difficulty, the Sun and the Moon moved and were placed in the sky. A carrier was selected to carry the Sun and another carrier was selected to carry the Moon.[1] The Sun Carrier and the Moon Carrier declared that every day, as they went on their journey from east to west, someone would die. This would be the price for carrying the Sun and the Moon. Mankind walks the earth at a price and that price is the death of people every day and every night.

Moccasin Game (Shoe Game)[2]

There is a place called *Hadahoniiye'bee Hooghan* (the House Made of Banded Rock). The people living there were visited by *Yé'iitsoh Łá'í Nanaháii* (One Walking Giant) who spoke and said, "My grandchildren, let us play the moccasin game." The people replied that they did not know how; so he went away.

The next day he returned and again said, "My grandchildren, I would like to play the moccasin game with you."

The people told him, "Grandfather, we do not know the game." Again he left, but he returned on the third day, making the same request, and once again the people said they did not know how.

After he had left for the third time a bird, *Tsé Náhálééh*, came to the people and said, "The person coming to you is called One Walking

Giant. When he comes again asking to play the moccasin game, tell him we will play the game at a place called *Tséłchíi'yi'* (Red Rock, on the eastern slope of the Lukachukai Mountains) where Big Snake lives. All the Holy People will be there."

One Walking Giant came back the fourth time, saying, "My grand-children, I have come to play the moccasin game with you."

This time the people replied: "It is well, Grandfather, we will play the game over in *Tséłchíi'yi'* (Red Rock) where Big Snake lives."

The Giant was very pleased and said, "That is good, my children, that is what I came for." The people said they would send word to the Holy People to gather in four days in Red Rock Canyon to play the Moc-casin Game.

All the Holy People assembled together. At the end of the fourth day, One Walking Giant arrived. He had a feather from an eagle which he kept laying against the palm of his hand. From this feather in the Giant's hand, to the moccasin where the *Tólásht'óshí* (little ball) was hidden, there shone a faint ray of light like an almost invisible rainbow. This would help him know in which moccasin the ball was hidden. He had 102 sticks of yucca with him. The number came from the sun's 102 trails.

There are 102 *k'et'ááz* (yucca counters) in the game. The *tólásht'óshí* (ball) is made from the inside of the yucca plant. The sticks are tied in a bundle and are used as counters to pay the points back and forth. When one side has all 102 points, it wins the game. The people on each side place four moccasins in front of themselves. A small ball is hidden inside one of the four moccasins, and the opposing side guesses where the ball is located. A stick is used to tap the moccasins and to select the exact location of the hidden ball. If the guesser taps once, that means he is guessing the ball is in the moccasin he is tapping. If he taps more than once, that means he is guessing the ball is *not* in the moccasin he is tap-ping. If the ball happens to be in the moccasin on which he tapped once, he takes the ball out and gives it to his side.

If he taps more than once on a moccasin, and the ball happens to be in that moccasin, it costs his side 10 counters.

The Giant explained the game to the Holy People and said, "This will not be a free game. All those who travel by day will play against all those who travel by night. The night will bet against the day. The night animals will be on the north side and the day animals on the south. If the night animals win there will be darkness always; if the day animals win there will be light always."

Coyote also came to the canyon to play. He said as long as he howled by both night and day he would be on the winning side, whichever it might be.

The side of darkness used the moccasins of *Shash* (Bear) and *Dahsání* (Porcupine), while the day people's side used the moccasins of *Na'azísí* (Gopher) and *Nahach'id* (Badger).

After explaining the game and its rules, the Giant took a thin piece of corn husk and painted one side black to represent darkness and one side white to represent day. He said he would throw the piece of corn husk into the air. The side of the corn husk which landed upward would tell which team would have the first chance to hide the ball. He let the corn husk fall and the day people called out "gray, gray, gray." The night people called out "black, black, black."

The gray or white side came up; so the day people had the first chance to hide the ball. For a while it looked as if the day people would win, but, finally, a certain night bird hit the moccasin where the ball was hidden and tossed the ball to the night side. Then Owl took the ball and hid it. One time Owl decided not to hide the ball in the moccasin but kept it in his hand. The Giant came over to guess, but he missed, because the ball was not in any of the moccasins. Tears came down his cheeks, and it looked as if the night people might win. As a last resort, the day people sent Gopher under the ground to tunnel up inside each moccasin to discover where the ball was hidden. Gopher reported that the ball was not in any of the four moccasins but rather was hidden in Owl's hand. One of the day birds, armed with this information, went to guess the location of the ball. He pretended to hit each moccasin, but before doing that he said the ball was not there. Finally, he hit Owl's hand and out rolled the ball.

The animals and the Holy People played the game all night but neither side could win all the counters. The animals knew that they must finish the game before daylight and that all night animals must be back in their homes before the sunlight hit them. The night was almost over and neither side had won all the counters. Preparations were made for the animals to return to their homes.

When Owl dropped the ball, all the birds and animals chose whatever designs or colors they wished to wear in the future. *Gáagii* (Crow) and *Shash* (Bear) had fallen asleep. At the last moment the people noticed the approach of dawn. They woke them up hurriedly and told them to get dressed and back to their homes before the dawn came. Crow was in such a hurry that he just dipped himself in the charcoal and became all black. Bear jumped up and reached for his moccasins. Dawn was almost breaking, and he was in such a hurry that he put his moccasins on the wrong feet (his left moccasin on his right foot and vice versa). Today Bear has strangely shaped feet. Then he ran to get into the woods before the sunlight hit him, but he was not quick enough. Just as he was going into the woods the sunlight hit his coat which caused Black Bear to have a reddish sheen to his coat.

Since neither side won, we have both night and day—not all one or the other.

Seasons

After the people had finished with the Sun and Moon, they began to consider dividing the year into various seasons. First Man and First Woman thought about growing things and animals and when they should plant and harvest. It was decided that the seasons would start with spring when there would be growing things. These growing things would grow, and that would be summer. Then they would get old, and that would be harvest time which would be fall. Then the growing things would be finished and that would be winter. Lightning People were given a time to come, which was in the spring and summer. After winter, they would wake everyone so that all would know that spring had come. It was the responsibility of Lightning People to warn the people, so that they would not tell stories at the wrong time of the year.

Harvest

First Man brought forth the white corn which he had. First Woman brought the yellow corn. They put the perfect ears of corn side by side. Turkey danced back and forth four times, and out of his feather coat dropped four kernels of corn which were gray, blue, black and red. Next Big Snake came forward, and he gave four seeds which were the pumpkin, the watermelon, the cantaloupe and the muskmelon. The harvest from these seeds was very large.

The First Adultery

After the harvest, Turquoise Boy visited and slept with First Woman. When First Man returned home he found his wife with Turquoise Boy and was very hurt. This was the first adultery.[3]

At that time there were four leaders: Big Snake, Mountain Lion, Otter and Bear. Usually, every morning First Man would talk to the people, telling them what to do that day. After he found his wife with another man he no longer would come out and talk to the people.

The leaders went to see First Man to find out why he no longer spoke to the people every morning. First Man answered and explained what had happened and why he was worried and deeply concerned. First Man also spoke to his wife, asking her why she had done it. Did she not know that he was responsible for all the good things they enjoyed together? She got angry with her husband, and the conversation led nowhere.

Yellow Fox, Blue Fox and Badger had developed bodily appetites which made them seek out other women, and they further introduced the practice of adultery.

First Man called the leaders and other men together, except those who were responsible for the problem. Together they discussed what should be done. Before a decision was reached, First Man asked for *Nádleeh* (the hermaphrodite) to come to him. He asked whether *Nádleeh* could cook and prepare food, weave and fix men's hair. He asked whether *Nádleeh* had the proper utensils to carry out those tasks. *Nádleeh* replied that he knew how to do these things, which usually were performed by women, and that he had the proper utensils.

The Separation

The leaders and First Man decided to separate themselves (the males) from the women. They decided to build a *Naashkǫ́ǫ́'* (raft) and take all the men over to the other side of the river. The place the men crossed was where water flowed together, and there was a rushing of water, which made it almost impossible to cross. With great difficulty, the men reached the other side. They wanted to prove that the women could not get along without them. The leaders decided to leave the four guilty men (Yellow Fox, Blue Fox, Badger and Turquoise Boy) with the women. It was thought that, since these men wanted the women so badly, they would be left behind.

When the men left, the women laughed and made merry. They said that the women did not need them and were happy to be rid of them. Besides, they had several handsome men still with them. At first the women did not mind being alone. They planted a small field just as the men planted a corn field on their side of the river.

The men who were left with the women soon became exhausted from trying to meet the sexual demands of so many women. Their desires, which had been so strong earlier, quickly disappeared. Later the men lost their voices, and even their noses became smaller as a result of the physical demands of the women.

On the other side of the river, *Nádleeh* ground the corn and cooked the food so that the men did not suffer. In a few years, however, the women became lazy. They did not take care of their small field, and it grew only weeds. At times, some of the women attempted to cross the river to rejoin the men, but the swift and strong current carried them off, and they were drowned. The women used strange objects to satisfy their lustful passions. The result was the birth, later, of giants and monsters. Some of the men also attempted to satisfy their desires through the use of the liver of a recently-killed deer. Those who took part in this practice were struck by lightning. On the other side of the river the women were very hungry, and their clothes were ragged. They called the men to show how thin they were, and they asked to be taken back.

The leaders held a council. All felt that, if women disappeared, it would be bad. As a result, the leaders decided to take the women back. Cleansing ceremonies were held to purify both the men and the women. After the proper ritual and sweat baths, both sexes were purified and returned to live with each other.

Monsters

First Man and First Woman lived near *Dził Ná'ooditii* (Huerfano Mountain). These two were the first Beings to appear like the people we now know as humans. The living things that came from the worlds below were similar to spirits; they were the Holy People.

The population began to increase, and the crops were good; but there were monsters who killed people and caused great concern. As mentioned above, they were the result of the actions of the women in the lower world during the Separation of the Sexes. The people were very afraid of the monsters.

At this time people were living at Pueblo Bonito, and these, like the early Navajos, were threatened by the monsters. *Yé'iitsoh* (Big Monster) lived on top of Mount Taylor. He would hit the people with his clubs of black, blue, yellow and varicolored flint. He used them for food.

Déélgééd (Horned Monster) roamed over the land. He had very keen eyesight and was similar to a rhinoceros. He lived in the valley where wild cotton grew. If someone passed near him, he would chase and kill the person with his horns or simply run over him.

The *Tsé Nináhálééh* (Bird Monsters) lived on the pinnacles of *Tsé Bit'a'í* (Shiprock). There were a mother, a father and two youngsters. The parents would fly and pick up people for food and drop them into the nest. The fall would kill the people. Then the youngsters would eat them.

Tsédahódzíítáii (Monster That Kicked People Off the Cliff) sat leaning back against Kicking Rock. As people walked by, he kicked them off the trail and over the edge of the cliff. Down below, the monster's children devoured the victims.

Biináá'yee'agháanii (Monster That Killed With His Eyes) stared at his captives until they were hypnotized. He then ate them.

There were many more monsters, too—*Tsé' Ahéénídiłii* (Crushing Rock), *Séít'ááṣ* (Moving Sand), *Jadí Naakits'áadah Náhiníléíi* (Twelve Antelopes), *Shash Na'aṣkaahii* (Tracking Bear) and others.

While all this was happening, First Man and First Woman were living at the foot of *Dził Ná'ooditii*, "Mountain Around Which Moving Was Done." They had been told that when the people had multiplied, Changing Woman would be born.

Asdzą́ą́ Nádleehé (Changing Woman)

One morning at dawn, First Man and First Woman saw a dark cloud over Ch'óol'į́'į́ (Gobernador Knob). Later they heard a baby cry. When they looked to see where the crying was coming from, they realized that it came from within the cloud that covered the top of Ch'óol'į́'į́. First Man searched and found a baby girl. She was born of darkness and the dawn was her father.

When First Woman decorated Changing Woman, she said, "Sit down here, my daughter." Then she spread out an unwounded buckskin. On it she placed a piece of turquoise, one of abalone, one of obsidian and a white bead. Then she put white bead moccasins on the girl's feet. She gave her leggings and a skirt of white beads. She designed her sleeve fringes with white beads and made her wristlets of white beads. Then First Woman decorated her neck with white beads, turquoise beads, abalone shell beads and obsidian beads. She gave earrings to Changing Woman, and she placed her hand on the girl's forehead and moved the hand over the length of Changing Woman's head. In this way everything was to grow in the future. Finally, she placed a white bead head plume in the girl's hair.

To the east the bluebird gave its call; from the south the dark small bird called; in the west the wild canary gave its call, and from the north came the call of the corn beetle. First Man and First Woman were pleased. The calls announced the coming of the Holy People for the fourth night of the ceremony.

First Man said, "This is Changing Woman who now is to be called White Bead Woman because she has dressed herself in white beads." Some of the Holy People objected to this and said they would continue to call her Changing Woman. A large cake was baked for the Sun, and this was given to him the next morning.

Talking God was asked to make some songs for the ceremony, and he replied, "My mouth is not used to it; so I will sing only four Hogan Songs."

Áłtsé Hashké (First Scolder) said, "What do you mean, just four Hogan Songs? Don't be foolish. You must sing more than four. Your tail feathers number twelve and you should therefore sing twelve Hogan Songs."

Talking God agreed and answered, "So be it." Then he placed a rainbow across the hogan from east to west and another rainbow from south to north. He made the hogan larger by blowing on each side, beginning with the east. On the east side Talking God planted a row of 12 white beads in the shape of tail feathers; on the south he planted 12 turquoise beads in the shape of tail feathers; on the west side he planted 12 tail-feather-shaped abalone shell beads, and on the north he planted a row of 12 tail-feather-shaped jet beads.

When this was done, all those present were very happy. Talking God sang his 12 Hogan Songs, and the others gave their own set of songs.

As time passed, Changing Woman felt lonely and wandered away from her hogan. She sat in the sun by a small waterfall. There she lay down and slept. When she awoke she felt tired, and she was sure someone had just slipped away from sleeping beside her. She saw tracks which had come from the east, and she saw where the tracks had left.

In time, she had twins. Both were boys. As the boys grew up, their mother adored them and gave them much love. When they still were small, they had their first bows and arrows. They would go hunting for small game and bring back rabbits and squirrels. The boys exercised daily, wrestling and running. They would race to the east to the top of a mountain in the morning. There they would breathe in the sunlight as it came out from behind the mountains to the east. When it snowed, they would roll in the snow, stripped of their clothing. Soon they were very strong.

As the boys grew older, they asked their mother who their father was. Their mother did not answer.

She always cautioned the boys not to go too far from the hogan because the monsters might catch them. Changing Woman was worried all the time. She was afraid the monsters might catch her boys and eat them. One day the boys were playing close to their home. Suddenly the earth shook, warning them that a monster was getting close. The boys quickly ran home to hide. The monster walked up to their hogan and demanded that the two boys, whose tracks he saw leading to the hogan, come out. Changing Woman told the monster that no one else lived in the hogan. The monster mentioned the tracks which led into the hogan. Changing Woman said that she had made the tracks herself. She said she was so lonely that often she would go outside and make children's tracks in the sand, using her hands just to make believe that there were children around. This satisfied the monster and he left.

Notes

1. In some of the stories the Carrier of the Sun was a man on a horse; in other stories the carrier was Turquoise Boy. There is no agreement on this point. The same holds true for the Moon Carrier. In some stories the carrier is a man on a horse; in others, White Shell Girl.

2. This story takes place before the destruction of all the Monsters.

3. The identity of the offending parties varies from story to story. In one, for example, the husband was Wolf and his wife was seduced by Handsome Yellow Fox.

How the People Came Out of the Underworld

ALAIKSAI!—Attention. Before anybody's memory the Hopi lived in the underworld, which was the original place of all human life. Here, in the beginning, all life and everything was good in peace and happy. The people were governed by the chiefs (*Mongwi*), village criers (*Chakmongwi*), priests (*Momwit*), and high priests and all their religious rites were ruled by the high priests. The people were classed as common, middle, and first class.

The time came when the common and middle class of people grew wise to the doings of the priests and the high priests. All the days of their lives these poor people had been cheated of their family rights by the upper classes of the people. At times the wives of the lower class were visited by these men and by the priests and high priests, while the poor husbands of the women were away. Now all this kept on from bad to worse.

By this time the wives of the priests and the higher class of men also grew wise to what had been going on for all these years, and they were greatly troubled. Then, gossip, quarreling and fighting started between the men and women. Some priests said that it was a joy to cheat and steal another man's wife and that they would pray hard and earnest for prosperity. The women in return said, "If this is so and true, would it be more joyful to you then if we did the same to you as you have done to us? Would you then pray harder still for prosperity?"

This question was, of course, asked by decent women brought up before guilty men and at this, every heart was troubled. The women turned their husbands away. They had no place to go but to their gathering places, called kivas, which were the underground houses—meeting places at times of ceremonies. In these kivas some hearts were sad and some did not seem to care so very much. They were all waiting and watching to see who would leave the kiva first to go to their houses to see if their wives would refuse to let them in. Some women had declared that they would not let their husbands in, so they put their belongings outside of their doors.

The men left the kiva one by one, going to their homes to try their

From Edmund Nequatewa, *Truth of the Hopi: Stories Relating to the Origin, Myths, and Clan Histories of the Hopi* (Flagstaff, Ariz.: Northland Press, 1967). Reprinted by permission of Northland Press.

wives, but finding their things outside, they had to go to the homes of their relatives. Even there, they were not welcomed and were not invited to eat, so they were forced to take two or three ears of corn to the kiva to roast. That was all they had for their meal on that day. The night came on. What were they going to do? This was the question. Some said they would stay in the kivas and live on roasted corn as long as they could, thinking that the women might get over this trouble and their anger.

While the wives were still feeling strong against their men, they called a council. Every woman was present. At this council it was decided that the men would be falsely forgiven and would be taken back by every wife. All this was followed out and the husbands were made happy. But knowing all this, the chief, Yai-hiwa, and village crier, and their families, were greatly troubled and were sad. A thought came to the chief's mind of what he should do and how he must punish his people. Now with all this he was troubled in mind. About this time, when the men had been falsely forgiven, the women were going around and running wild after the unmarried boys, so that they might break the hearts of their husbands and so be revenged. Their families were neglected and their fires and cookings were left unattended. Among both men and women there was not a soul who could be happy in such sinful days, for there was murder, suicide, and every other wicked thing that made the days darker and darker.

All this worry and sorrow was on the chief. What could be done? Nobody knew. So he went calling on his wise men (*Posi-wiwaimkum*) personally, and broken hearted as he was, he could not help but shed tears at every call. These wise men were named Kotiwa, Tani, Sootiwa, Komay, Seytiwa, Nawiki, and Kowisa, and they were the best of all wise men, with high ideals. But everything was for the chief to say in those days, so he asked every wise man to come to his counsel on the fourth day, out at a distant place away from the people.

The day came and the chief was out early that morning. With his bag of tobacco and pipes he was waiting for his wise men to come to the appointed place. One by one they came, each with his bag of tobacco and his pipe. The village crier was the last to arrive, and now everyone had come who was expected. Here they kindled a fire and being weary and sad they were rather quiet, sitting around their fire. The chief filled up his pipe with tobacco, lit it and smoked, then passed it to Yai-owa, the village crier. He puffed the smoke four times, then looked up to the chief, saying, "Father." In return the chief said, "My son." The pipe was passed on around in the same manner to every man. After the chief's pipe was all smoked out, every man filled his own pipe. Every pipe was first handed to the chief. Here they had their fatherly and brotherly smoke.

When the smoking was done the chief said, "My dear fellowmen, I pray in hopes that the gods, our fathers, get the smell of our smoking that they may have mercy upon us. With their power, I pray we will succeed and win because of what I have planned to do. My dear fellowmen, it is this. We must find a new place somewhere and we must find some way to get out of this sinful land, either below or above. I am in hopes to save some of you people if you only could realize this and feel as grieved as I do, about the trouble we are having this very day. I pray you to help me." Everybody was silent, arms folded, heads down over their knees while the chief was speaking. Every word was heard.

Then they said, "Our father, our chief, we pray with all our hearts and we are ready to help you. We will stand with you. We will walk in your path and whatever you ask of us we will do."

"Very well," he said, "be watchful and look ahead in my path that I may not mislead you. I pray you all and hope that the words you have spoken are from the very hearts of you and are true."

"We pray you, chief, that the words we speak are from every heart, and they are true."

"Very well, my fellowmen, I thank you. We will get busy at once. Tomorrow we will make *pahos* (prayer offerings) for our gods asking for the mercy and blessings that they bring upon us. I, the chief, Yai-hiwa, again thank you all. Be here earlier tomorrow."

The men went to their homes with the hope of success in their hearts, for they were true, honest men and were loyal to their chief.

The next morning being the second day of the meeting, the chief and all his wise men came to the same place where they had met the day before and here they smoked, as usual. Every man had brought his material with which to make pahos, or prayer sticks.

"Now," said the chief, "my dear fellowmen, let us start our work, and let every heart be in earnest. Let no soul be discouraged for we must work till we succeed."

"Yes, here I am," said the bird, "Why do you want me?"

"It is I," said the canary, "Without you and your magic songs nothing could be done."

"Certainly, being noted for my songs I feel that it is my duty to be here and help you," said the mocking bird.

Before getting things ready for the ceremony, the two birds flew back around the rocks and there they changed their form into human beings. When they came back, the Hopis saw that they were handsome tall men with long straight black hair.

Now all this time the men were getting the things ready with which the Birdmen were to work and perform their ceremony. In laying the altar they spread out the sand in a small square and in the center they placed a sacred water bowl and for each direction an ear of corn was placed. Each ear of corn was of a different color—yellow for the north, blue for the west, red for the south, and white for the east.

When the altar was set up, they were ready for the mocking bird to take the lead in singing. The first songs were for making up the medicine water in the sacred water bowl. After the medicine water was made, the calling songs were to be next, but the questions arose: who would they call first? Who would have the courage and strength to go out to find a place for these Hopis to go, where they might rest and live in peace? The two Birdmen knowing all things, the Hopis left everything to them that there might be no more trouble. So they first called the eagle, *Kwa-hu.* At the end of every song the sacred water was sprinkled to each direction.

As they were singing the eagle came and sat in the midst of them and said, "Why do you call me? Why do you want me?"

"Welcome," said the men. "You being strong on the wing that is why we call you. We want you to help us. We think that you might find a place for us that we may be saved, and we pray that you will."

"Even though being a bird of the air and strong on the wing it is a hard undertaking. But with all my heart I am willing to help you, so let us hope for the best and pray our gods that I may come back to you alive. To be sure, which way must I go?" asked the eagle.

"We wish you would go up into the skies. There may be an opening and another world up there," said the men.

When the eagle was ready to fly and the prayer feathers were tied around his neck and upon each foot, the eagle said, "Pray that I may find a place up there and bring good news." Then off he went up into the skies. He circled round and round above these men and they watched him as he went up, till he was no more to be seen. At last it was getting late in the day and the people felt rather uneasy about him, but finally he was seen coming down, and now it was very late. It seemed as though he was just dropping down, and sure enough he was. He was hardly alive when he came and dropped in front of them all, exhausted, and they rushed to him and rubbed him till he came to. Soon he was quite well and had come to himself again. Then he was ready to tell the news.

"I know you are anxious to hear how far I have gone and what I have seen. Well, my dear good men," he said, "to tell you the truth, the way up there is rather discouraging. When I left here and kept going higher and higher, not a living thing was to be seen above the clouds. As I went on going higher I began to wonder where I would rest, but there was nothing to light on and nowhere to get a rest. When I looked up, it seems as though there is an opening up there, but I was getting very tired already, and if I didn't start to come back I might not be able to return here alive and tell you this news."

After hearing all this they were very much troubled and deep in sadness, and they wondered what else must be done. The eagle then received his prize of many prayer offerings and was asked to stay with them to the finish, and, of course, he was glad to be with them.

By this time the two leaders—canary and mocking bird—thought of someone else to call. Again they were singing the calling song, and in singing the song it was mentioned who they wanted. Before the fourth song was half sung, a hawk, *Ki-sa* came and circled above once and sat down in the midst of them and said, "Why do you call me? Why do you want me?"

"We call you because we are in trouble and we need your help," said the men.

"Yes, I do know that you are in trouble," said the hawk. "All who have a heart wish to help and save you, and I am willing to do whatever you will ask of me."

"Very well," said the Hopis, "we want you to search the skies for us. You are strong on the wing and can fly high, so we feel that you might be able to find a way out of this wicked world."

"Very well," said he, "I will try."

So they made ready for the hawk to fly and put prayer feathers on him as was done to the eagle—around his neck and on his feet.

When he was all ready, he said, "Pray with all your hearts that I may find a place for you and bring you good news."

"We will," said the men, "for we want to save our families and many others who have good hearts, so may our gods take care of you while you are on the journey."

Up the hawk went and circled round and round overhead, as the eagle had done. For a long time he could be seen up in the air till he was gone above the clouds. All this time the men were singing prayer and luck songs that nothing would happen to the hawk.

It was getting late and everybody was rather uneasy again, and they kept watching for him very anxiously. Finally, he was seen again, but he did not seem to be alive and the eagle did not wait to be asked but went right up to meet him. Then every heart was troubled because they thought that he was surely dead. Now, before the eagle knew, the hawk had dropped past him, and then he just dived for the hawk, to catch him, and when the eagle did catch him his mouth was wide open but his heart was still beating a little. When the eagle came down with him in his claws he laid him down on a white robe and every eye was full of tears. Soon one of the men started to rub him, while the mocking bird sang the "life returning song." When he came to he was quite weak, and earnest prayers were shown by smoking many pipes for the hawk. Now by this time he was ready to tell his story.

"I know," said the hawk, "you are all anxious to hear what I have found out for you up in the skies. When I left here, the first part about going up is the same as what brother eagle had seen and told you. I had gone as far as he did, then I took the courage upon myself and went on up as far as I could see up there. I am quite sure that there is an opening up there, but I was tired out and was not able to go any further before I knew that I was dropping down. I tried to turn myself over, but could not make it, for I was exhausted. Finally I felt something hurting me on my sides. I opened my eyes and found myself in the sharp claws of brother eagle. Then, I do not know how we got here, but now I thank the gods and you all that I am alive again. But let us not be discouraged, we might find someone that will make it up there and find out for us all about what is up there. I know every heart is in trouble. My heart is in trouble too because of you."

After hearing this story of the hawk, there was very little light in the hearts of the men. But the thoughts with the men were still very deep of what is to be done next, or who would be the third to try the skies for these Hopis. Everything and everybody was very still and quiet—prayers were being said by the smoking of many pipes.

The next morning being the fifth day of their ceremony, the wise Birdmen—canary and mocking bird—called the men to attention, to come around the altar and fill up their pipes by which to say their prayers again to the gods. After this was said and done, they started singing the calling ceremony again, but they did not know who they were calling this time. Before long something came and just went "whip," sounding like a whip over their heads many times and then sat down in the midst of them, and he was a swallow, *Powvowkiaya*.

He said, "Here I am."

"Welcome," said the men.

"Why do you call me? Why do you want me?" said the bird.

"Yes," said they, "we need you. We want you to help us out of the troubles we are having. We want to be saved."

"I know you do," said the swallow. "I was anxious and longed to be called, but I know your minds are full and of course I know the way things have happened, so I have no envy against those who were called first, because I may not be able to equal what they have already done, but do understand that I am willing to help you."

"Yes," they said, "you being strong and swift on the wing, we pray in hopes that you will make it up through the skies to find a place for us, and here we have these prayer feathers made for you to wear on the way."

"Thank you," said he, "I would be happy to have them, but all those might be in the way so I will go without them."

"Very well," said the Hopis, "you know best of how you go in the air. May our gods bless us and have mercy upon us so that nothing will happen to you and we pray that our gods may take care of you on your journey and bring you back safely to us, so pray that no heart may be discouraged."

"You have all said well. I thank you all," said he.

Then he went off and in a little while he was out of sight. The men filled their pipes and were smoking. Those who were not smoking were singing the prayer songs of good luck. Again it was getting late in the day and the men were still strong with smoking and singing, while the eagle and the hawk were looking up into the skies with their sharp eyes. Finally they saw that the swallow was coming and they hesitated not, but flew right up to meet him. When they reached him he was nearly done and with a faint voice he said, "Catch me." They made a dive for him and did catch him and brought him down and right away they gave him some water and started to rub him up till he had come to himself. While he was resting the gift of prayer feathers was given to him.

When the chief handed all this to him, he said, "This is our gift to you, from us all. We are glad that you have returned to us again."

"Yes," said the swallow bird, "and I know you would like to hear what I have seen and done. It is too high up there. What these two brothers and I have seen is too great and wonderful, and to anybody without wings it is dangerous because the wind is strong up there. Going into the opening I got scared of the wind and was afraid to go any higher for fear I may not be able to come back. If I did I might not be alive to tell you this. What all I did see I could not begin to tell you all about it."

Now the Hopis were wondering who would be the next one to fly into the skies for them, so rather hopelessly they filled their pipes again to smoke and to pray some more, and of course they were very silent.

Finally the canary bird spoke up and said, "My dear fellowmen, we will make our last try so we will call brother shrike, *Si-katsi* and see what he can do for us. He is pretty wise too, so cheerfully come to the altar and we will sing again."

They all moved up around the altar and took up a little more courage, hoping down in their hearts for success. Before many calling songs were ended someone came flying very close to the ground and sat down on top of a nearby bush and from there into the midst of them.

"Welcome," said the Hopis.

"Yes, yes, here I am," he said. "Why do you want me in such a hurry?"

"Yes," said the mocking bird. "Here we are in trouble. Brother canary and I have been working here with these Hopis trying and hoping to find a place and a way to save them from this sinful land. These three brothers here have done their best up in the skies and they all seem to be very certain about an opening somewhere up there. This is why we wanted and called you, hoping that you can find another world and save us."

"With all my heart," said the shrike, "I am here to help you. I know and feel that it must be a hard undertaking because these three brothers were not able to make it. But to be sure, you must all tell me if you are all earnest in the hope to be saved. Somebody's heart must be bad here and he is the one that is holding you back and keeping you working so hard. Every heart must be true and honest. Let us all be one if we really want to be saved."

The chief of course was most troubled to think of all that time he had spent and had not yet accomplished anything, for he, himself, had good faith in his men and trusted them. Anyway, he asked the people then if there is any one of them with a false heart and who is intending to forsake them and they declared themselves to their chief and father to be all true men.

"No fault having been found in you, it gives me courage to go on and take the trip," said the shrike, "so pray for the best while I am away." He went off on a slow flight and as he went higher, he kept going faster. Soon he was no more to be seen. The men then took their pipes, filled them up and smoked with all their hearts, while the canary and the mocking bird were singing their prayer songs. The eagle and hawk were keeping their sharp eyes looking up into the skies.

Praying for many days with their pipes, every tongue was burning with the taste of the tobacco, but their courage was still strong for they were hoping for good news with all their anxious hearts. The day seemed very long.

It was very late when the shrike was seen high up in the sky and he was very slowly coming down. The eagle and the hawk saw that he was still strong so they did not go up to meet him for his little wings were still holding him up. As he was coming down nearer everybody was asked to hold their heads down with high hopes that he may land safely. As he landed they felt that their prayers were answered and they were filled with much joy. The shrike was asked to be seated in the center of them and be resting while the men joined in prayer by smoking their pipes.

When this was done the chief said to the bird, "I am more than glad and happy to see you come back to us again and it is not only I, but every-body here who is anxious to hear the news of what you have for us, so let us hear you."

"It is the same story," said the shrike, "from here on up to where these others had gotten to. When I passed that, I could see the opening and from there on the passage looked rather narrow. As I went on higher into the narrow passage, in there I found many a projecting rock on which I could light and rest myself. Then, at last, up through the opening which is just like a kiva you have down here. The light and sunshine is much better than here, but there is no sign of human life, only the animals and birds of all kinds. Now the question is, how are we going to get you up there? Because even the strongest birds carrying you one by one could not get you all up through there."

"So it is," said the chief, "that is another hard proposition, but let no heart be discouraged. Let us all be strong and we will succeed and leave our troubles behind here in this sinful world for I am more than glad and happy to know that there is another and better world up above, so if there is anyone present to give us advice of what is to be done next, I would like to hear him."

"It is I, who am called Kochoilaftiyo (the poker boy)," said a boy who was sitting way in the back. They did not even know that he was with them all this time, for he was ranked and considered as of the low class people.

"Come forward to my side," said the chief.

And he was seated on the left side of him. Being only a poor boy it was rather doubtful to the others that he would know of any advice to give, but he was treated like the others and so they smoked their pipes together. When this was done, the chief asked him of what he had in mind.

"It is not much of anything," said the boy. "But I am with you and with all my heart I wish to help you. You know and everybody knows that I am not recognized nor respected half as much as the others."

"You have spoken the truth, but you must forget that now," said the chief. "You who are with me here, I refuse no one."

"I thank you," said the boy with eyes full of tears. "I know a little crea-ture, kuna (chipmunk), who lives on the nuts of the pines. I think he knows how to plant and grow those pines and he may have some seeds. If

me down he told the people that the tree had gone
ing. Now the chipmunk was very glad that it had gone
course you know that he was overjoyed. Then the chip-
that it would be rather impossible to climb up on the
em that this tree was hollow inside and he started to
bottom of the tree to cut an opening into it. While he
way all the men circled around the little fire and started
gain by smoking. After all this was done the chief said that
r late in the day they would start their prayers and songs
le at dawn. Now they were all very anxious to see the
ne and before it did come the chief had appointed two
agle and the swallow, to be on the look-out, so that no
le might pass.

this day, before they started out, the chief said to the wise
hey must give an order for some kind of a guard that would
the bad people and the witches and wizards that would try to
way into the reed with the rest of the people. So the chief told
en to make their pahos for each four directions. These were to
the closing of all the different trails from all directions. When
e made he sent out the One Horned Society or priests who were
to guard the North and West, and the Two Horned priests to
e South and East. When they got to the four directions they
ur lines out of sacred corn meal about six feet long and on both
the lines they set a paho falling backward—not toward the
b. Whoever steals their way into the bamboo and crosses this line
erish, which means that they will drop dead. Of course, many
tried to cross from different directions and were found dead.
his is how two of the societies or religions were started; *Kwakant*
Horned Society) and *A-alt* (Two Horned Society), which are stil'
istence today. Whoever came to the bamboo by the set path car
y to the chief, to join in going to the Upper World.
The time came for them to sing their calling songs and before t'
ted to sing they renewed their altar on which they had laid
yer offerings. They made four of these prayer offerings and set th
four sides of the tree to hold it up. These prayer offerings were
e span of a man's hand. When they started to sing they had

---

he would come and plant and grow us one of those tall trees it might reach
the sky so that we may climb up on it. He lives in the rocks and pines."

"Very well," said the chief, "let us call him." At this he turned to the
mocking bird and asked him to sing his calling song for the chipmunk. At
the altar the mocking bird picked up his rattle and started to sing. It was
not very long before the chipmunk appeared over the rocks with his usual
chip-chip voice, and when he did come up he ran in front of the altar.

"Why do you call me, and why do you want me?" he asked.

"It is because we are in trouble. We need your help."

"I am ready," he said.

"As you are noted for your tree planting and know how to make
them grow so fast we would like you to plant one for us that will reach
up to the sky and into the new world. We have been here many days
trying to find out how we can get up there."

"Yes," said the chipmunk, "I do know how to plant trees, but I cannot
be very sure and promise you that I could make it grow up to reach the sky,
but for your sake I will try, so let us pray to our gods who really have power."

They filled up their pipes and smoked again, to carry their earnest
prayers to the gods. After this was done, the little chipmunk reached into
his bag for his tree seeds. "This," he said, "is a spruce. We will try it first."
He put it in his mouth and sang four of his magic songs. Then he took it
out and set it in the ground in front of him, watching it very closely.
Again he reached into his little bag and drew out his little rattle of sea
shells with which he sang over his planted seed. Soon the tree began to
grow out of the ground, and when it was about three inches high, he spit
all over it and around the roots. With that it began to grow faster. Now,
he kept this up as he was singing and his mouth began to get awfully dry
so he asked for some water to increase the moisture in himself. Finally
the tree was as high as a man stood and when it got this high he would
run up on it and with his little paws would pull it upward at the very top.
With songs and pulling it up, the tree was growing very fast indeed. The
little creature kept this up till it had grown to its full height, but it did
not reach the sky.

"I have done my best," said the chipmunk. "The tree will grow no more."

The high hopes of the chief sank again because the tree did not reach
the opening up in the sky.

"Being called to help you," said the chipmunk, "I will try again, so keep your hopes and do not be discouraged. I think it has weakened this tree making it grow too fast, so this time it will be a little slower."

And he reached into his little bag for another seed which was a fir-pine. This he planted, with the same performance as the first time. Again, the little tree began to grow and the chipmunk repeated his same songs with new and strong hopes that he might make it reach the hole in the sky. Going up on this tree he would take his sacred meal and at the very top, with his prayer, he would throw this meal upward as high as he could, hoping that this would make it grow up through the opening.

While he was busy growing his tree every man was smoking his pipe and they were making their earnest prayers from their very hearts. Finally the chipmunk came back down to the ground again and said, "My tree has stopped growing again, although it has passed the first one by four men's height, but be not discouraged, I will try again. First, I must have prayer."

He reached into his bag and out he brought his little pipe and smoked. While he was smoking he kept a seed in his mouth which was a long-needle pine. When he had finished he set the seed in the ground again, and started his performance in the same manner with all the hopes of making it reach the sky, but this was also in vain, though it did pass the two first trees.

Now not only the chipmunk, but all the rest of the people were very much troubled and crying in their hearts to think that the trees had failed to reach the opening in the sky. The chipmunk, with a broken heart, filled up his little pipe and smoked, thinking very hard of what he could do next, because he thought himself powerless and knew that only his gods had unlimited power so with his smoking he prayed the gods for more wisdom. He could see that every heart was sad for the men were sitting around with their heads down upon their folded arms over their knees.

A thought came to him now, so he slowly raised his head and said, "We are all very sad but I will try again, so I wish to ask you from your very hearts if there is someone here who is not very willing to go and hates to leave behind the ones he loves or there may be some of you that still have evil thoughts in your hearts. All this work and many sleepless nights are getting heavy on our father, our chief. We must confess ourselves to him and to our gods that we will do right and will try to live the right kind of life in the upper world."

"We are all true," said ... stayed to this day with our ...

The chipmunk left them ... grows. Here he took a little ... brought a tiny piñon shell full ... and smoked his pipe over it, whi... in the same manner. When this w... the ground, at an arm length deep... shoot and he covered it up. He too... and stood over the plant and said hi... meal high up toward the sky. Then t...

"Now," he said, "this being the l... we must give all our hearts to our god... our prayers and make this tree grow u...

When all their preparations were ... was thrown up toward the sky, the tw... magic songs and the rest all joined with t... knew the songs so that they could follov... songs were ended, the little chipmunk ran ... to the top he pulled on it and he ran back ... Then he came down and filled up his pipe a...

He was always keeping time with the sing... to run up the tree, and he just kept this perfor... high enough, and still they were singing an... singing, they asked the four other birds that ha... go up into the sky to find the opening, to fly up ar... had gone up, because by that time, the little ch... couldn't run up the high tree again.

Now these birds, that is, the eagle and the hawk ... and the shrike, made their trip up into the sky to the ... times and each time, when they came back they tol... was coming nearer to the opening. Toward the last, it w... that could go up and he made this trip up four times. B... made he stayed up on the top limb, and with him on the ... went through the opening. Of course, the old shrike felt v... he knew he could come back down, resting on the limbs o...

When he ca... through the ope... through, and of ... munk told then... tree. He told t... gnawing on th... was gnawing a... their prayers a... as it was rath... for the peop... morning co... birds—the ... wicked peop...

Now o... men that t... hold back ... steal their ... the wise ... represent... these we... suppose... guard t... made f... ends o... bambo... will p... peopl...

... (One... in e... safe...

... sta... pra... on... th...

around the altar and the two birds were watching the opening at the bottom of the tree so in case the wicked people should start to come through they could drive them away. The two birds were appointed because they had sharp claws. When they started to sing their calling song, being a magic song, it took effect and they found the names of men who were in this ceremony following one another because the calling song as it began, named all the wise men who were serving in the ceremony. Before long the people were coming up one after another—that is, one family after another family.

When the people were gathered there, the chief had his prayer offering ready and at the foot of the tree he set this little prayer offering down in front of it. Then with his sacred corn meal he made a line pointing into it and then he walked in and his family followed and the rest of the royal families came after him, like the family of the village crier and the families of the others who had a high position, such as the high priest.

As they were going up through the tree the shrike started outside, because he was rather light and he could rest on the limbs. They didn't know how far they were going up. It took them quite a long while and the chief was rather anxious to get up to the top and after a long time they finally came up to the opening. When the chief got up there the shrike was waiting for him and when he crawled out of the tree the rest followed and as some of these people came out they started to sing the same songs that they were singing down at the bottom. These songs were limited and they were only to be sung four times, because they were awfully long songs. In a ceremony like this everybody was so anxious to get to the top it didn't seem so long and before all the people were through, the songs were ended and there were still some more people gathered around the tree. Then everywhere there was trouble down below, for those who hadn't been able to get up while the songs were being sung had to stay at the bottom, because the ceremony couldn't be sung any more.

Then the One Horned Priests who remained below had to cut the tree down for fear that someone might steal their way up, so they cut down the tree and this tree still had some people in it, so that is why the bamboo is jointed—because the people in there stuck in the tree and the tree kind of shrunk in between them.

GLORIA CRANMER WEBSTER:
THE CONTEMPORARY POTLATCH

In 1951, the Indian Act was revised and the section prohibiting the potlatch was simply deleted, not repealed as the Kwakwaka'wakw had continued to hope. During the dark years of potlatch prohibition, the people had persisted in carrying on their ceremonies in secret, accepting the changes in form and content that such secrecy demanded. It was a time of fear and confusion for people who believed that "It is a strict law that bids us dance. It is a strict law that bids us give away our property. It is a good law." These words were part of a speech made to Franz Boas when he first visited Fort Rupert in 1886. Almost one hundred years later, one of the two survivors of the 1922 potlatch trials expressed similar feelings when she said, "When one's heart is glad, he gives away gifts. It was given to us by our Creator, to be our way of doing things, we who are Indians. The potlatch was given to us to be our way of expressing joy. Every people on earth is given something. This was given to us."

The causes for the drastic changes in our way of doing things include a period of rapid population decline due to introduced diseases and alcohol. As well, the zealous efforts of the missionaries to "Christianize the heathen" were partially successful. The white teachers of several generations of Indian children devoted most of their energies to "civilizing" their students, rather than providing any useful education. "They were trying to make white people out of us," one woman said in reflecting on a time of her life when she knew little and cared less about who she really is. She, along with others who shared similar experiences, is now trying to make up for those lost years.

Although clandestine potlatches were held before the revision of the

From *Chiefly Feasts: The Enduring Kwakiutl Potlatch*, ed. Aldona Jonaitis (Seattle: University of Washington Press; New York: American Museum of Natural History, 1991). Reprinted by courtesy of the American Museum of Natural History.

Indian Act, it was not until 1953 that the first public "legal" potlatch was held. It was held in Coast Salish territory, a long way from the homes of the Kwakwaka'wakw. From 1952 until his death in 1962, Chief Mungo Martin worked at the British Columbia Provincial Museum, carving totem poles and teaching young carvers. One of his projects was the construction of a big house. When the house was completed, he hosted a potlatch, inviting many people from our area. In a speech to his people, he expressed his feelings about what he was doing, following a rehearsal:

> Now, we are finished. That is the way I wanted you to come. Thank you. Thank you, chiefs. You have put strength inside me, for I was very weak all by myself away from home. I almost cry sometimes, when there is no one here to help me. And you have come to help me, you with your famous names, you chiefs. You have strengthened me. Your fame will spread because you are here. You have strength, for you know everything. You, too, have been left to take up the duties which have been passed on to you. So you will help me to finish what I want to do.

The triumph of Mungo Martin's potlatch is evident from the speeches made by the chiefs who were his guests, as recorded during the event. That there were no repercussions from the authorities was a relief and added to the satisfaction felt by those who had participated.

In all probability, the success of Mungo Martin's potlatch encouraged people in Alert Bay to think about building their own big house. Various tribes contributed to the design and construction. The big house was completed in 1963 and was opened with a potlatch hosted by Chief James Knox of Fort Rupert. He was one of twenty people who had been imprisoned for two months in 1922, for potlatching. Many people attended, some out of curiosity about something they had only heard about, but had never seen.

Since then, there have been potlatches every year, with most of them taking place in Alert Bay, although a few are held in big houses in Kingcome Inlet, Gilford Island, and Comox. For villages which do not have big houses, potlatches are held in community halls and people often comment that "it's just not the same without a fire and dirt floor."

The reasons for giving potlatches are the same as they were in the past—naming children, mourning the dead, transferring rights and priv-

Everyone works together with incredible energy and enthusiasm to ensure that everything will be ready on time. While the food and big house crews are finishing their jobs, others are loading trucks with potlatch goods and ceremonial gear to deliver to the big house. Such cooperative effort seems to surface only during potlatch time and is probably indicative of another change in our lives; that is, we are no longer able to help each other in any kind of ongoing way. However, it is of some consolation that such cooperation has not completely disappeared and that it does emerge for the right reasons.

While all the other activity is going on, the old people meet to decide on the dances to be performed, the order in which they will appear, and the names to be given. At this time, representatives of various branches of the host family may announce that certain dances and their names will be transferred to the host, explaining the kinship connection and the history of the dance. Relatives and friends may contribute money, varying in amounts from one hundred to one thousand dollars, to show "how I feel in my heart for you." The chiefs present all express their appreciation for the host's determination to follow the path of his ancestors. Food is served, while the host or an older member of his family thanks everyone for attending and expresses the hope that everything will go well. There is an appeal for all to work together, because we are now so few, so poor, and so weak in our world that what we are able to do is only a shadow of what used to be. These statements in Kwakwala reinforce our painful awareness of how much we have lost over the years. At the same time, the strong words of our old people inspire us to hold on to what we have left.

At last, it is time to go to the big house. As soon as you enter, another difference between past and present is clear. There is no longer any strict seating arrangement, with people sitting according to their tribal and individual rank. People now sit anywhere, except for the host family, which is always seated on the left toward the back of the house. Chiefs and singers sit on either side of the long drum, with the overflow occupying a row of chairs in front. In earlier times, only those who had received proper names were permitted to enter a big house for a potlatch. Today, anyone may attend. There may be quite a number of white people, some of whom have been invited, others who have not. A few of the white people are anthropologists, who are friends of the host family.